Alcohol Ink

STEP-BY-STEP TECHNIQUES FOR INK-BASED FLUID ART

DESIRÉE DELÂGE

DAVID & CHARLES

www.davidandcharles.com

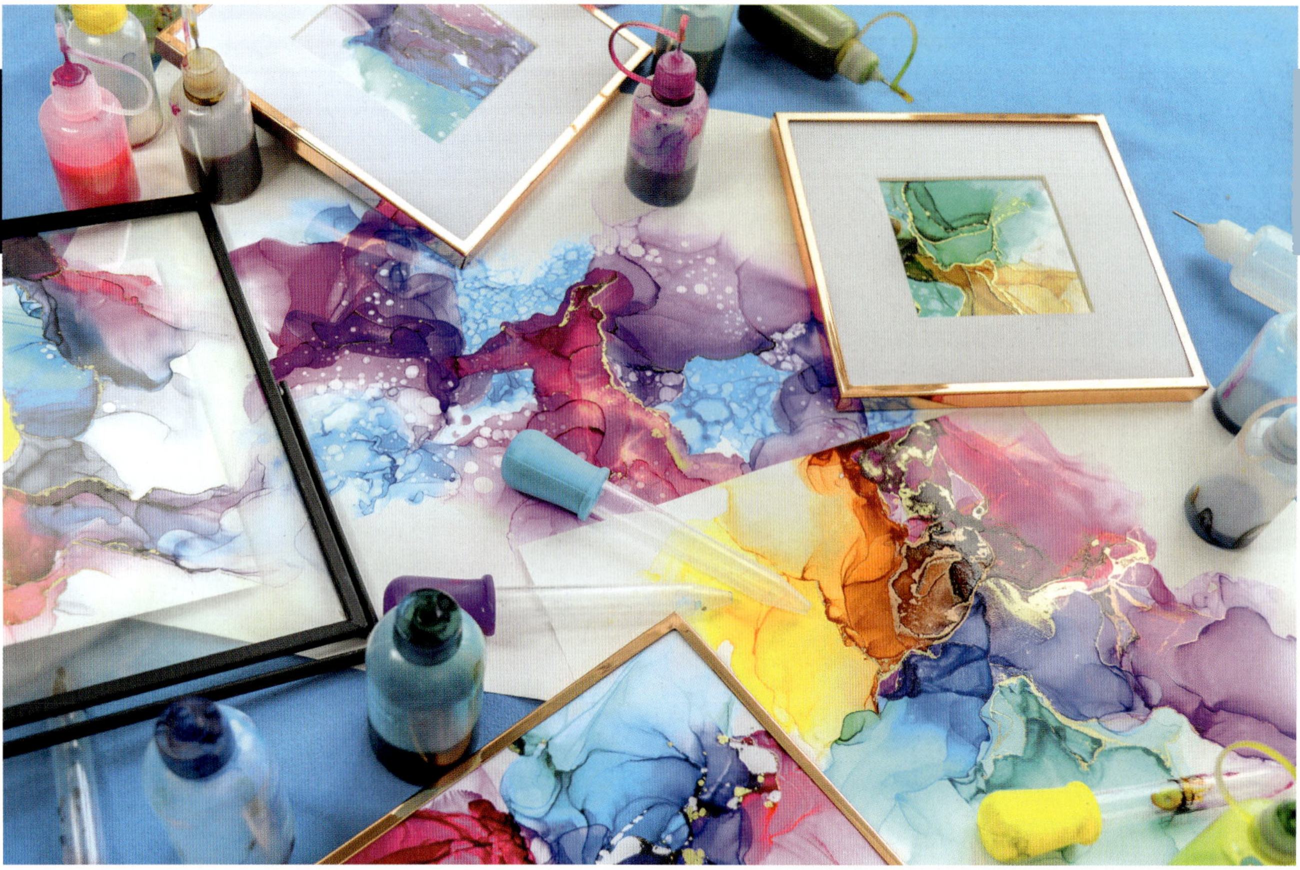

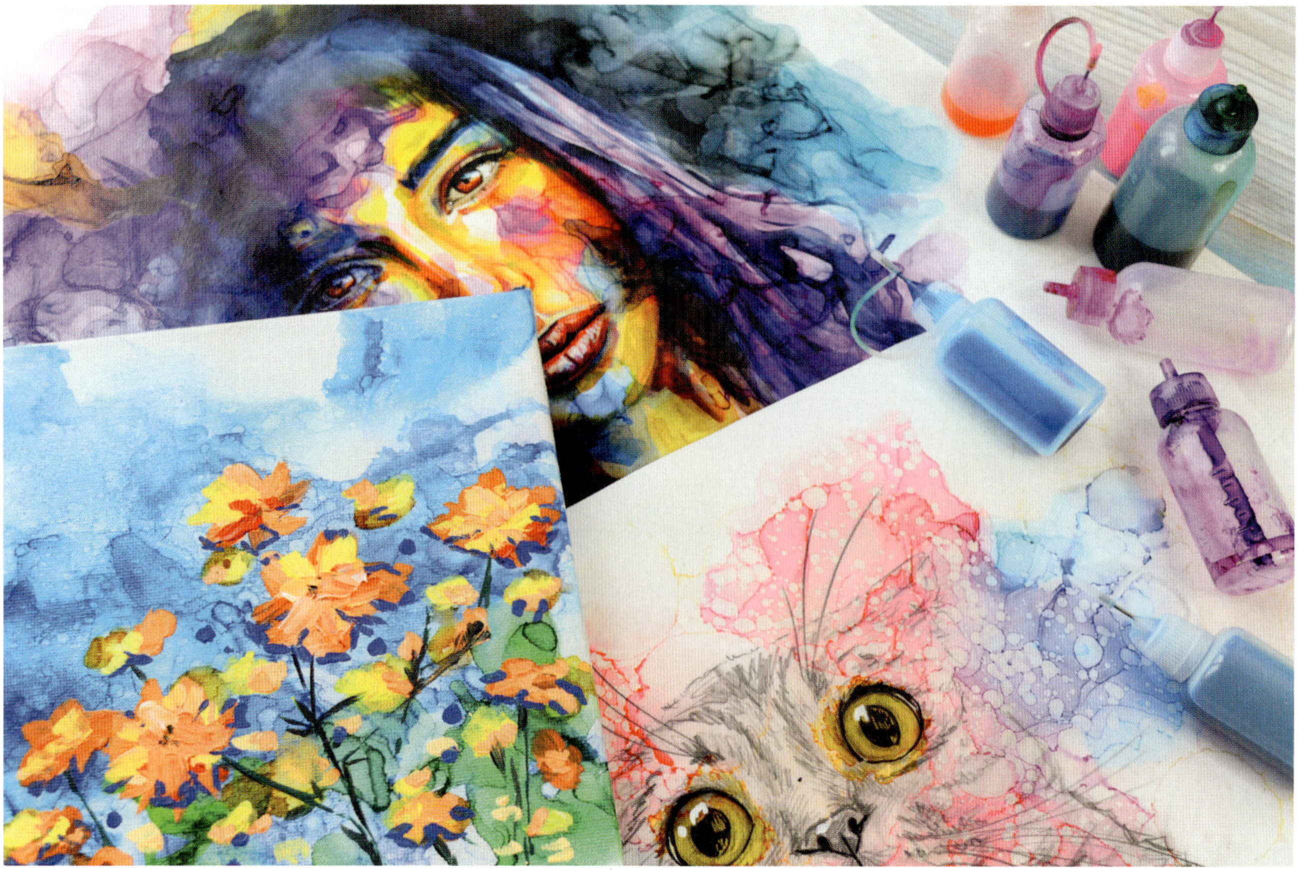

Contents

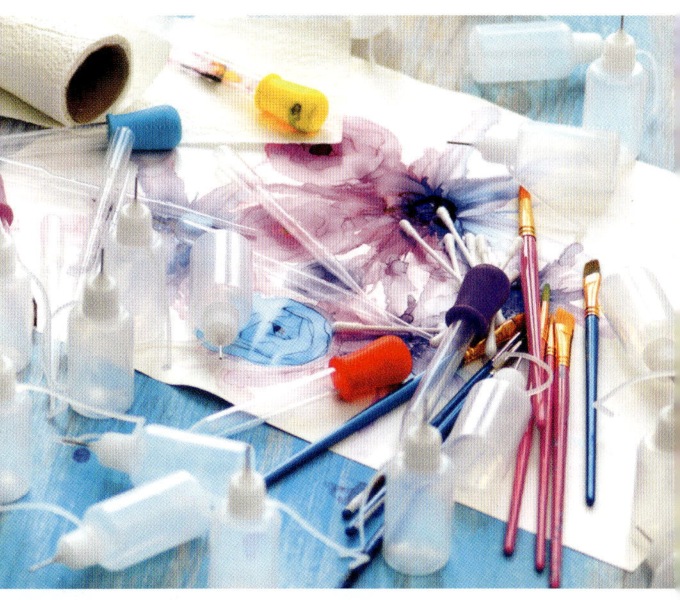

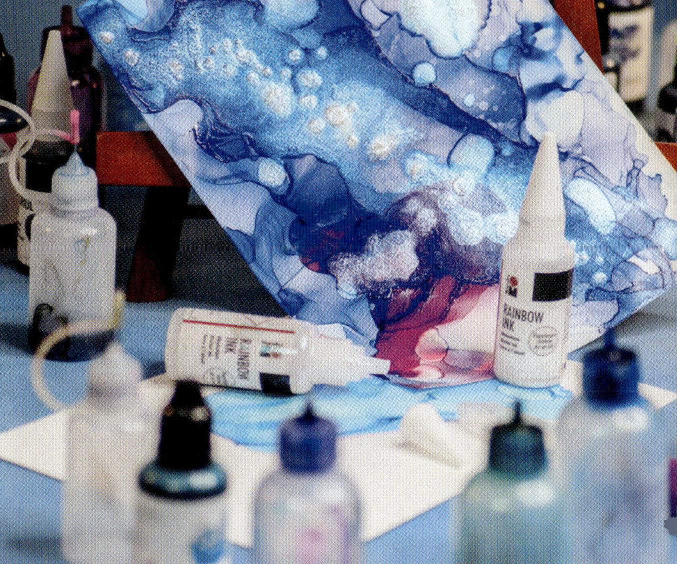

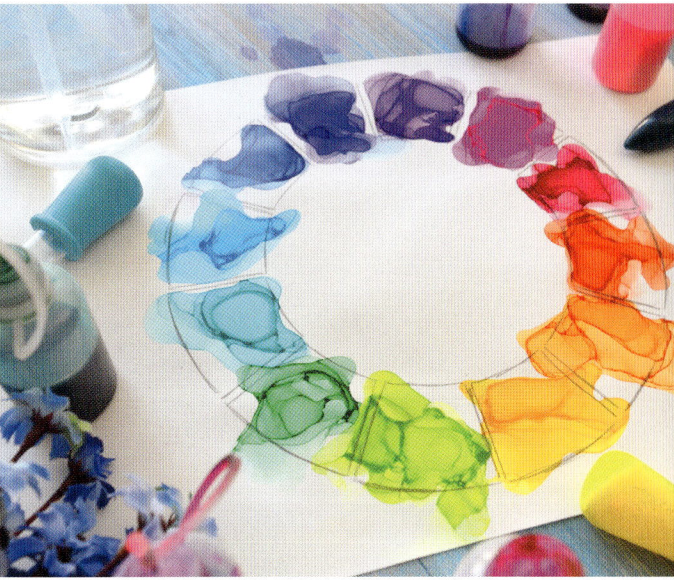

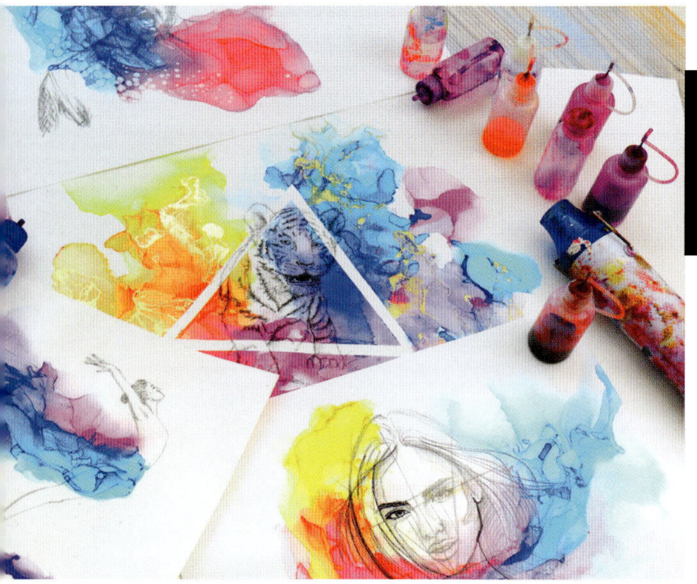

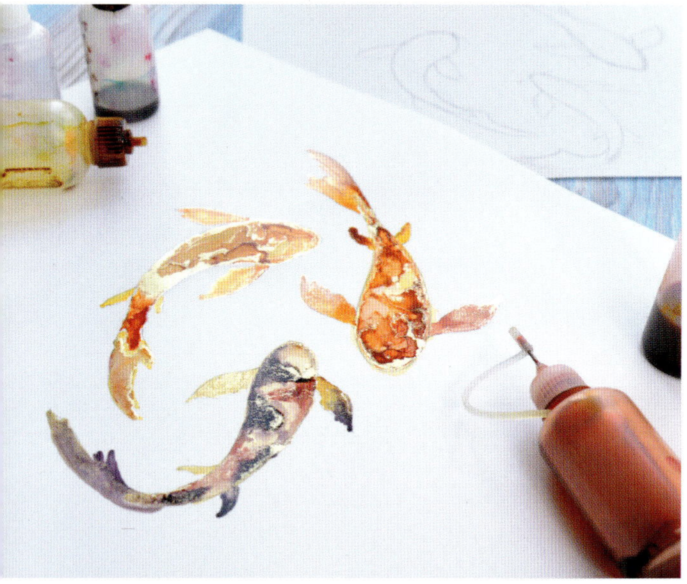

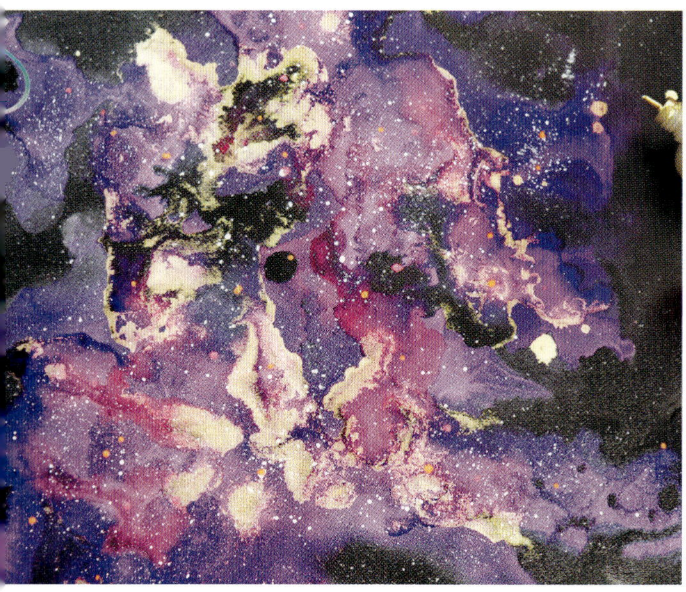

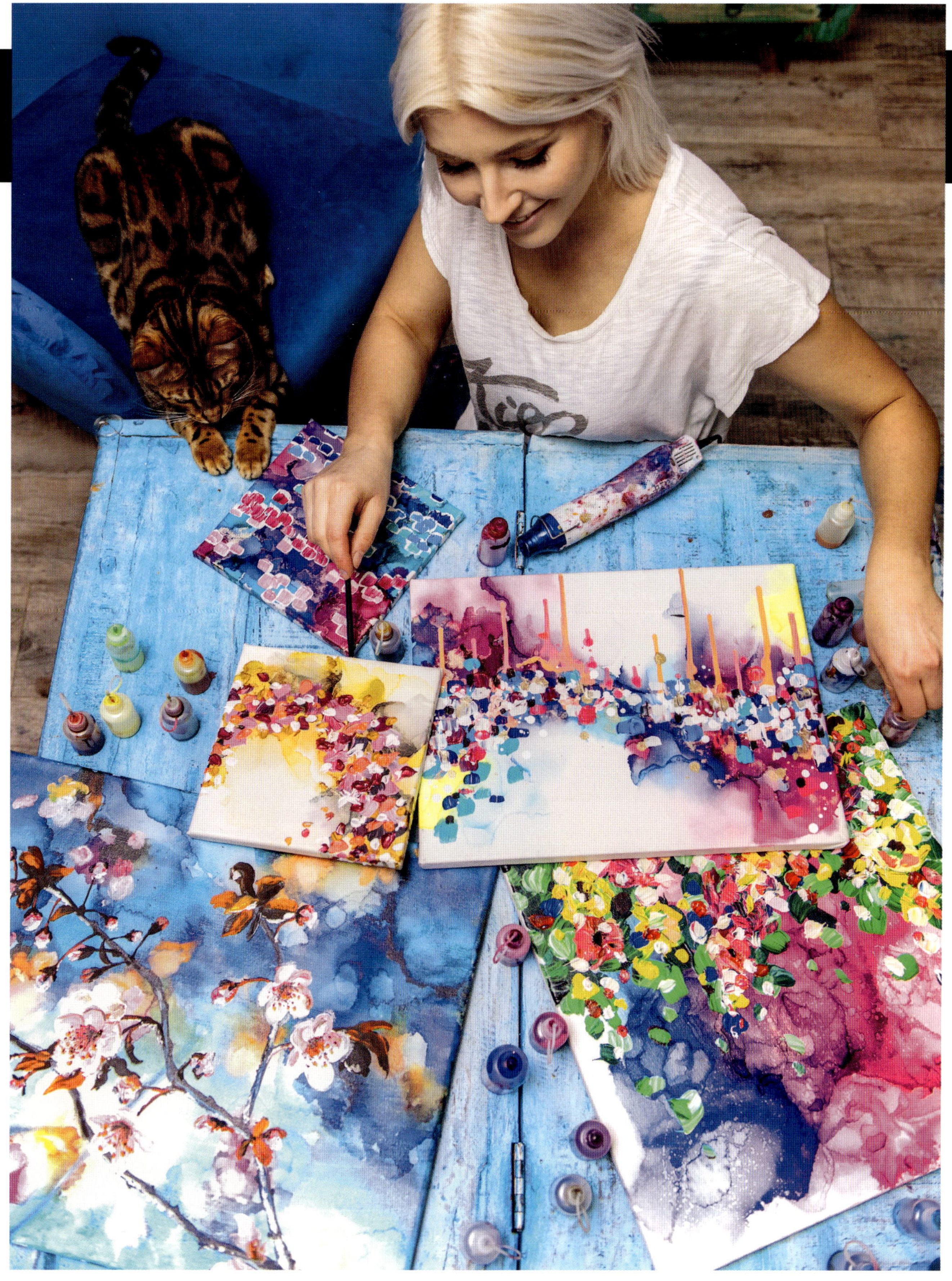

"PAINTINGS DON'T HAVE TO BE PERFECT - IT'S MORE IMPORTANT TO HAVE FUN."

Foreword

I'm so excited to share this book with you. This was the first book on the subject of alcohol ink in the German-speaking world, and it has now been translated into English. I rarely beam from ear to ear, but I'm definitely beaming now. I hope to be able to do justice to this colourful subject, because painting with alcohol ink is simply amazing!

Writing this book was great fun. It also proved to be a very intense period of painting. I barely saw the summer of 2019, especially as I also held my first major exhibition of paintings in alcohol ink and acrylic that year. So how did I get into alcohol ink?

In 2016, I came across alcohol ink at a craft workshop with my friend. Instead of using the ink to stamp like she did, I painted with the alcohol ink and started playing around with it. I left my abstract designs behind and only remembered them much later. Through Instagram, I felt inspired and encouraged by the works of many like-minded people in the US. Painting with alcohol ink is really random and abstract, as if from another world, and I wanted to continue and develop it even more.

Originally, I studied communication design and worked as a self-employed freelancer for companies and agencies. I gave all that up to start my blog "Krigelkragel", specialising in painting advice and inspiration, and DIY projects involving painting. With the blog, I want to make learning to paint simple for everyone through instructions, workshops and online courses.

Paintings don't have to be perfect - it's more important to have fun. When you're not under pressure, creativity comes naturally and makes things beautiful. Hence the name "Krigelkragel", which means 'scribble' in my native German.

To paint with alcohol ink, you don't need any classical training in art. In fact, you don't have to be able to draw or paint at all. You can start completely freely and let the alcohol ink paint along with you. You'll create beautiful, abstract images with it. It's fascinating how chance becomes a factor.

Even if you're a pro in one or more creative fields, alcohol ink can offer you thousands of new possibilities. It combines very nicely with other techniques and media, and will enrich your art.

I've packed a lot of my knowledge about alcohol ink into these pages. You will find more detailed explanations in my online courses but this book will work as a beautiful reference that opens the door to a new creative world!

Have fun with the book as you explore the amazing art of alcohol ink.

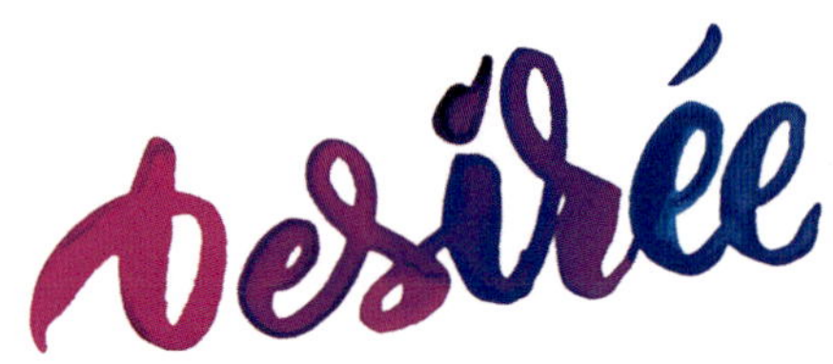

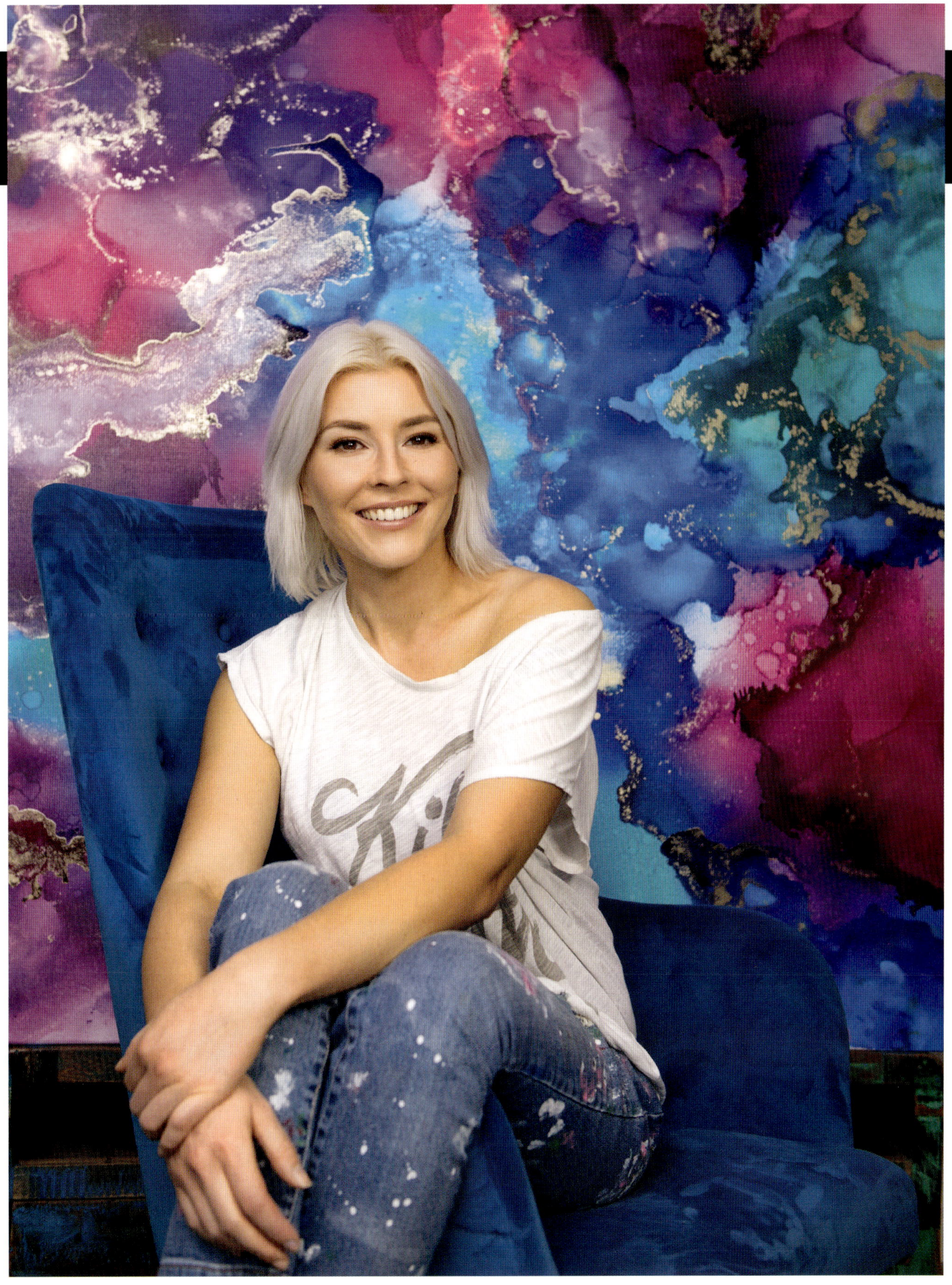

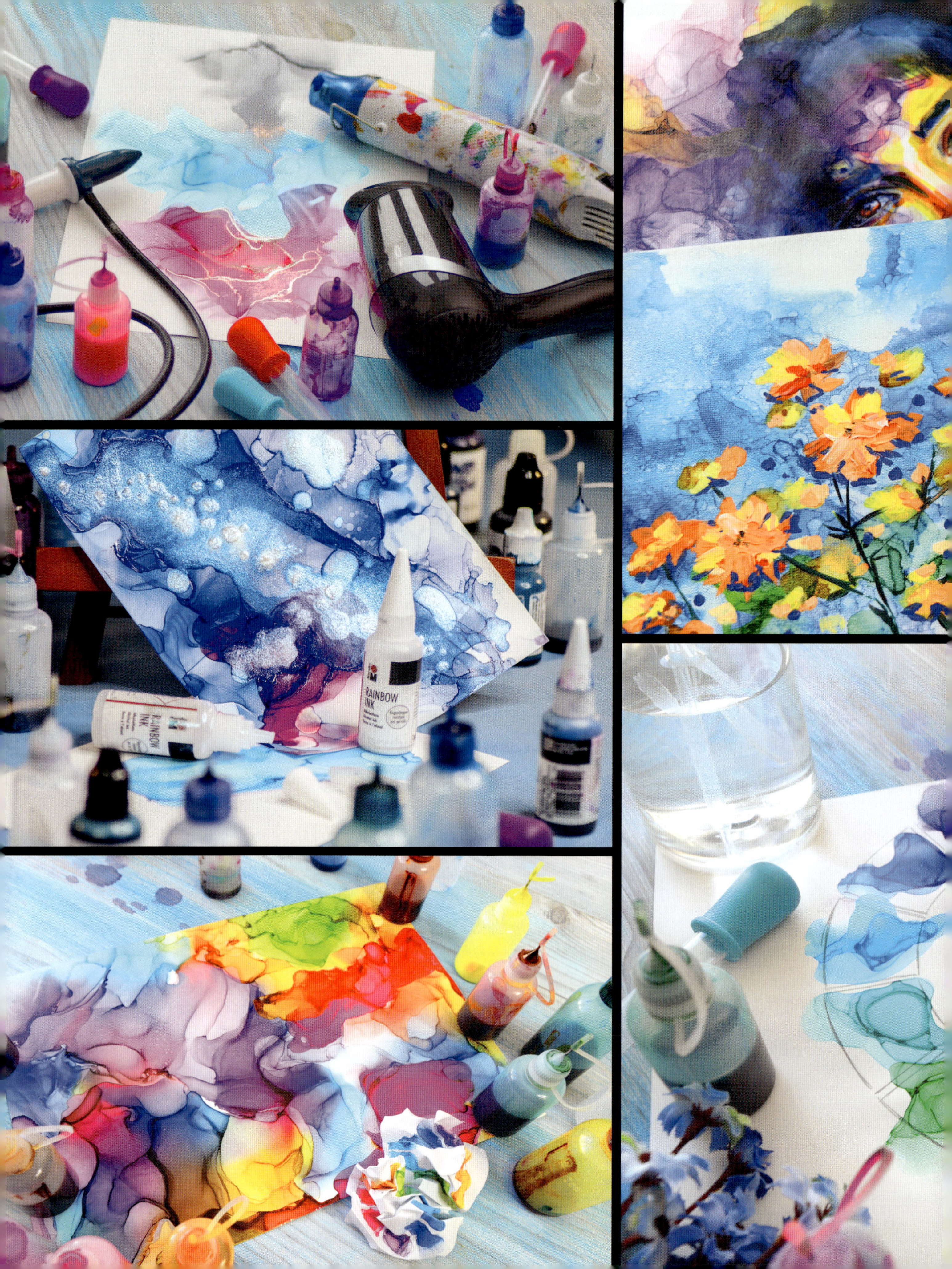

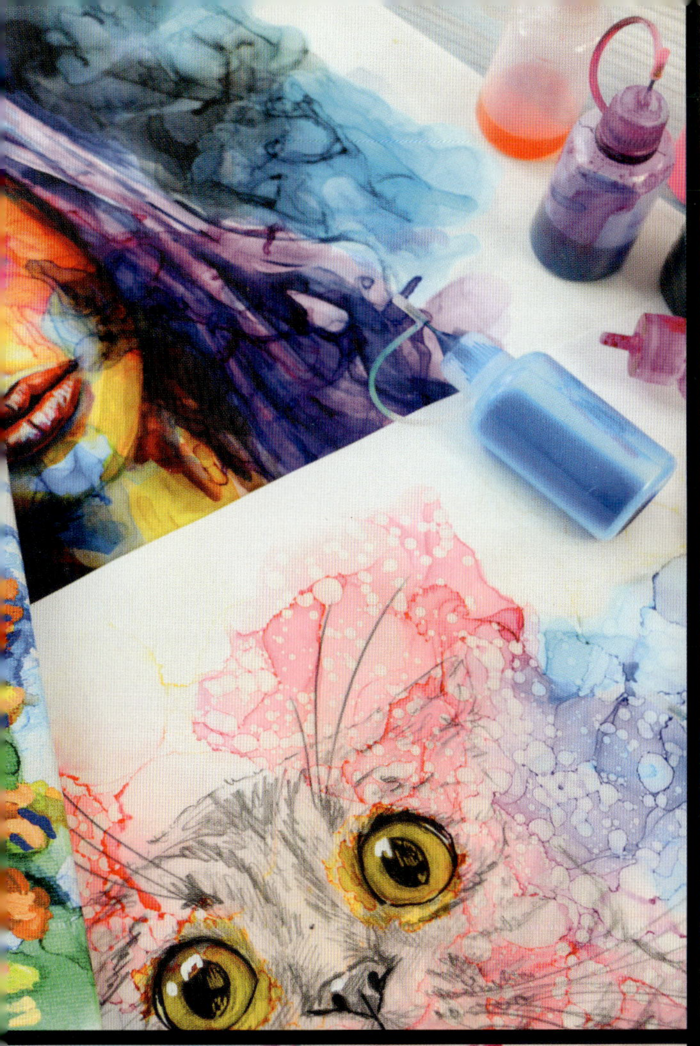

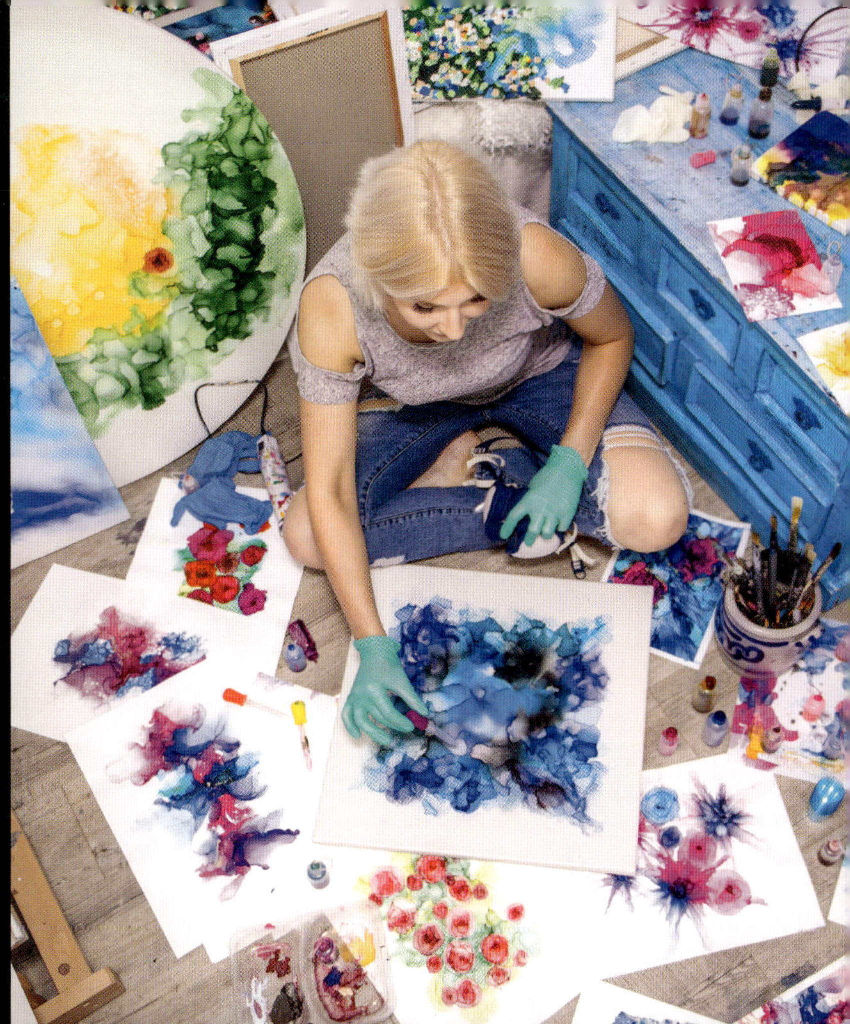

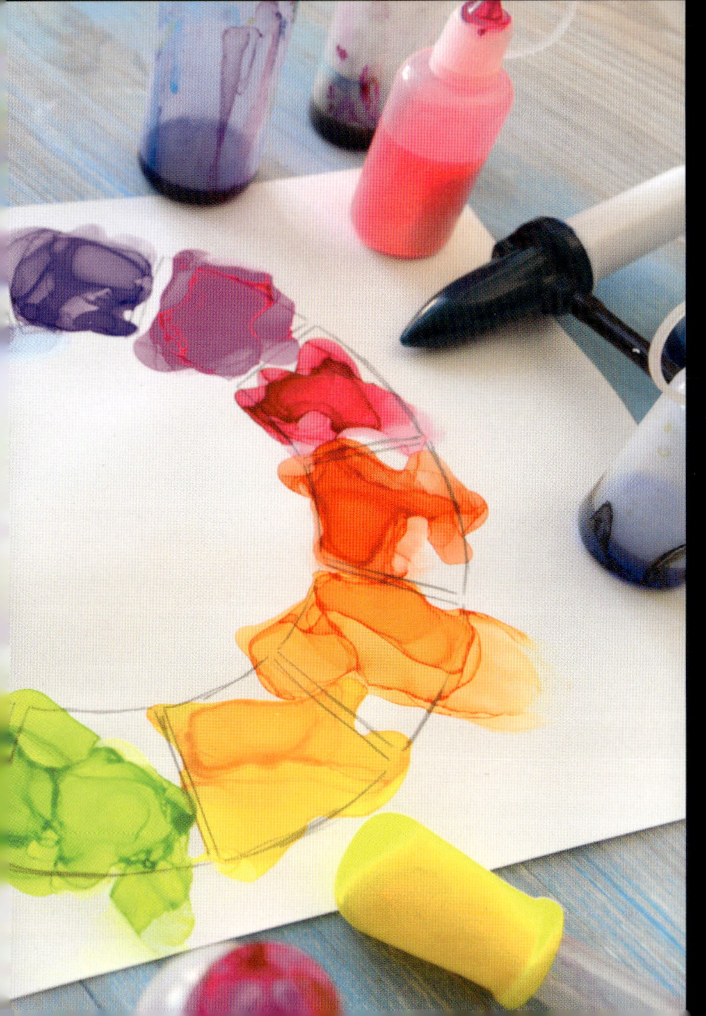

BASICS

WHAT IS
Alcohol Ink?

As the name suggests, alcohol ink is alcohol-based ink; yet what seems so simple is actually the gateway to a huge, creative and infinite universe of painting, always full of new ideas and possibilities. However, before we begin our journey of discovery, there are a few things you need to know in advance!

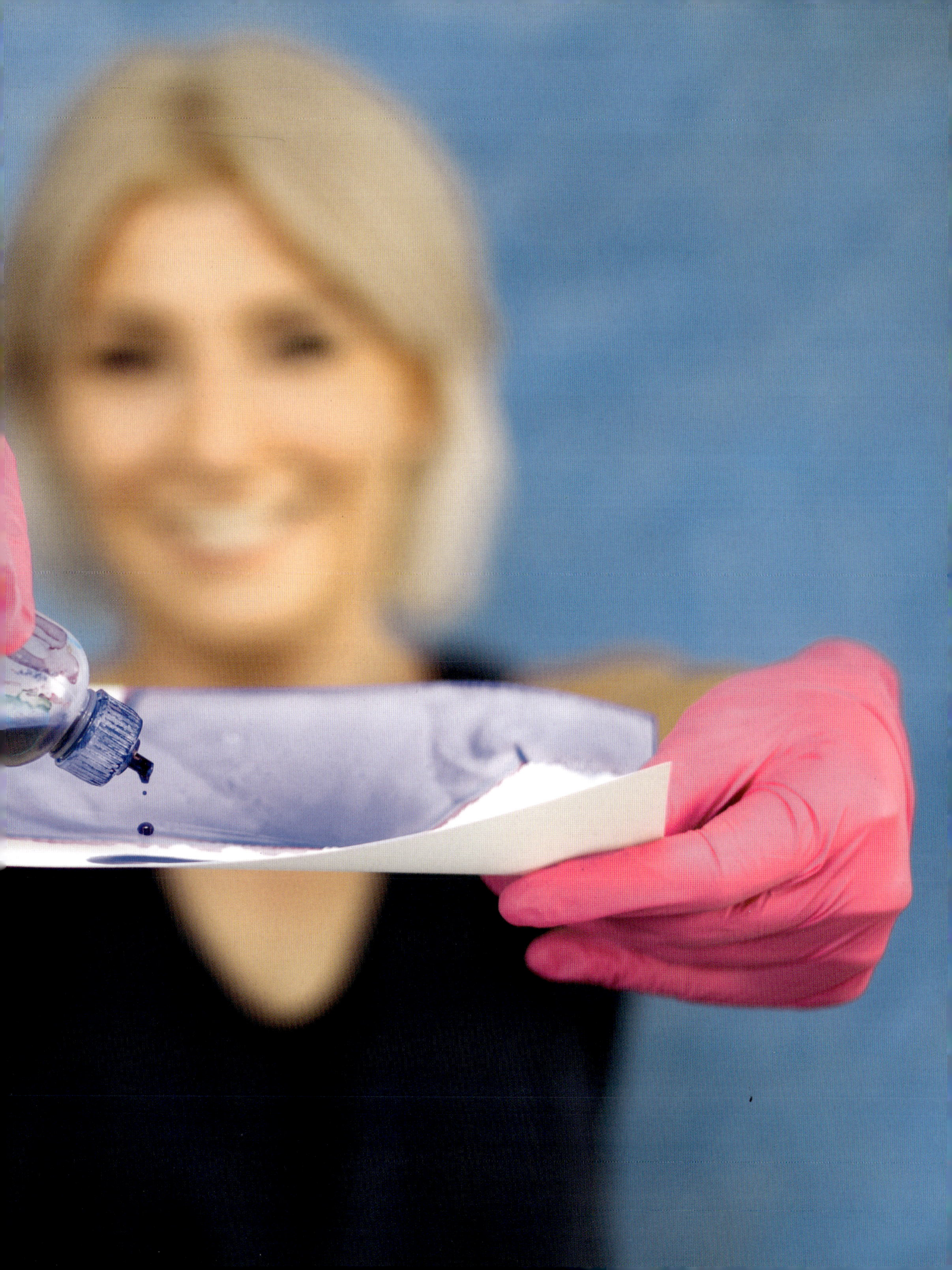

DON'T WRITE – PAINT!

Alcohol ink is a very fluid paint medium, usually used to paint abstract, colourful images, and the techniques I will describe in the following pages could be said to fall into the category of 'fluid art'. The principle of fluid art is to paint in a 'flowing' and completely wet state. Alcohol ink is moved over the painted surface with air using a hairdryer, hot-air blower, airbrush or similar. It's fascinating how chance plays a role in every painting.

This form of painting originates from the US, where alcohol ink is used for rubber stamping, in the world of card-making and scrapbooking, was used in a different way.

PAINTING WITHOUT PRESSURE

It's no wonder that the technique is so popular. With alcohol ink, anyone can create beautiful, abstract paintings without any classical training in art. You don't even have to be able to draw or paint in proportion, or have the loveliest handwriting. Everyone can do it, including you.

AMAZING VERSATILITY

You may be wondering, 'And where are we heading with it now?'. The answer lies in the complexity and versatility of alcohol ink. In this book, I'll show that with alcohol ink you can paint not only in an abstract style, but in many other ways too. You can paint objects with it, colour in illustrations, and combine it with hand lettering. Finally, I'll show you how awesome alcohol ink is for DIY projects, painting on to a variety of surfaces other than paper.

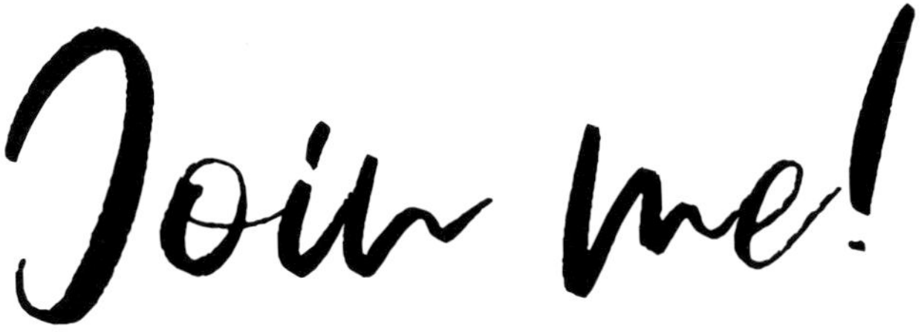

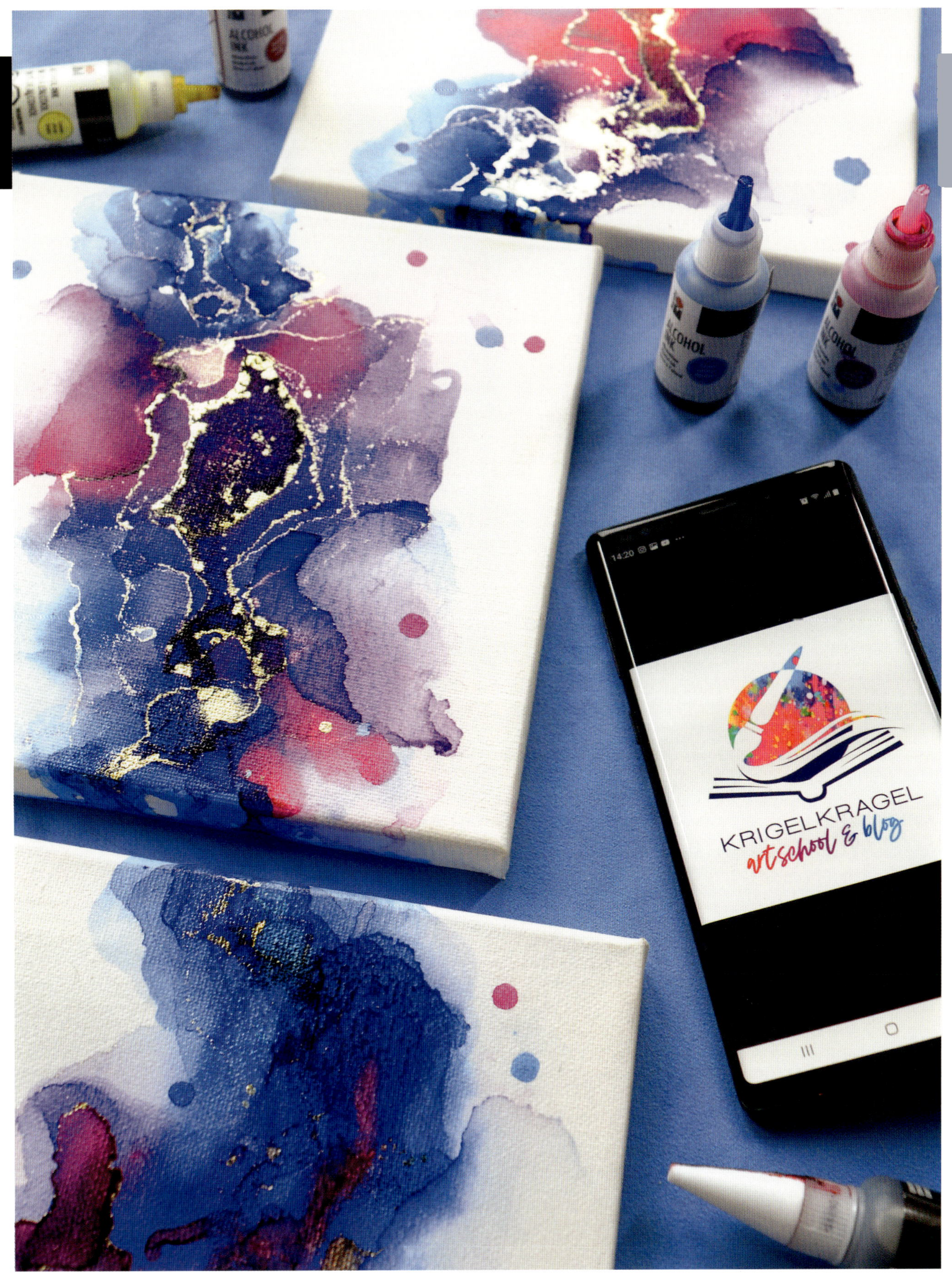

KRIGELKRAGEL
artschool & blog

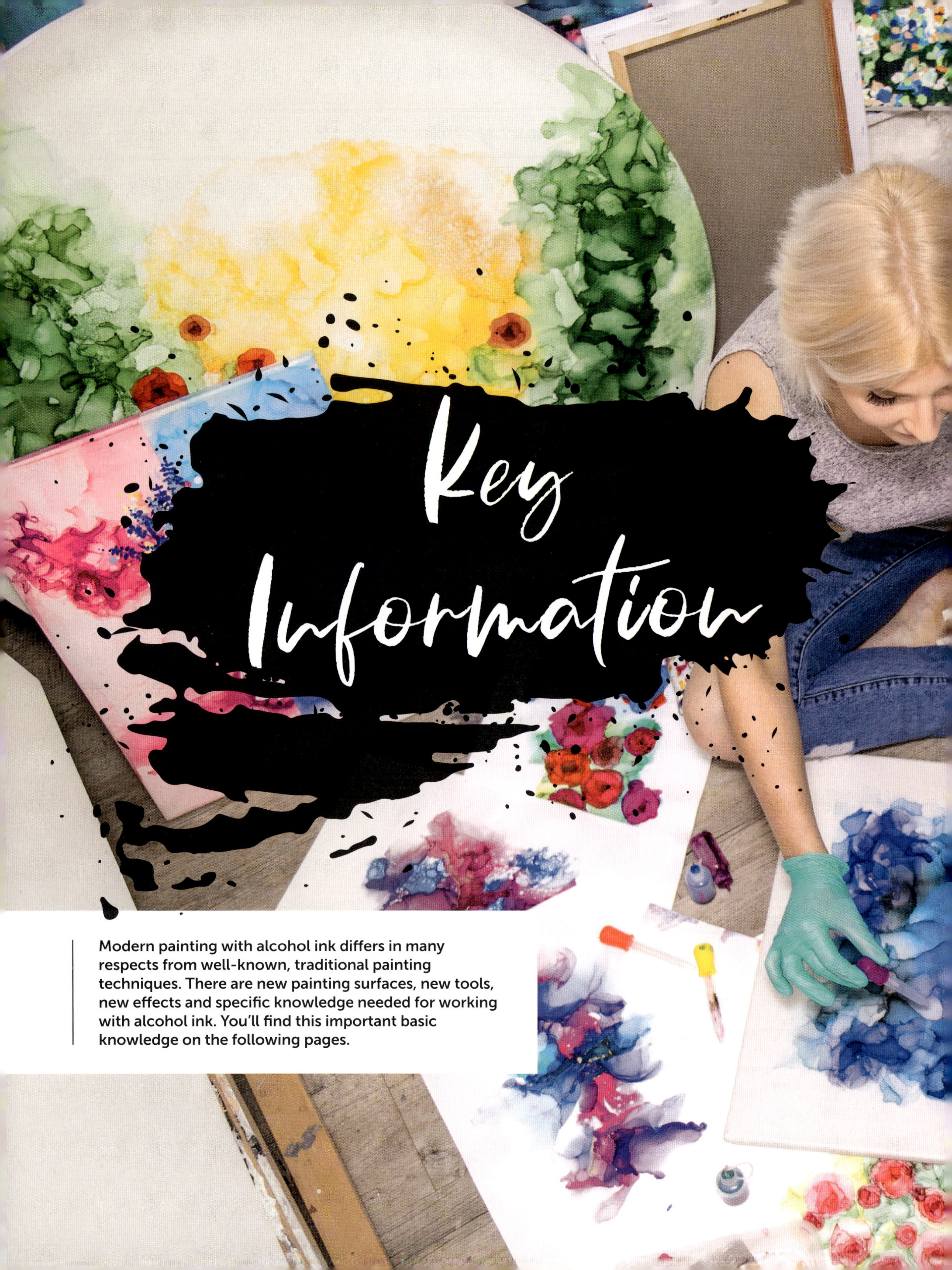

Key Information

Modern painting with alcohol ink differs in many respects from well-known, traditional painting techniques. There are new painting surfaces, new tools, new effects and specific knowledge needed for working with alcohol ink. You'll find this important basic knowledge on the following pages.

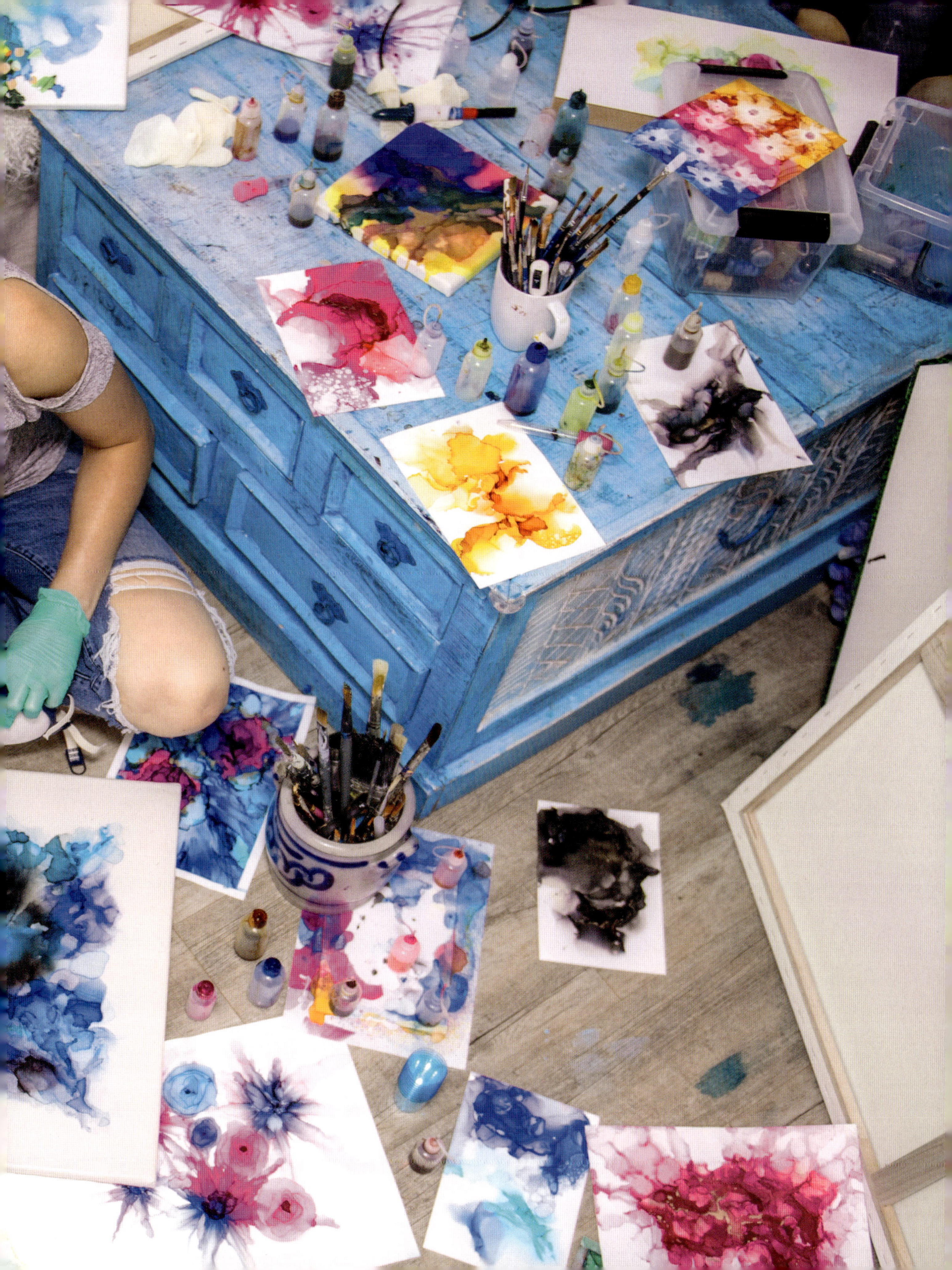

INKS

Alcohol inks usually consist of highly concentrated dye and therefore a little goes a long way. The colours available cover the entire spectrum, and are extremely intense. These inks are transparent to semi–transparent.

As well as the pure colours, there are also metallic inks, such as gold and silver. White alcohol ink is available too. Similar to the metallic colours, white is more opaque and has a slower flow than the coloured paints, which contain pigments. I'll explain later how to apply these colours.

In addition to these basic inks, there are also various paint effects, such as 'rainbow' glitter ink!

The inks are either used neat or mixed with alcohol in small applicator bottles. Each bottle can contain just one colour or a mix of colours to create a new shade entirely. As a little ink goes a very long way, I recommend mixing your own right from the start. That way, you can prepare individual colours with your chosen intensity for a much more rewarding painting experience. I practise this regularly for different styles; sometimes you need diluted alcohol ink, sometimes it's just right left neat.

The qualities of alcohol ink make it very special when compared to other painting media. One feature that is particularly important is that it can be re-dissolved with alcohol. This means that after you have created a design, the result can be further edited, decorated and designed. If something goes wrong, you can just wipe everything away with alcohol.

ISOPROPANOL

The alcohol that is used with these inks is called Isopropanol. This is high-percentage alcohol in concentrations of 90% or more. I mostly use 99.9% alcohol. You need to be very careful when working with these inks (see Precautions).

There is also a special alcohol-based paint medium for use with alcohol inks. Whether its use is relevant to you is down to your application purposes and requirements. For all the paintings and projects in this book, I have just used isopropanol.

SURFACES

To achieve the desired effects, the surface used for alcohol ink must not be absorbent. It's best when your surface is smooth and water-repellent. You can use Yupo paper (a brand of synthetic paper), matt stone paper, film and any other material with the properties mentioned. You can also seal porous or rough surfaces and discover completely new possibilities. I will explain how to do this later.

TOOLS

For painting with alcohol ink, the equipment has less to do with paintbrushes, and much more to do with air. In the Materials & Equipment section, I explain in detail about using a hairdryer, hot-air blower, airbrush and all the other aids.

SEALING

Protecting your finished work is extremely important to shield it from ultraviolet (UV) light that could cause fading over time. Apply a layer of varnish to the work; in some cases, a layer to protect against scuffs and damage is also useful. You can do this by applying a coat of clear varnish or epoxy resin - this protects your work and also refines it. You will find a section on epoxy resin finishes later in this book.

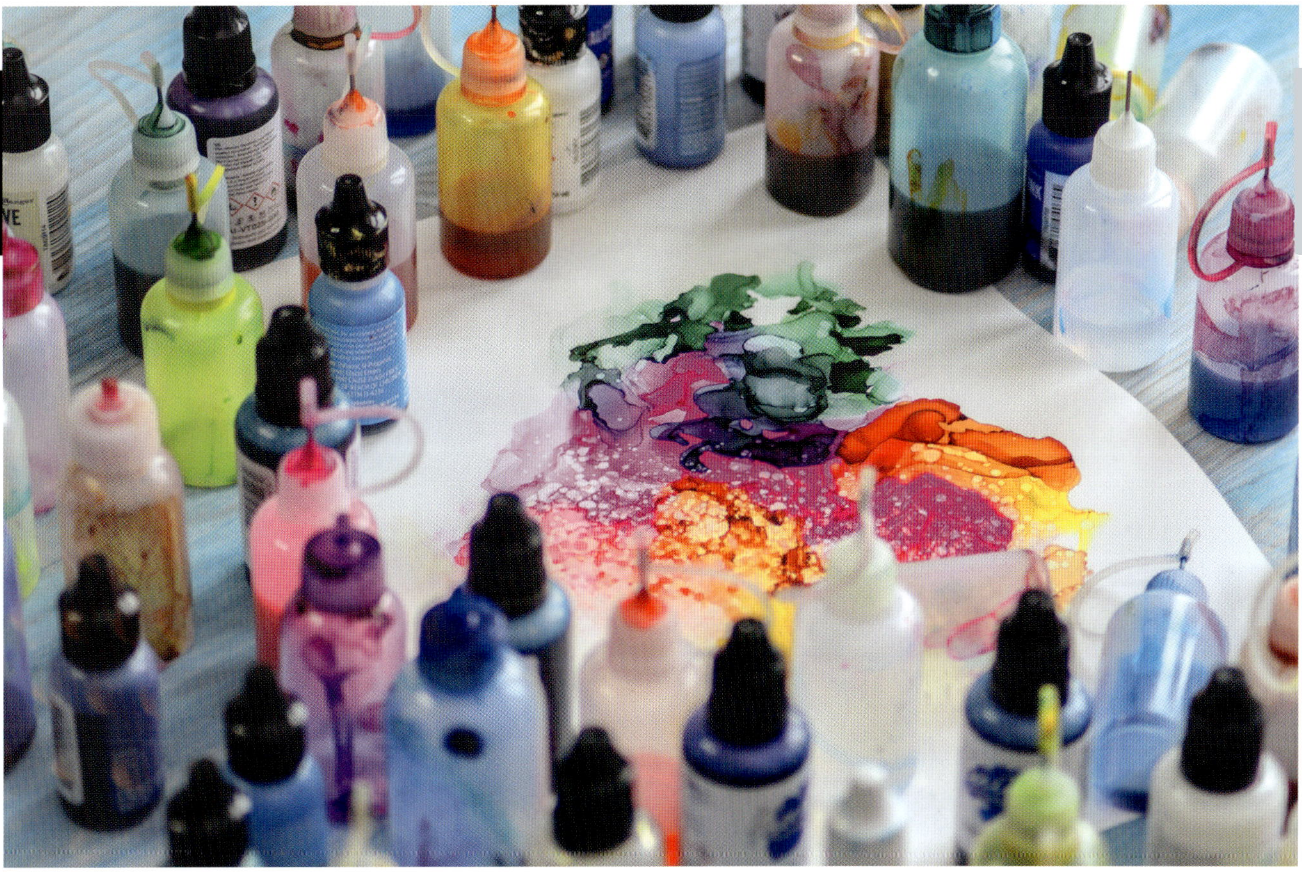

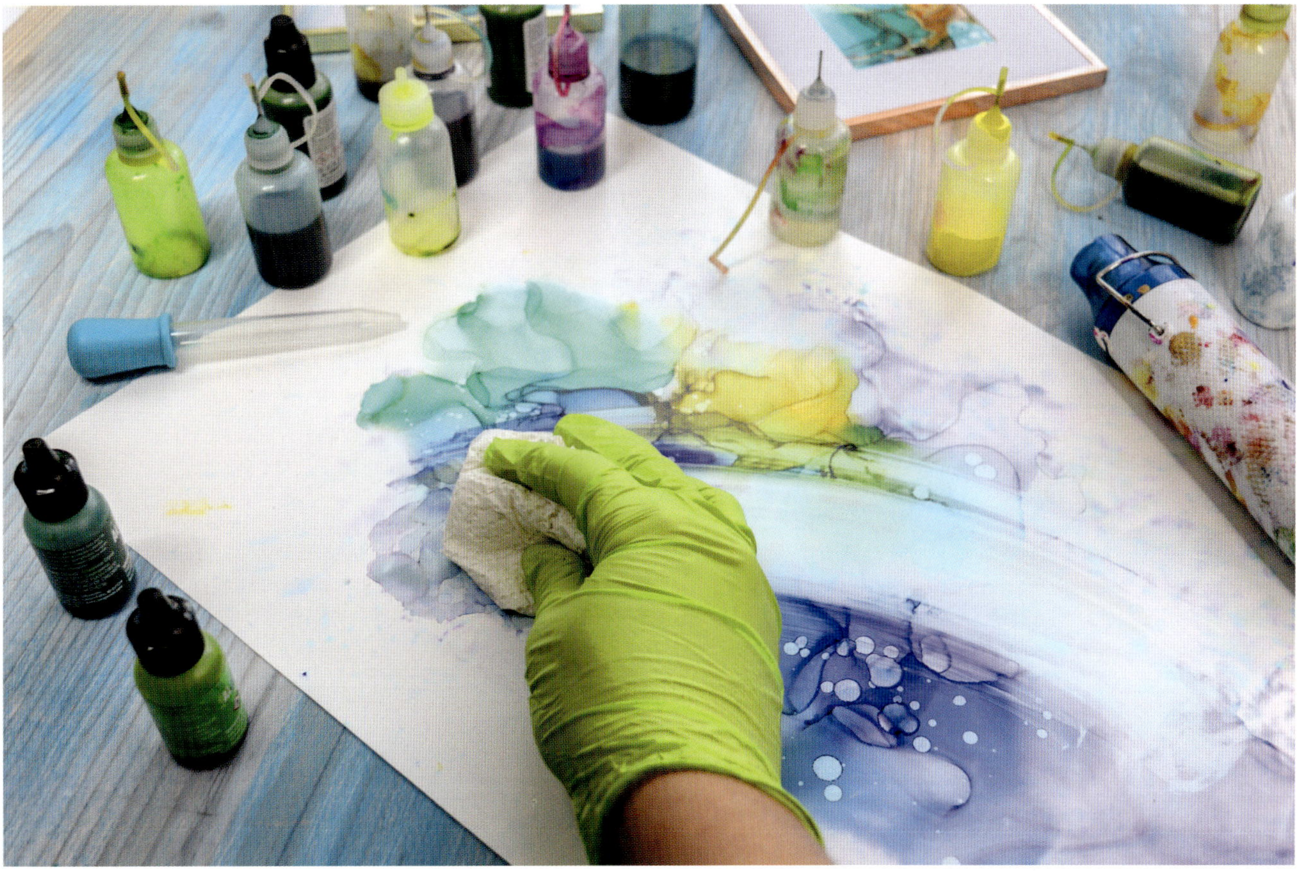

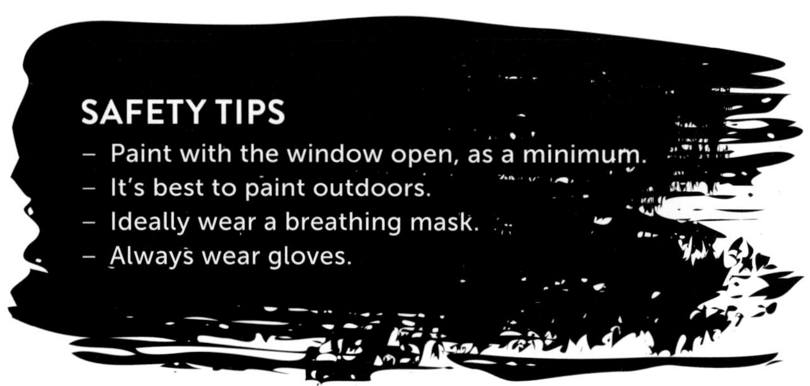

PRECAUTIONS

You should be aware that painting with alcohol ink is something that is only suitable for adults. The paints should only be used with protective measures in place, such as wearing gloves, opening a window (as a minimum), and preferably also wearing a breathing mask. The same caution applies here as for painting with varnishes. Under no circumstances does alcohol ink belong in children's hands. Even under supervision! Even the presence of children when you're painting with alcohol ink is best avoided.

The reason for these precautions is that alcohol evaporates at much lower temperatures than water – even at room temperature, even when it's liquid. Because of this quality, it means that when you paint with alcohol ink, there are always vapours around you. This isn't bad in itself at low concentrations, but with alcohol ink, you usually paint wet on wet. The wet alcohol ink is blown with a hairdryer or airbrush, which speeds up the drying process, creating more vapour in the air. Also when you're painting, you're inevitably positioned above your work. Our body absorbs alcohol not only through our stomach, but also through our skin and mucous membranes in our noses, mouths and eyes. Alcohol vapours enter the blood and have similar effects to drinking alcohol. Of course, the effects depend on how long, how intensely and how often you paint with alcohol ink.

This explains why your workspace should at least be well ventilated, and why a mask that filters vapour, not just particles of dust, and gloves are essential. See more about the safety kit in the Equipment and Workspace section. It therefore follows that children should have nothing to do with painting with alcohol ink! Similarly, pregnant women should refrain from painting with it too.

Despite the requirements to take these precautions, there are thousands of enthusiastic alcohol ink painters. The small effort needed for your own protection is more than outweighed by the captivating painting experience and the ingenious results. Alcohol ink is a vibrant painting medium that always challenges and surprises creative people.

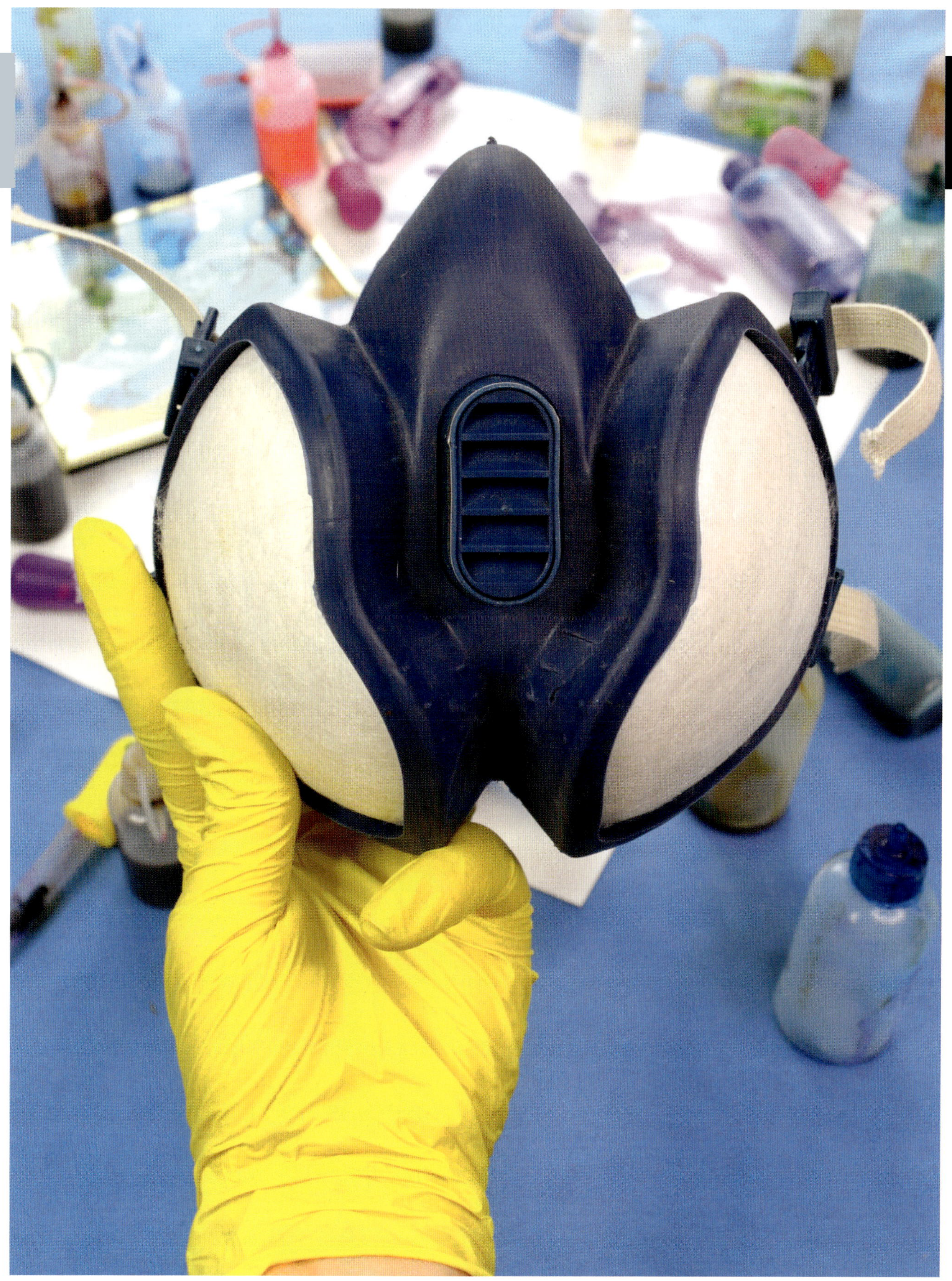

Materials & Equipment

When painting with alcohol ink you will need special materials, which you should have to hand, in order to be able to start your new works of art quickly and easily. I have summarised the standard equipment needed for alcohol ink and for your painting environment in this chapter.

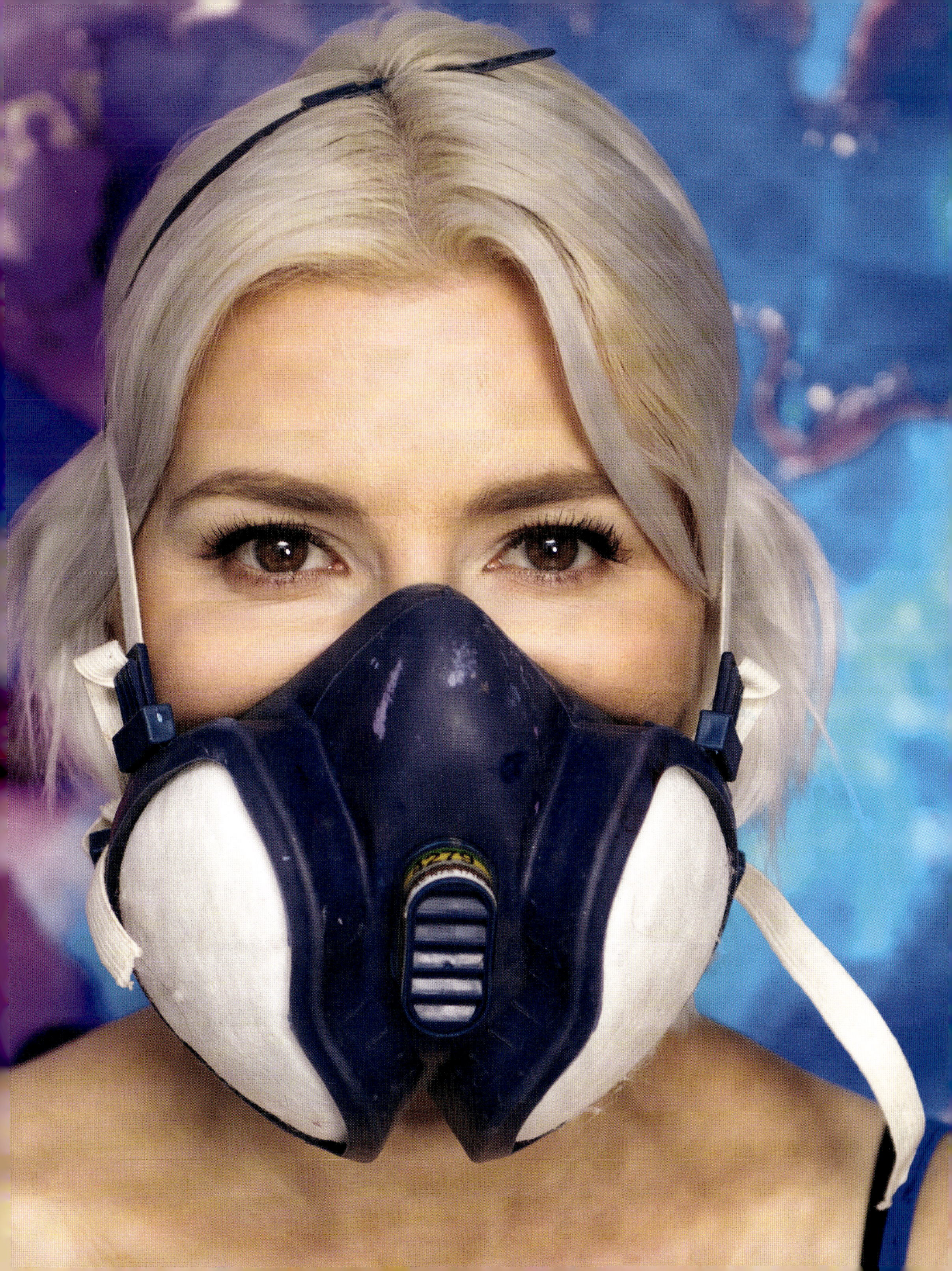

PAINT

To start with, you only need one colour. It then gets more interesting with two complementary or analogous colours. I'll explain more about this in the Colour Combinations chapter. If you're as enthusiastic about painting as I am, you'll quickly realise that you simply need all the colours!

PAINTING MEDIUM

You can obtain isopropanol from manufacturers and retailers who specialise in flow medium, or you can buy neat isopropanol. Either way, the alcohol is just as important as the paint itself. This is what will allow you to achieve the various effects. Paint and alcohol go hand in hand in this painting technique. You don't need water.

PAINTING SURFACE

The effects you can achieve with alcohol ink are most easily created on smooth, non-absorbent materials, such as the following:

YUPO, STONE PAPER AND FILMS are perfectly suited. Yupo paper has a slightly shiny surface. Stone paper is matt. I have tested other materials and have found that transparent film, lamination film and over-head projector films also work very well. They're ideal for practising, but if you want to sell your work it's best to use Yupo paper or something similar that is acid-free and will stand the test of time.

GLASS, PLASTIC AND CERAMIC are also suitable painting surfaces for alcohol ink. After painting, items for daily use should be sealed with varnish that protects against knocks, as well as with UV protective varnish. Some varnishes are adequate for this purpose, but epoxy resin is ideal. However, bear in mind that both products are no longer certified as food-grade. This applies to surfaces covered with alcohol ink too, so don't put food on a painted surface.

NORMAL PAPER AND CANVAS can also be painted with alcohol ink. To achieve the desired effects, you need to prepare these surfaces. In the Paint Surface Preparation section, I'll show you, among other things, how to properly seal watercolour paper, so that you can paint on it with alcohol ink. You'll find instructions for designs on paper and canvas too.

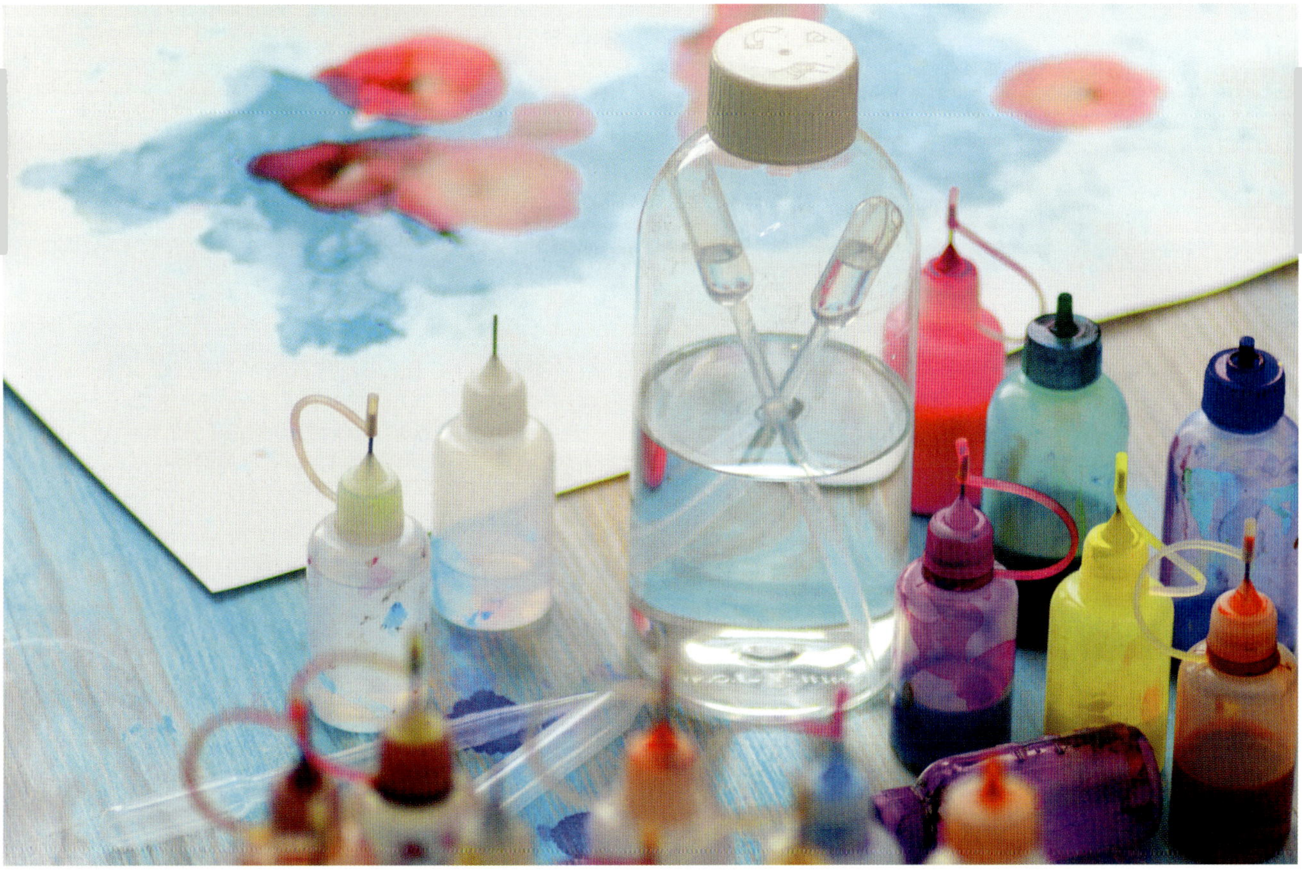

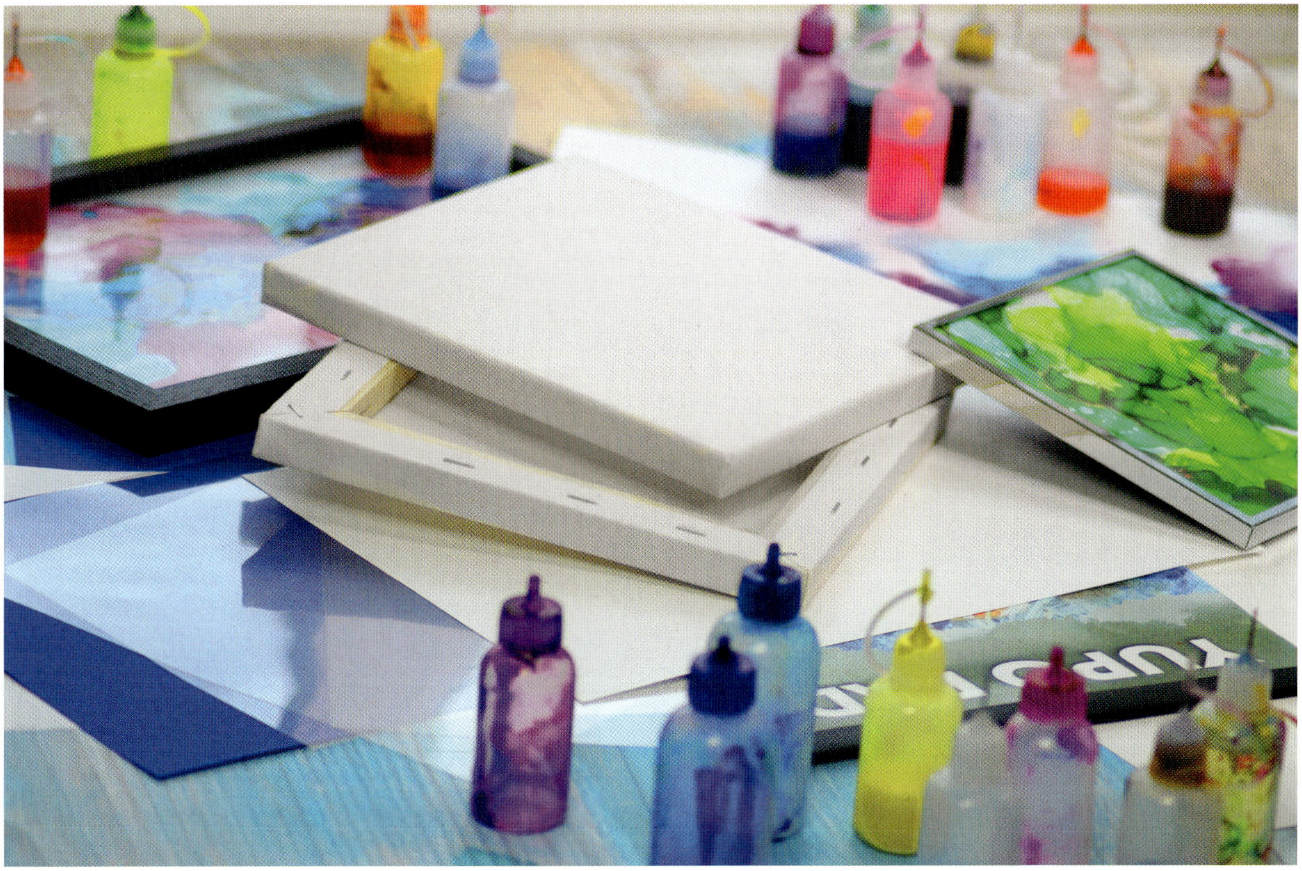

TOOLS

PIPETTES, also known as droppers, are needed to mix the ink and make drops or special effects on your painting.

APPLICATOR BOTTLES are very useful for holding ink at your desired intensity. They allow you to paint more sparingly, have more control over the result at the start and achieve different results from those of more direct, neat applications.

PAINTBRUSHES are used for creating effects when using alcohol inks. Simple, fine tip brushes are best - pointed, flat and slanted heads achieve very interesting results.

SPRAY CANS FILLED WITH ISOPROPANOL are needed for surface preparation, effects or to erase your painting. In my opinion, isopropanol is just as important as the ink.

KITCHEN TOWEL AND COTTON BUDS are often useful for wiping up excess ink and for creating different effects.

A HAIRDRYER, HOT-AIR BLOWER OR AIRBRUSH are your air painting tools. You can use them to direct the colour over the surface. A small travel hairdryer is an ideal first tool. The hot-air blower is my favourite. My airbrush is an inexpensive model designed for children, and works well.

It makes a difference whether you're blowing cold or hot air – I'll explain more about this in the Paint Application and Painting Process section.

NB Although you may be tempted to achieve the same air-blowing effect using a straw, I strongly advise against it! Most importantly, you will not be able to wear your mask as you work. In addition, you have far less control over how the paint moves. Please don't use straws!

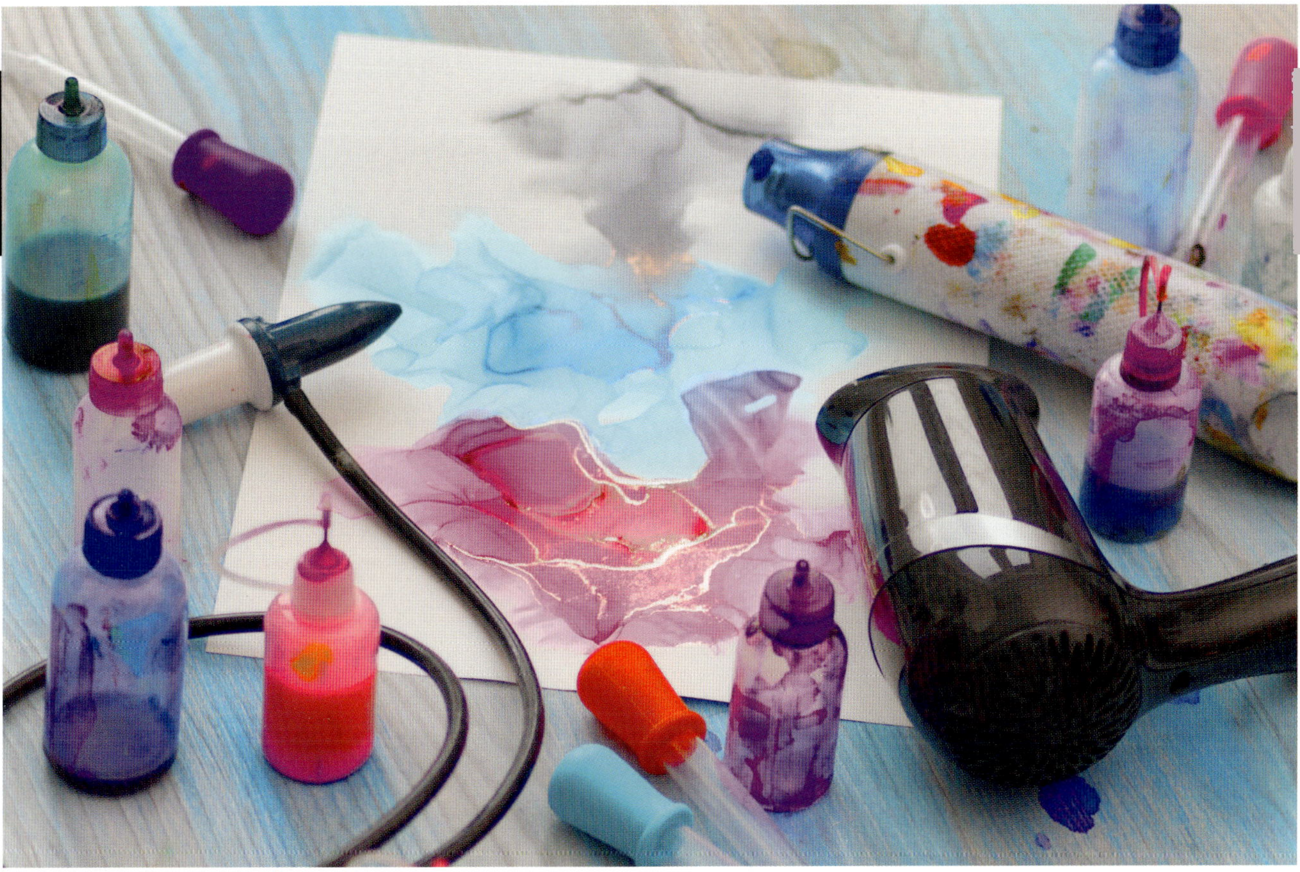

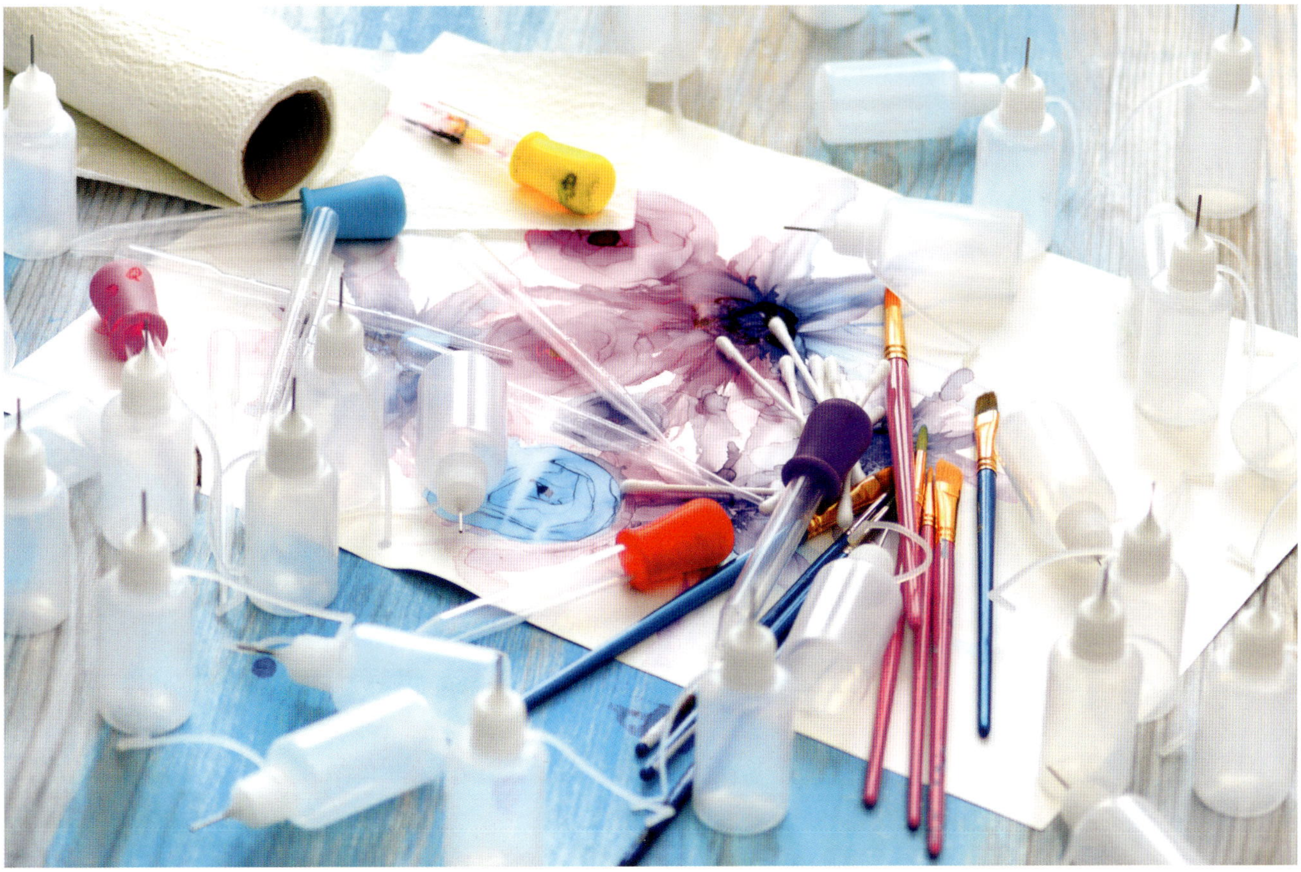

SAFETY AND YOUR WORKSPACE

Painting with alcohol ink requires certain precautions due to the nature of the paint and medium used:

A WELL VENTILATED ENVIRONMENT for painting with alcohol ink is a prerequisite. At least one open window and one fan. In the warmer months, I prefer to paint outdoors.

GLOVES are a must to protect the skin on your hands from absorption of alcohol. They also prevent hard-to-remove ink stains. Therefore, when painting with alcohol ink, please always wear gloves.

A BREATHING MASK is essential when painting with alcohol ink, especially if you paint frequently and for longer periods. In my painting courses, the rooms are well ventilated and equipped with simple breathing masks. As a permanent purchase for home, I recommend a mask that can filter both organic and inorganic gases and vapours. I always use this kind of mask, whether I'm painting for a short or a long period.

With these materials and this equipment, you're now well equipped to become an alcohol ink artist!

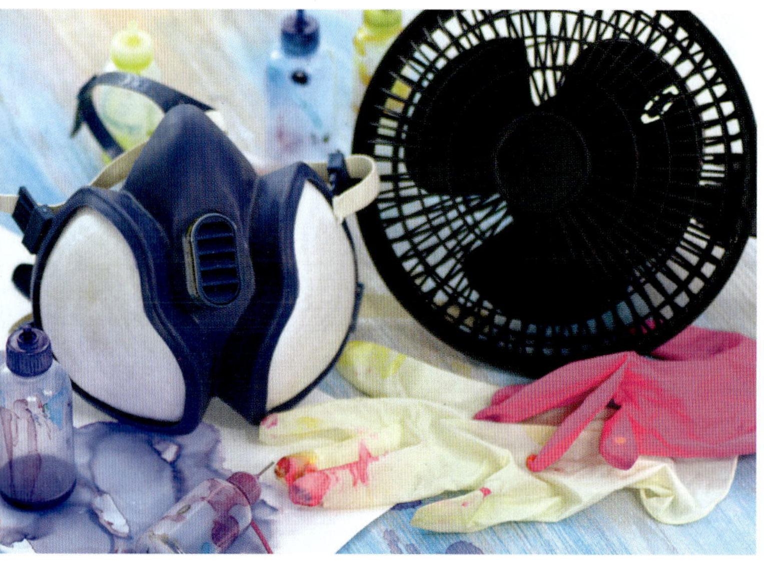

A LITTLE TIP FROM EXPERIENCE

Back at the very beginning, I tried painting with alcohol ink without a mask and in a poorly ventilated room. After a short time, I could definitely feel the effects – the lack of adequate air circulation combined with not wearing a mask meant that I inhaled and absorbed a significant amount of alcohol fumes in a relatively short space of time! It definitely wasn't fun and I learned my lesson very quickly. So work outside, or at least open a window, and always wear a mask. It's worth it for the joy of painting with alcohol ink!

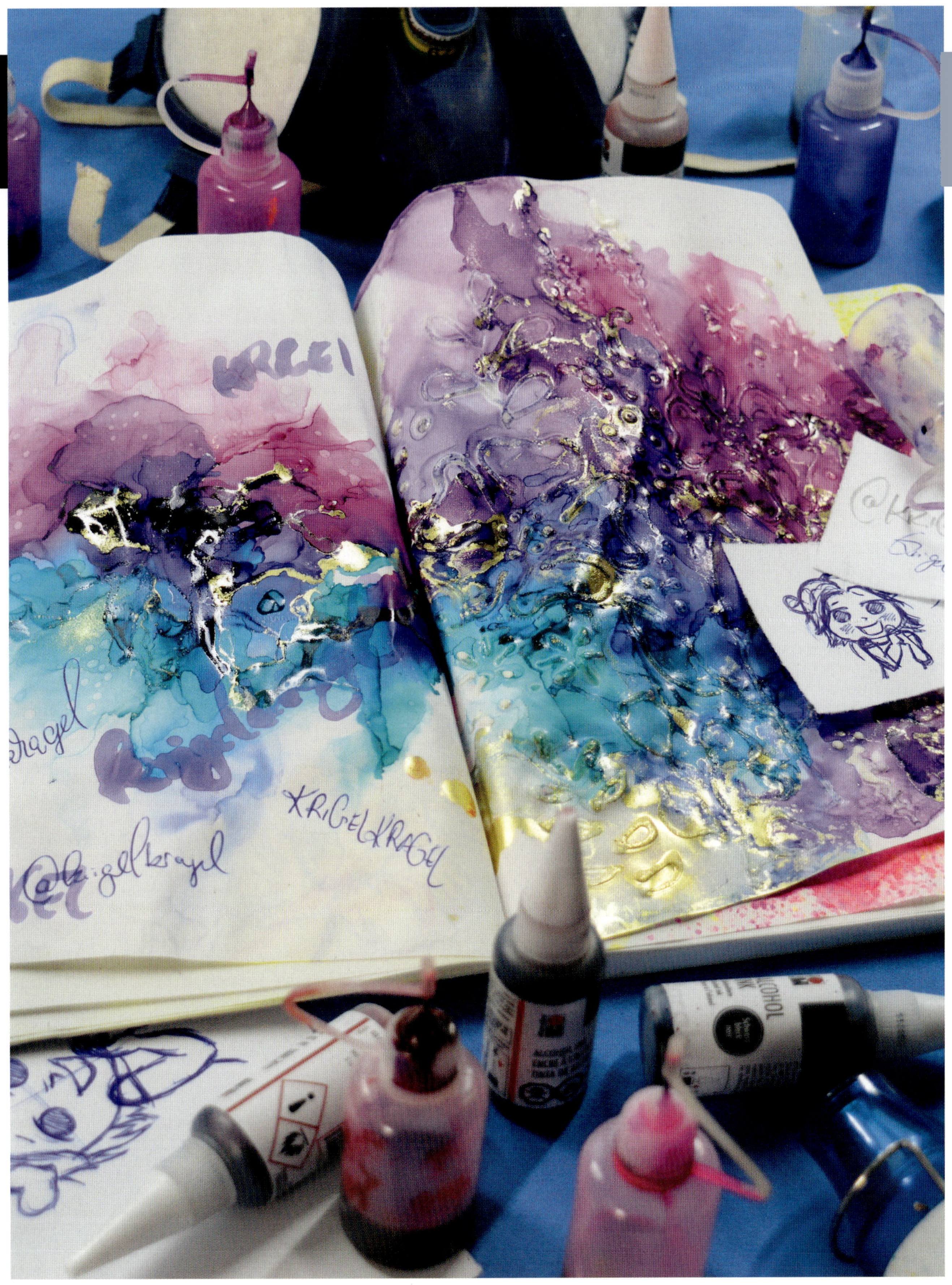

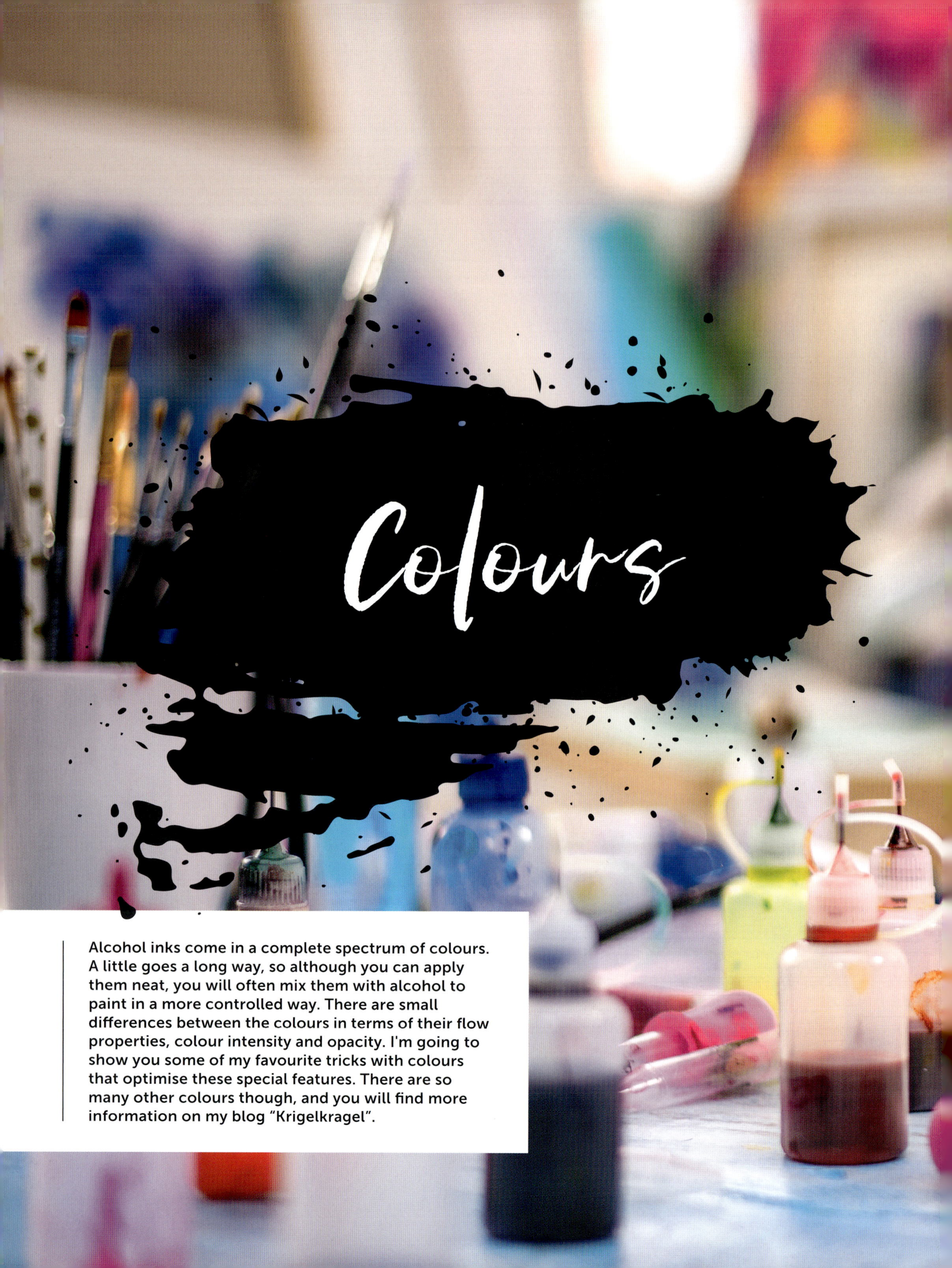

Colours

Alcohol inks come in a complete spectrum of colours. A little goes a long way, so although you can apply them neat, you will often mix them with alcohol to paint in a more controlled way. There are small differences between the colours in terms of their flow properties, colour intensity and opacity. I'm going to show you some of my favourite tricks with colours that optimise these special features. There are so many other colours though, and you will find more information on my blog "Krigelkragel".

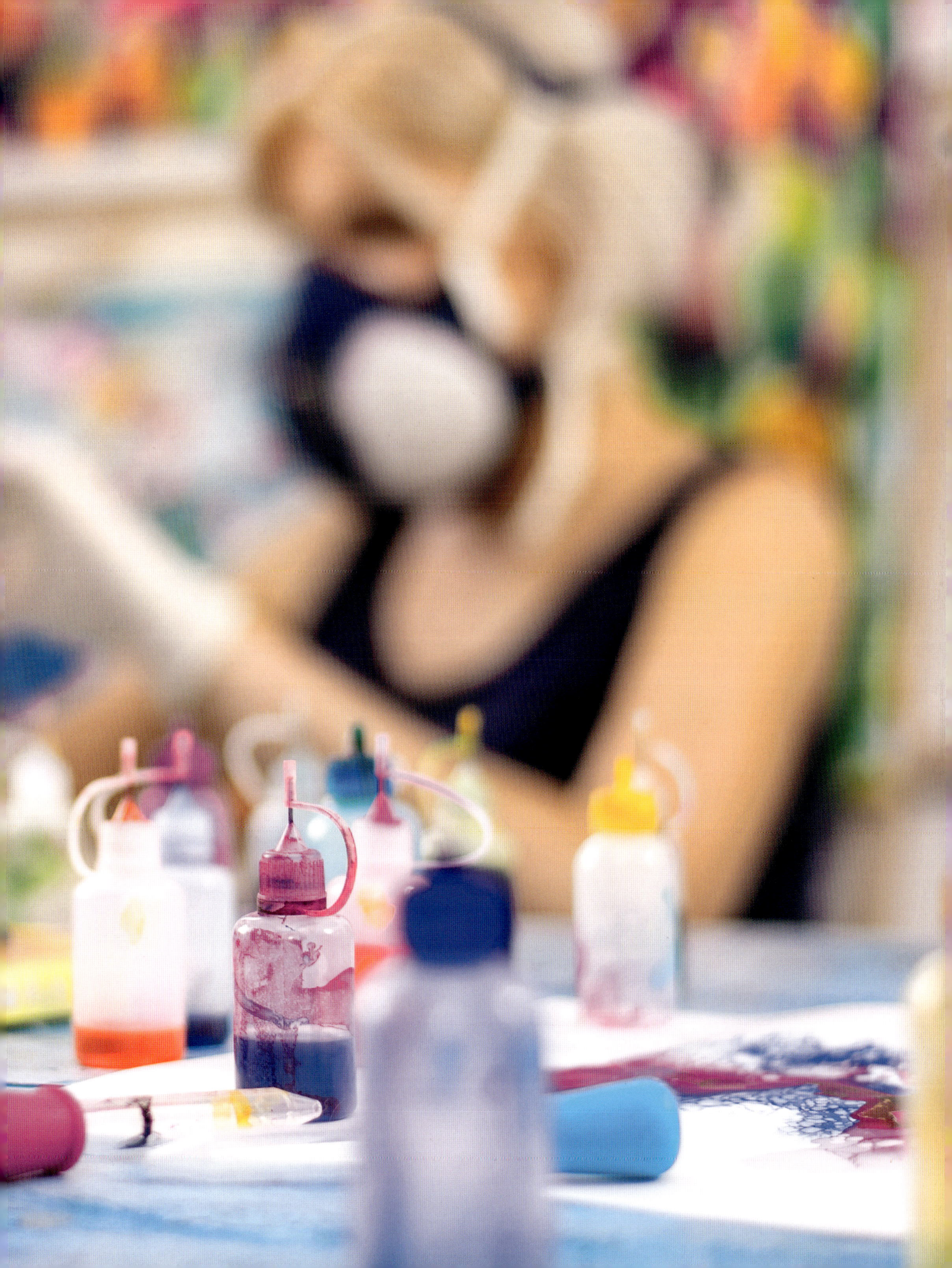

BASIC COLOUR TOOLKIT

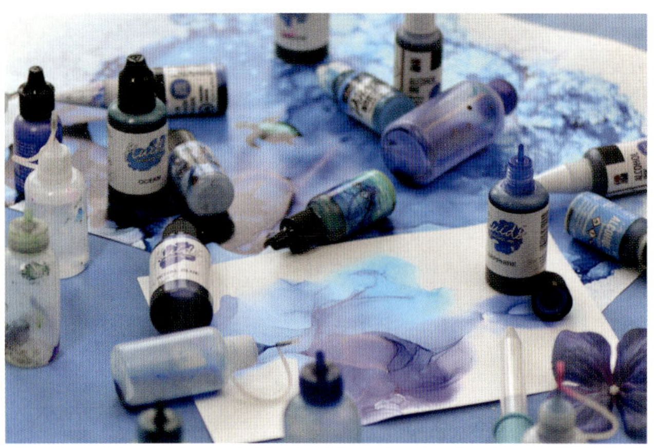

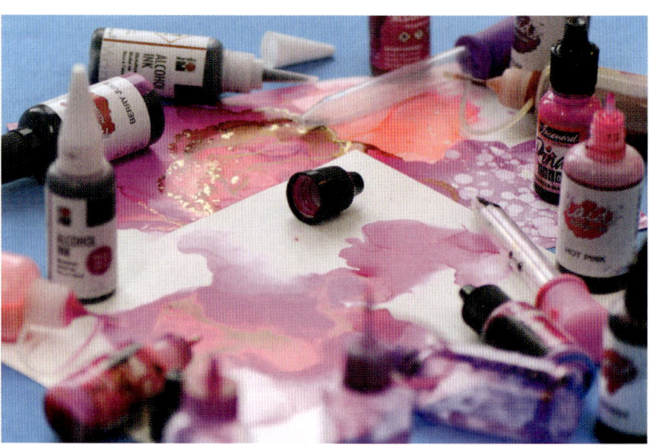

SHADES OF BLUE

Blue forms part of your basic toolkit of colours. There are shades of blue that err towards turquoise, and those that border on violet. With alcohol ink, these nuances are particularly visible.

SHADES OF MAGENTA

Sometimes the liquid alcohol ink in the bottle appears pinker than it actually is when it's dry. When dry, the shade can err towards purple. I recommend that you test and create colour charts for your pinks.

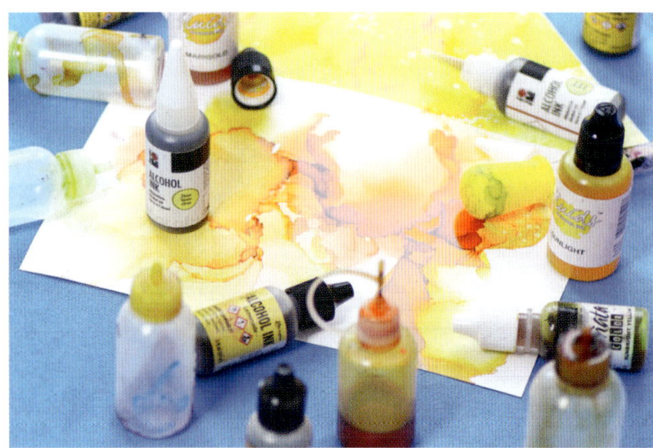

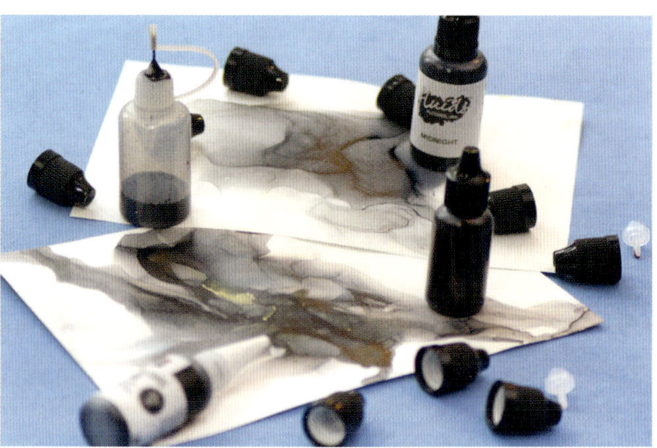

SHADES OF YELLOW

You will need at least one yellow in your essential palette, because you can use it to mix with blue to get green and with magenta to get orange.

BLACK

A little black will go a long way. It's virtually a given that this ink should be diluted. Without mixing it the Wispy effect, explained later, barely works at all.

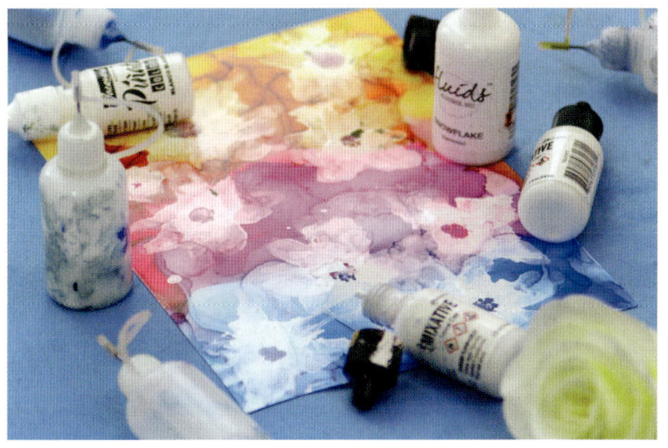

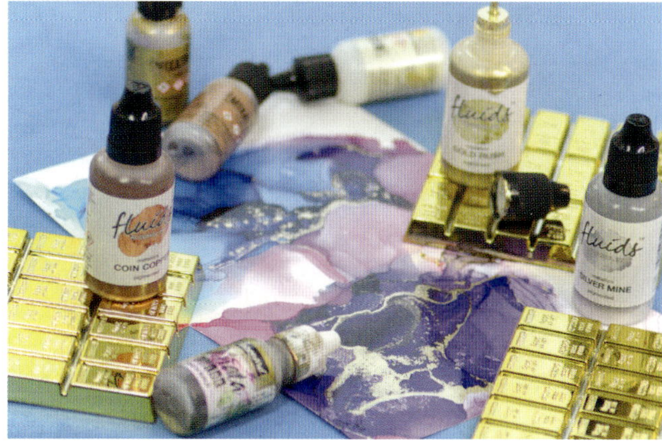

WHITE

Neat drops of white behave similarly to thin acrylic paint. White absorbs pigments from underlying layers, and is usually used as a colour effect for details. In the Special Materials chapter, I'll show you how to use white alcohol ink.

METALLIC PAINTS

I love the effects of these colours! In the chapter on Special Materials, I'll explain step by step how you can apply them in your artwork. Anyone who understands alcohol ink knows that metallic paints are of crucial importance.

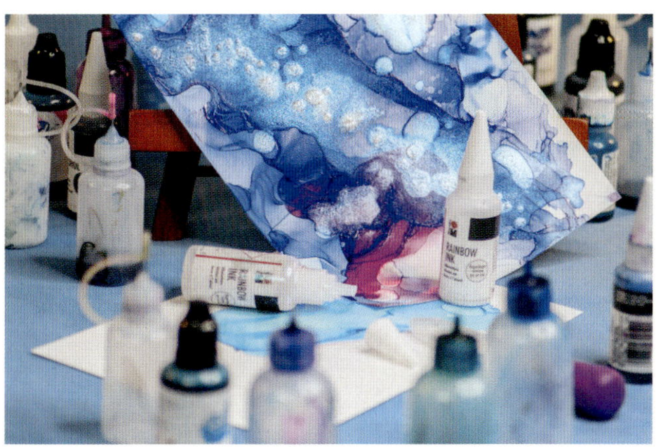

The colours I've introduced you to are just the basic palette. Besides these, there is every imaginable intermediate shade in ready-to-use bottles. Plus, you'll find every possible shade of brown and cream, purple, turquoise and grey in surprising variations ... and much more.

GLITTER PAINTS

Paints like these are used add sparkle to special projects. They can behave differently from the metallic paints, so just experiment with them.

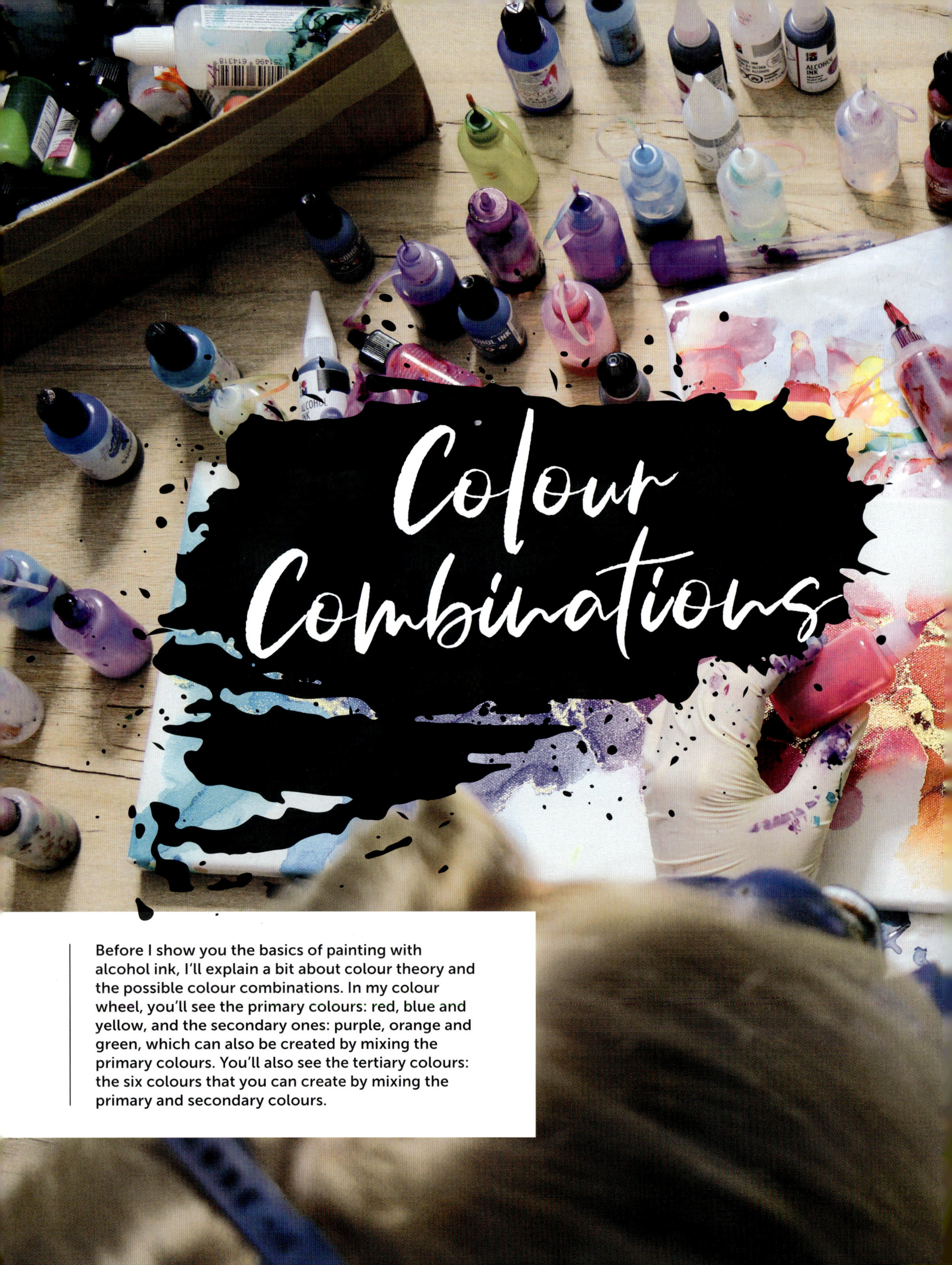

Before I show you the basics of painting with alcohol ink, I'll explain a bit about colour theory and the possible colour combinations. In my colour wheel, you'll see the primary colours: red, blue and yellow, and the secondary ones: purple, orange and green, which can also be created by mixing the primary colours. You'll also see the tertiary colours: the six colours that you can create by mixing the primary and secondary colours.

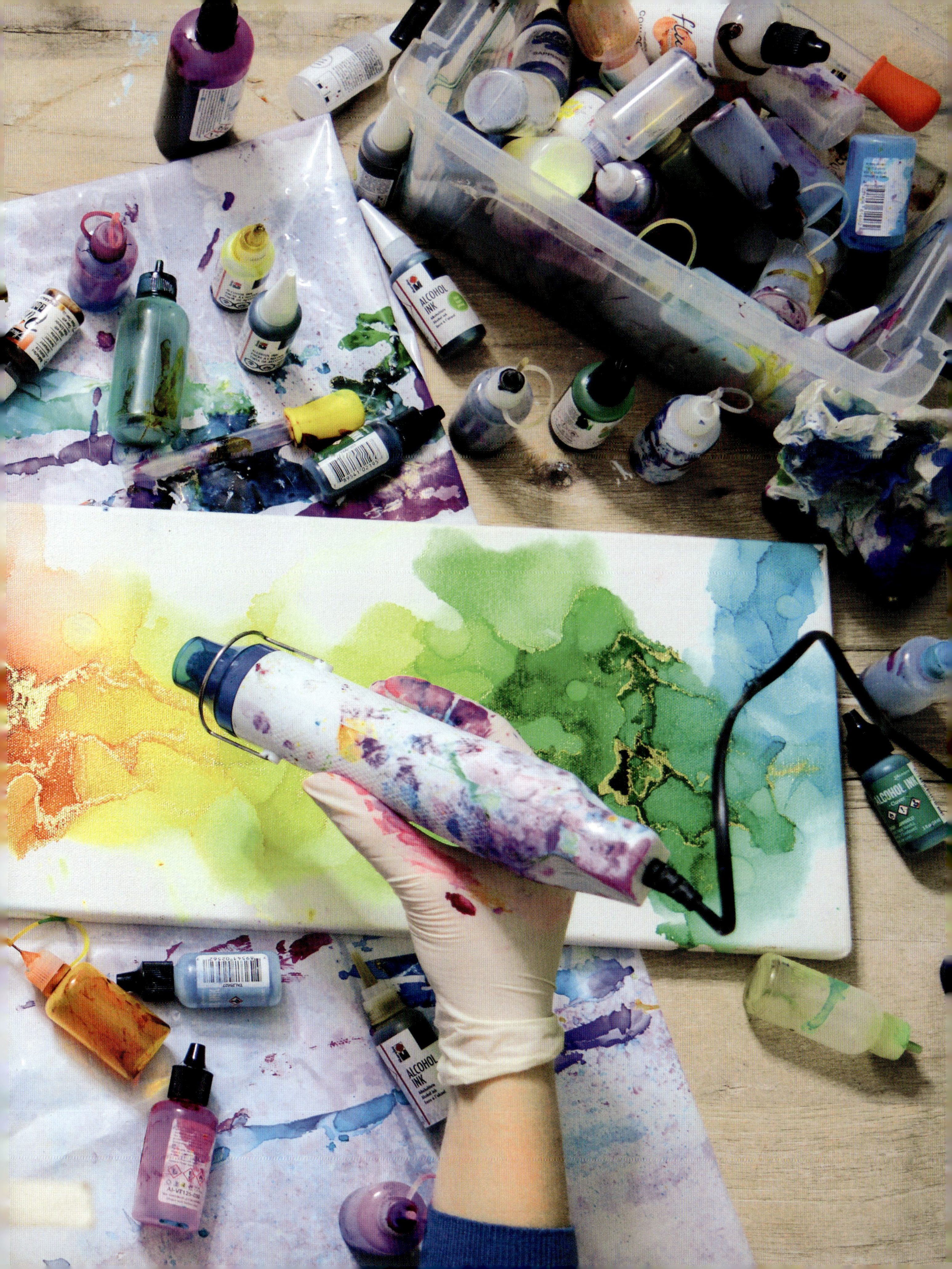

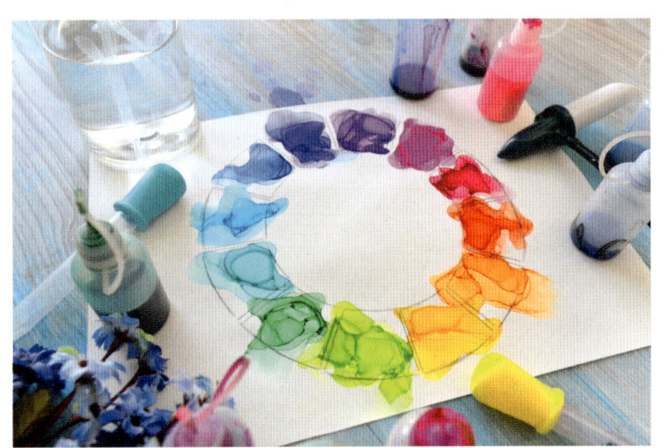

WARM AND COLD COLOURS

My colour wheel in the picture groups the warm colours on the right and the cold colours on the left. If you want to create certain effects or moods with your painting, then choose your colours from just one side of the wheel, or choose a focal point using a specific temperature. It's all about our associations with colours. Warm tones, such as red and yellow, are often associated with energy, happiness or love. Cold colours are associated with tranquillity, orderliness and intensity. A mix of temperatures can also be very effective, depending on how you position the colours. Below are classic colour combinations from the colour wheel.

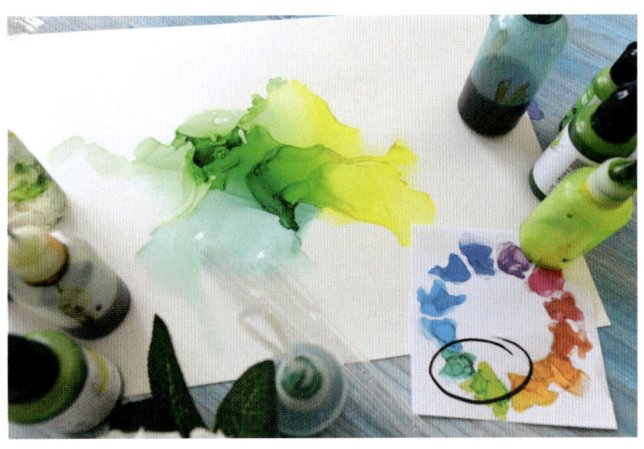

MONOCHROMATIC COLOURS

In this colour composition, you paint with only one colour or two very similar colours. For example, with a warm and a cool green. The yellow part errs towards warm, the blue part towards cool.

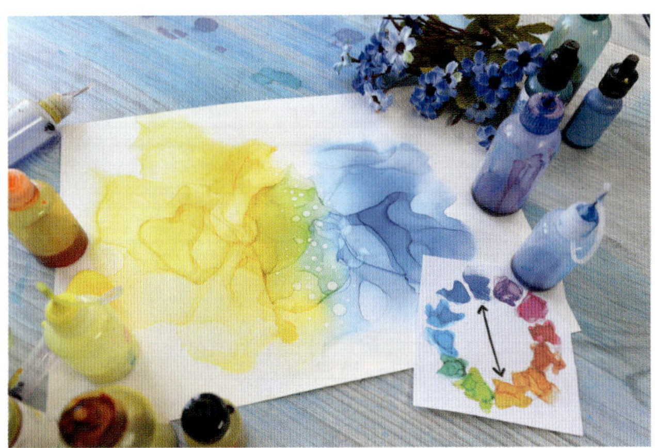

COMPLEMENTARY COLOURS

Opposite colours on the colour wheel are called complementary colours. When placed together, colours like blue and yellow, or green and red, make each other appear more vibrant.

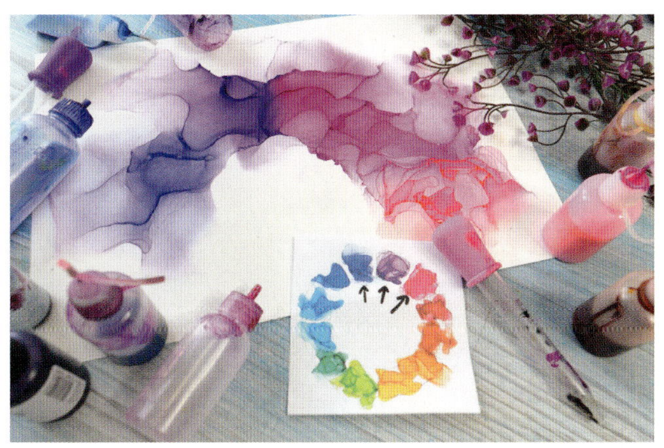

ANALOGOUS COLOURS

With an analogous colour selection, you create your palette using neighbouring colours from the colour wheel for a harmonious effect. An alternative option to the violet shades that feature in my illustration would be shades of green and turquoise.

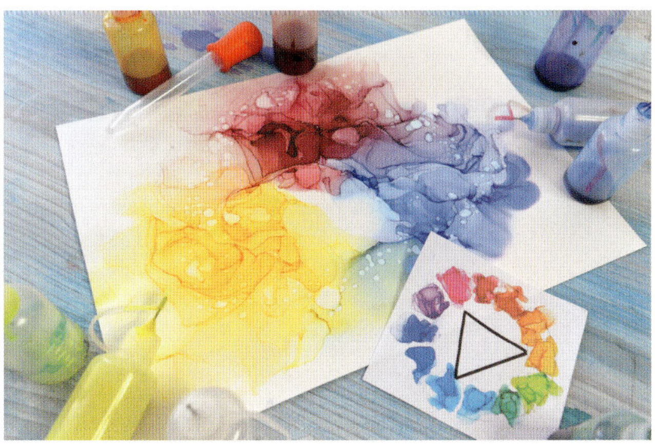

TRIADIC COLOURS

A triadic composition combines colours that lie at the tips of an equilateral triangle placed in the centre of the colour wheel. Continue to spin the triangle to find new, interesting combinations!

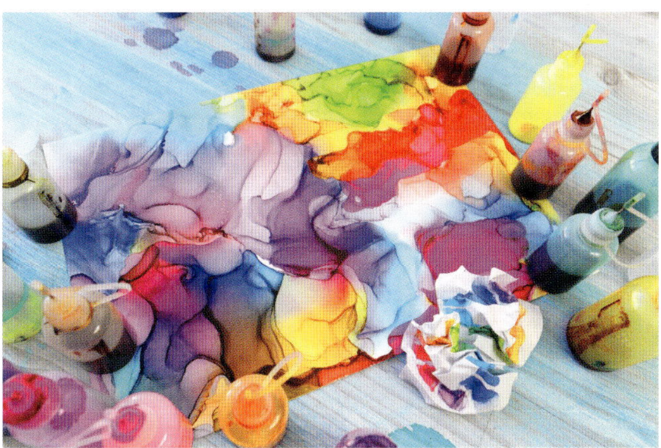

CHAOTIC COLOURS

A complete mixture of seemingly indiscriminate colours can create a pleasing chaos. Such combinations can be thoughtfully made or chosen purely intuitively. Either way, the result is very exciting due to the element of chance involved with the selection.

These combinations are a start, but you could try out something completely different. You can do whatever you want when it comes to art!

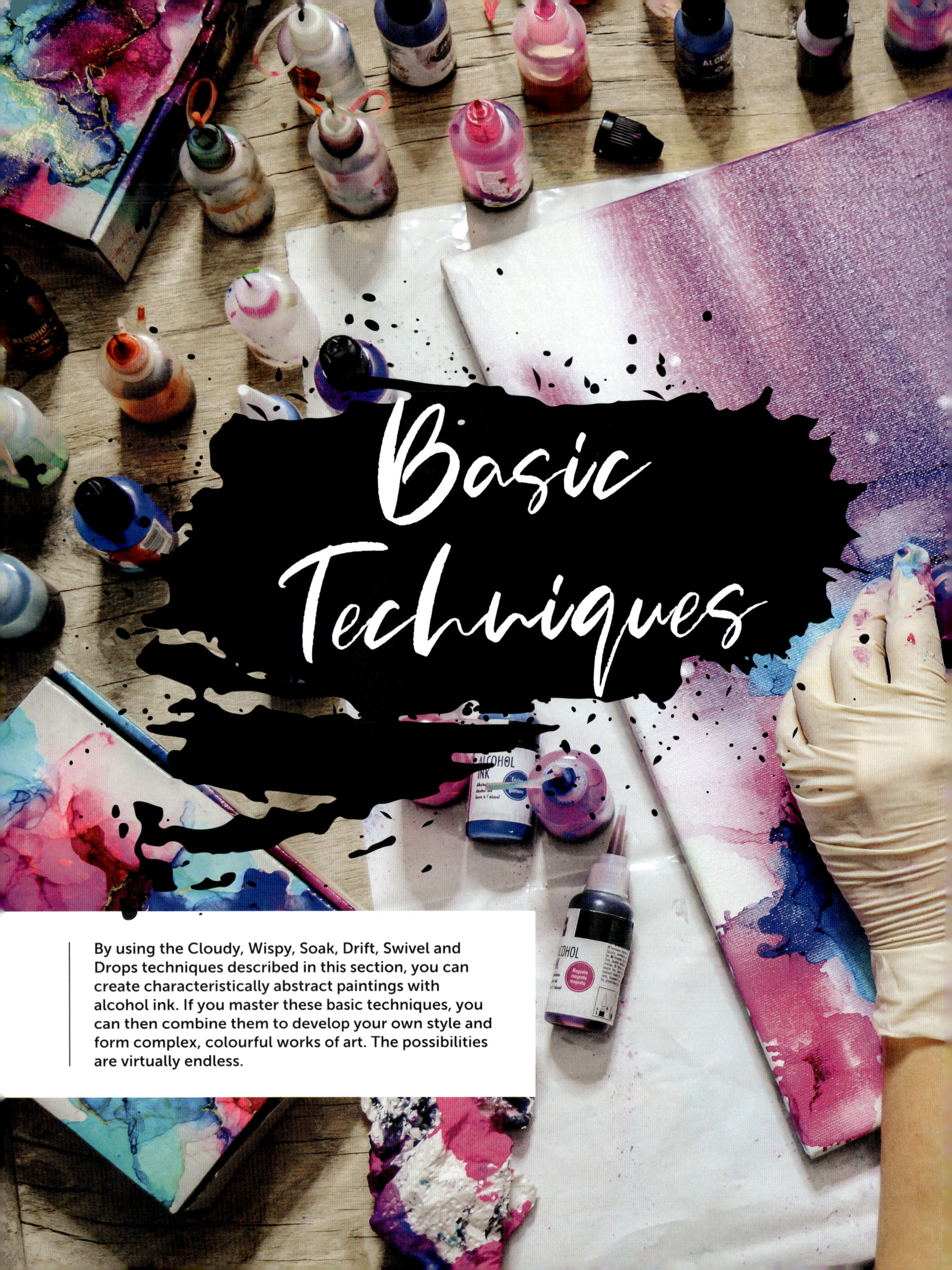

Basic Techniques

By using the Cloudy, Wispy, Soak, Drift, Swivel and Drops techniques described in this section, you can create characteristically abstract paintings with alcohol ink. If you master these basic techniques, you can then combine them to develop your own style and form complex, colourful works of art. The possibilities are virtually endless.

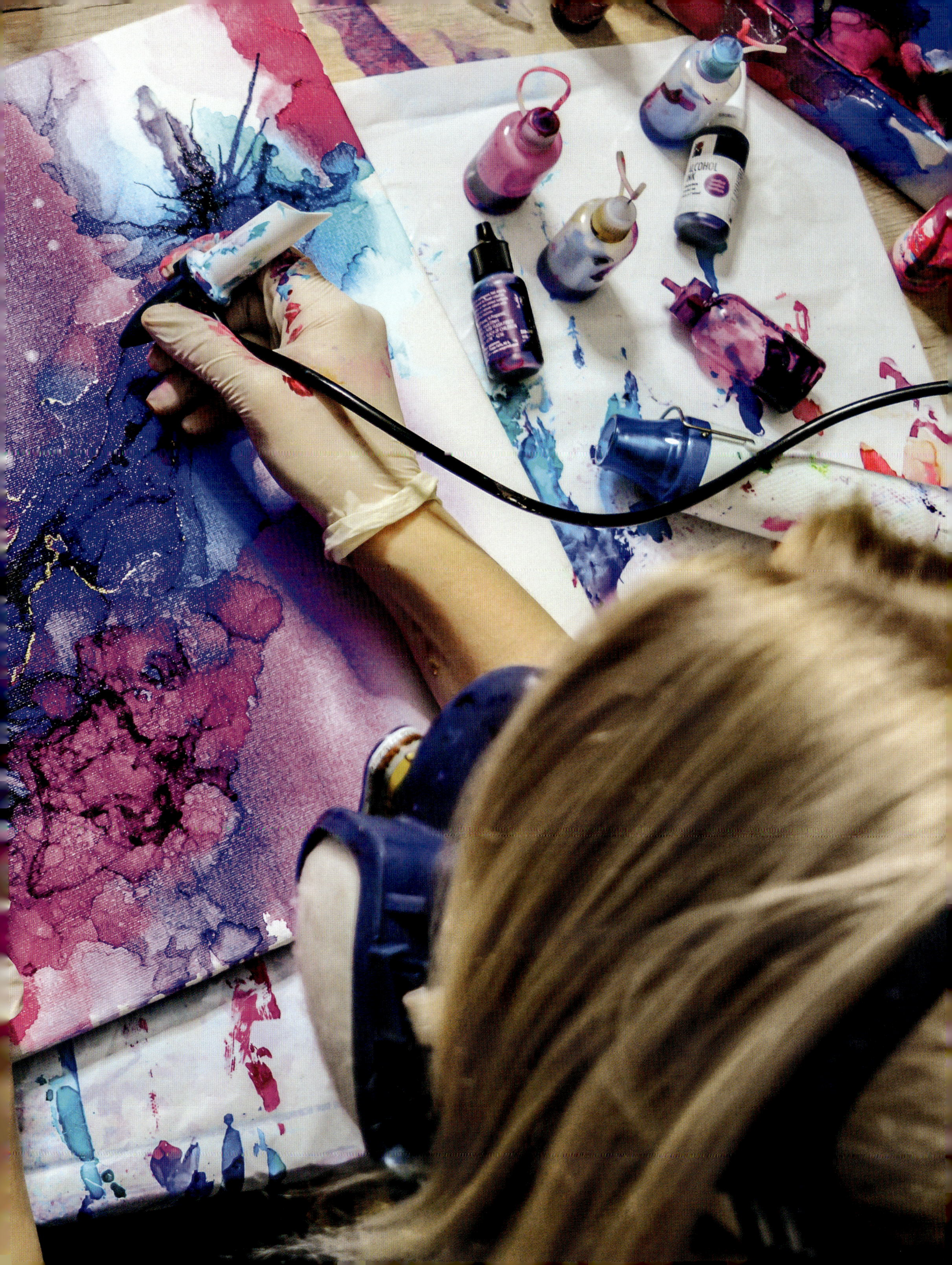

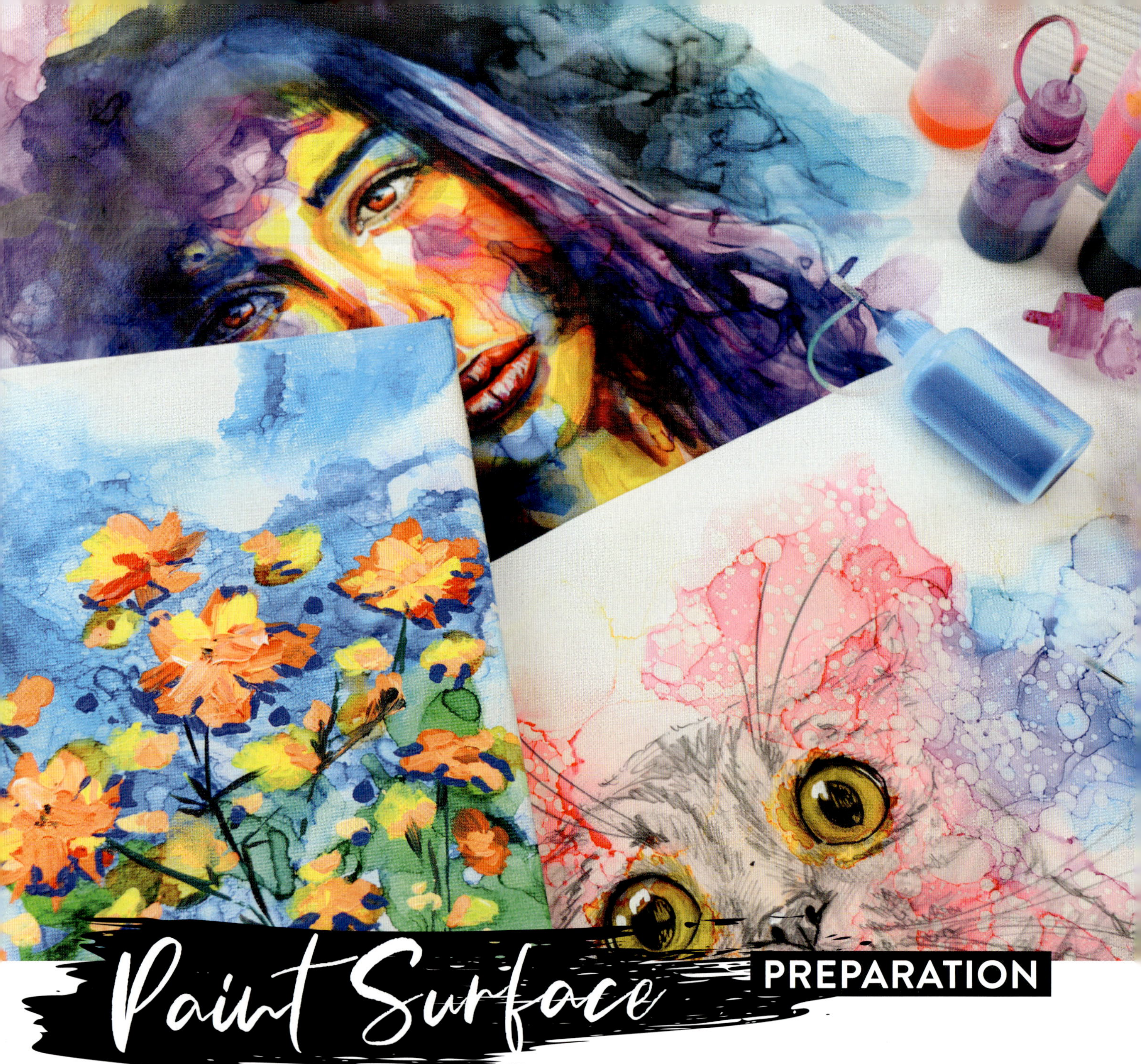

Paint Surface PREPARATION

I could name thousands of painting surfaces for alcohol ink! The only requirements are that they must be smooth and non-absorbent and as such, need to be pre-treated. In this section I'll show you how to prepare flat surfaces for painting with alcohol ink.

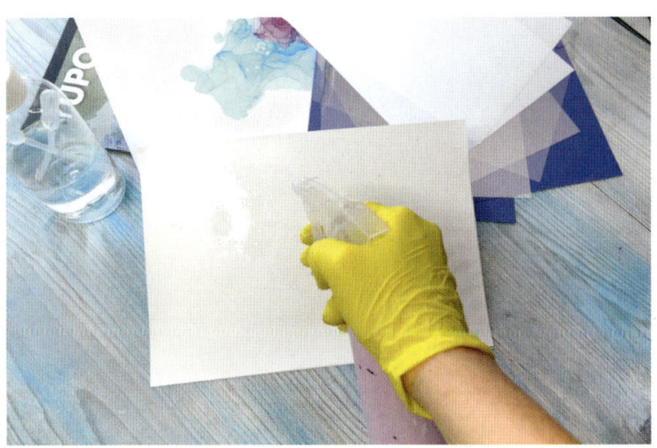

SMOOTH, NON-ABSORBENT MATERIALS such as Yupo paper, films, plastics, glass or metals can be painted straightaway. Most of the time, however, it is important to first spray them with alcohol and wipe them over. The effects are usually much easier to achieve once this has been done – some are only possible once the surface is wiped. In many cases, a generous layer of alcohol remains on the surface. The alcohol ink is then dripped on to this and painted.

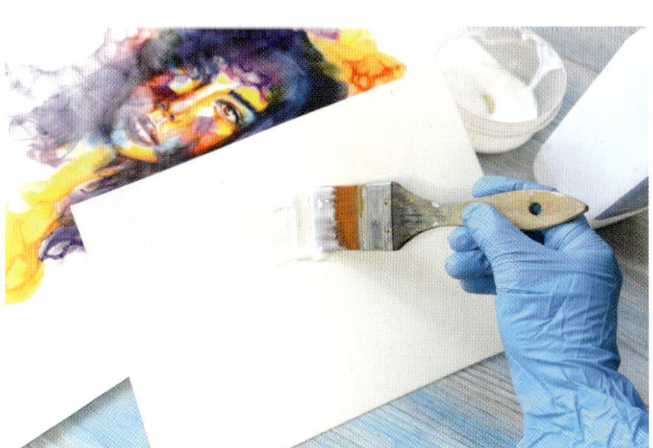

ABSORBENT PAPER SUCH AS WATERCOLOUR PAPER, stronger mixed media papers, card and cardboard can be sealed with transparent acrylic binder. It's best to use at least two layers, letting each one dry thoroughly. A few hours will be enough drying time. This technique can be used on other absorbent surfaces.

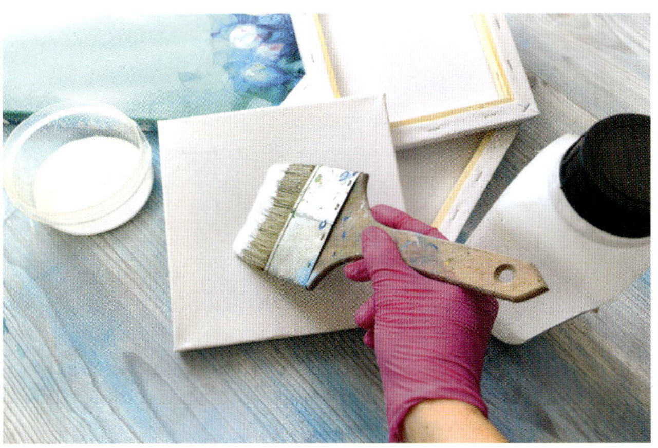

ABSORBENT MATERIAL LIKE CANVAS can also be sealed with transparent acrylic binder to make it suitable for alcohol ink. Again, it's best to use two layers and dry each one thoroughly. If you buy a canvas it will usually have already been treated with white gesso as a primer, making it suitable for use with alcohol ink or acrylic and oil paints.

Using this basic technique for preparing painting surfaces for alcohol ink, you can paint the effects straight onto the paper or create beautiful mixed media pieces. I'll give you some ideas about what's possible in the Mixed Media section later in the book.

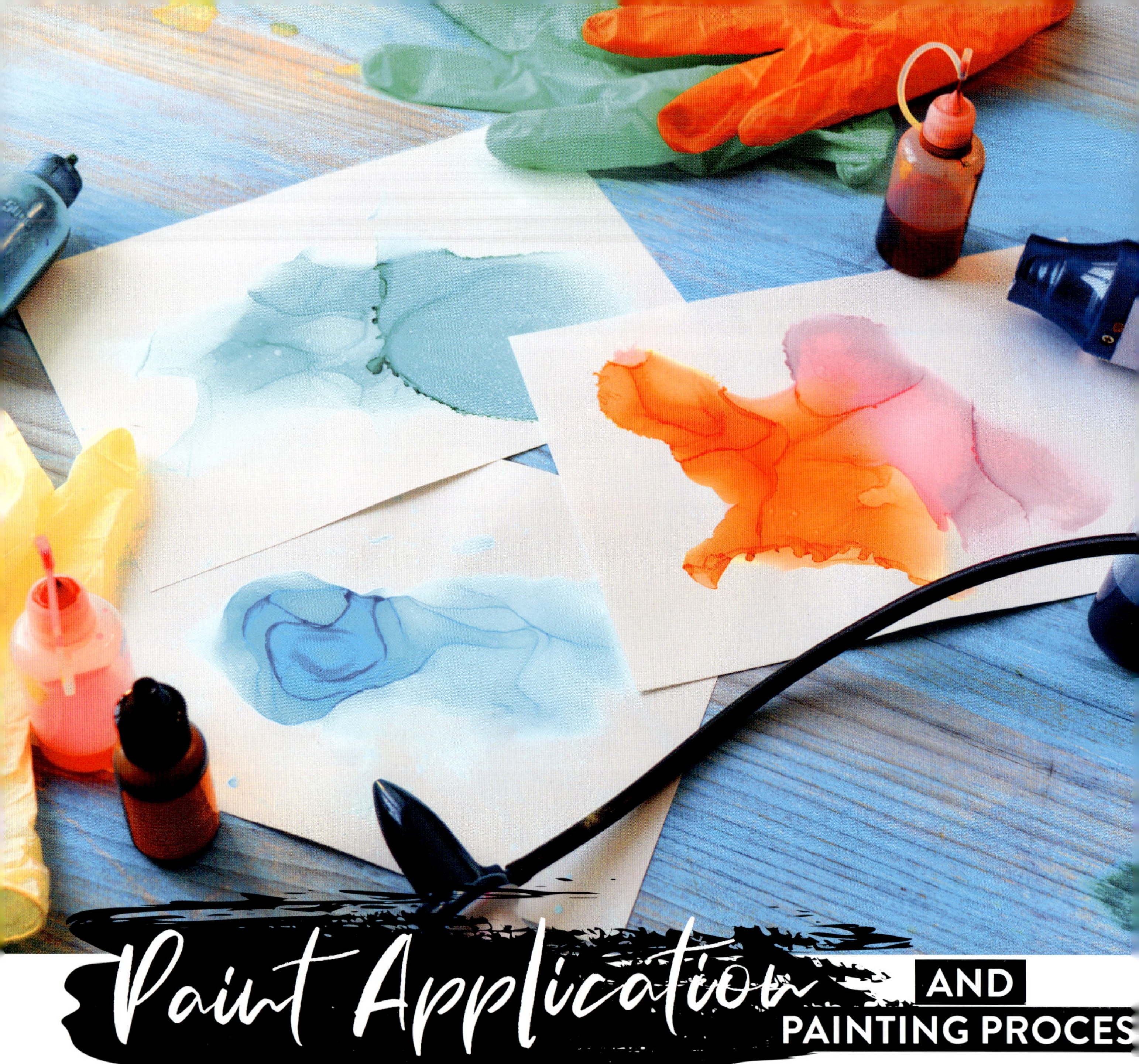

Paint Application AND PAINTING PROCESS

As with other painting techniques, there are different ways of achieving specific results when painting with alcohol ink. You can test how different inks behave using drops on Yupo paper, similar to creating watercolour swatches. However, real abstract painting with alcohol ink begins with the following basic processes.

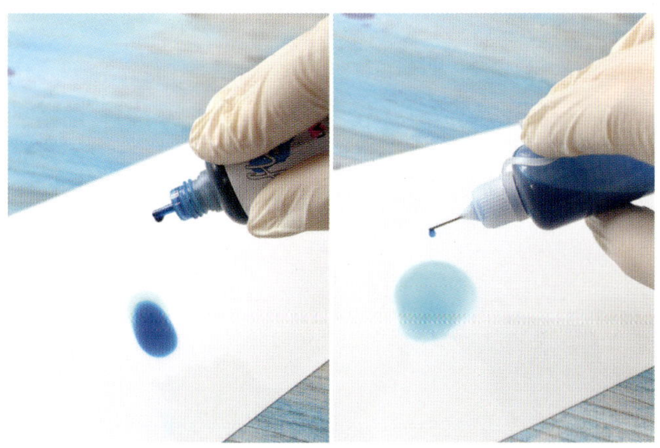

APPLY NEAT AND DILUTED

Depending on the manufacturer, inks differ in
intensity and dye concentration. This, together with
what different effects and appearances you want to
achieve, determines whether you should use your
alcohol ink neat or diluted. As you can see in my
photos, I often mix inks to my own desired intensity.
For large areas, however, I also use them neat. With
the help of this book, and with experience, you'll get
a feel for the right choice.

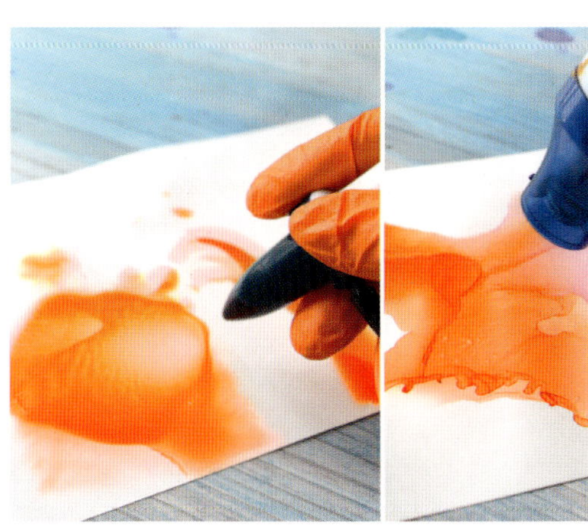

HOT AND COLD PAINTING

Temperature has a direct effect on the flow of the ink.
A hot-air blower pushes the alcohol ink quickly over
the surface whilst drying it at the same time. With the
cold air of an airbrush, you have more time to shape
the ink's movement and can get closer to it. The air
flow from the different-sized openings of the devices
also has an effect. This is particularly clear in the
Flowers section of the Painting Ideas chapter, later in
this book.

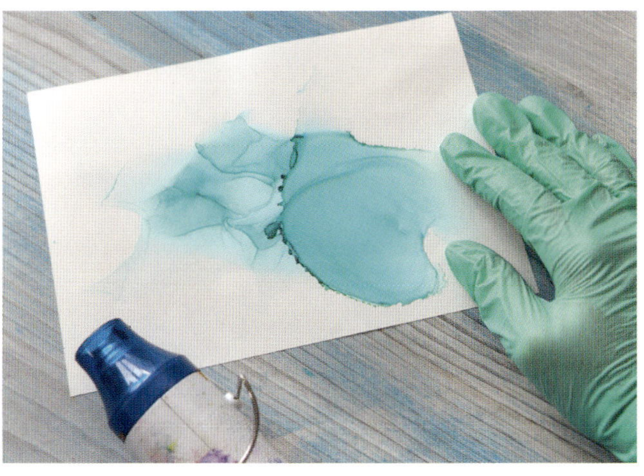

ACTIVE AND PASSIVE PAINTING

While you can steer and direct the alcohol ink for
your painting, the ink itself then has a life of its own.
Whereas acrylic paint simply stays where you put it,
alcohol ink comes alive without any assistance.
Actively 'paint' your picture with a hairdryer and then
apply diluted alcohol ink to one specific point or leave
an area untreated. The alcohol ink will form its own
shapes, and paint islands, shores and streams. You
can leave them like this or reshape them yourself.

The information about the basic application and
processes is important for the techniques that follow.
You'll find it's the basis for everything you need
to know.

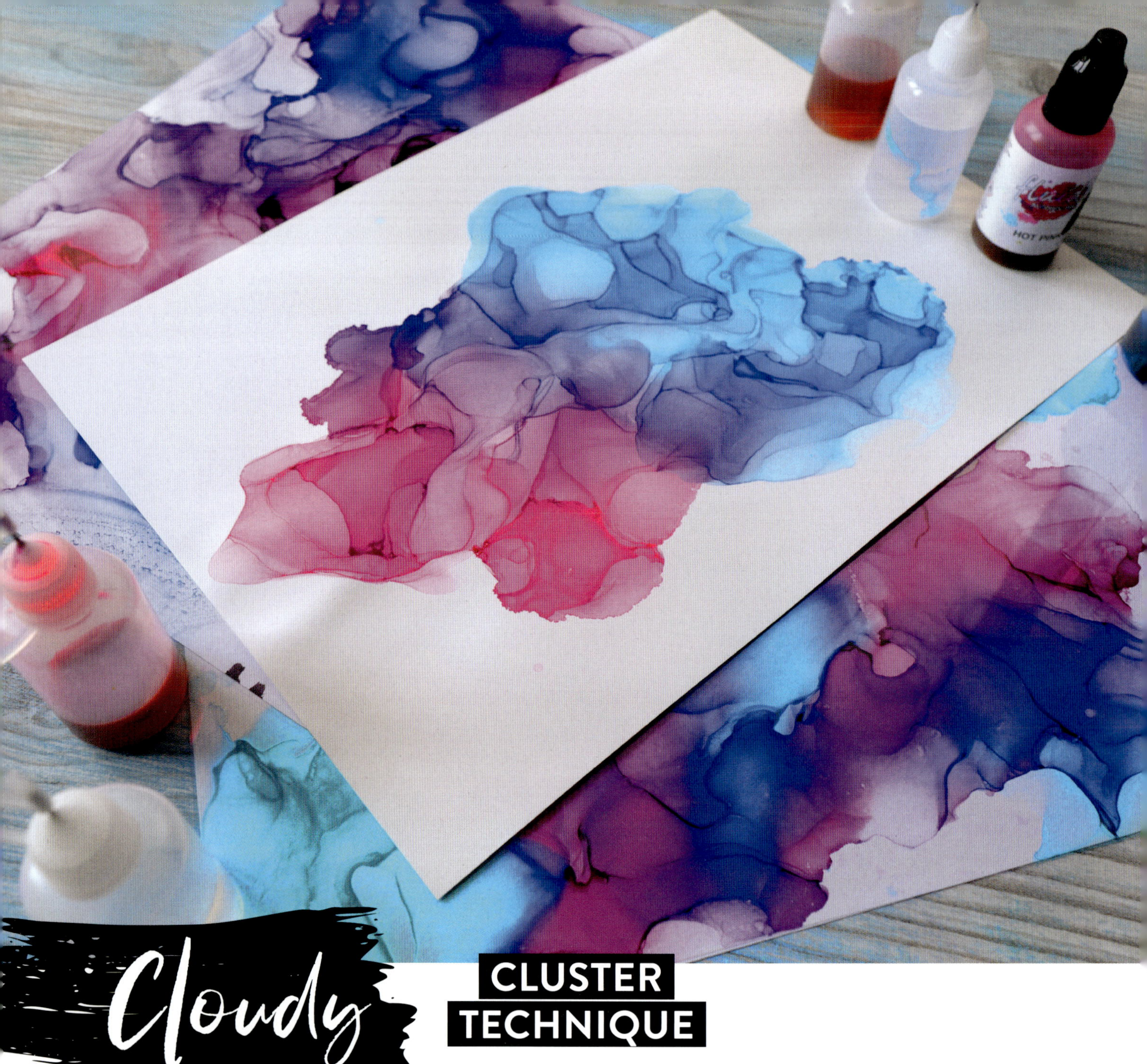

Cloudy CLUSTER TECHNIQUE

You'll come across the basic 'Cloudy' technique time and again when painting with alcohol ink. In this technique, you push the pigments away from the edge of the paint to distribute the colour. This creates cluster formations that look like clouds.

YOU'LL NEED

- Small hot-air blower or airbrush
- Non-absorbent surface
- (Diluted) alcohol ink; preferably two colours to achieve colour gradients
- Isopropanol (alcohol) in a pipette or applicator bottle

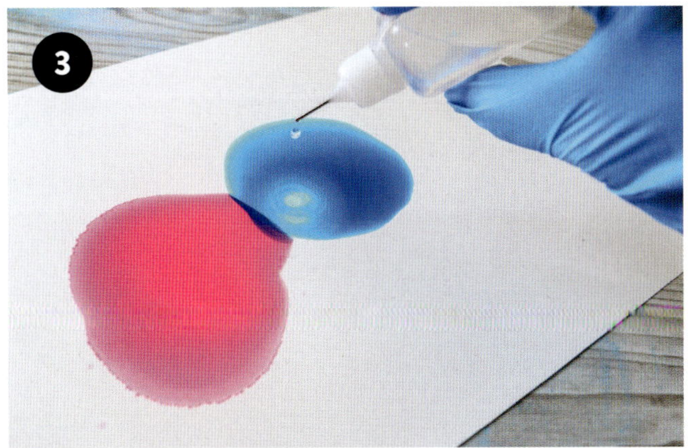

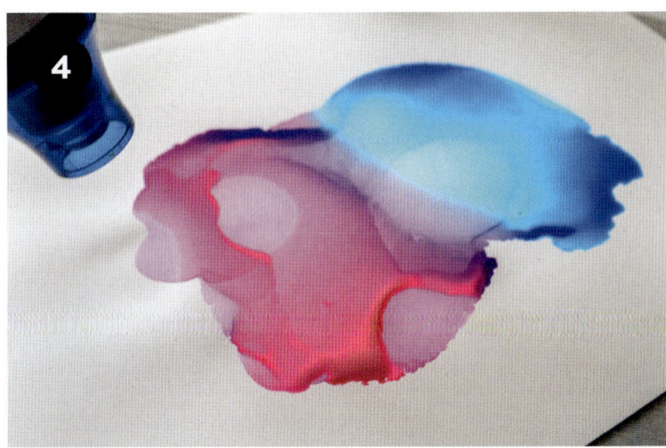

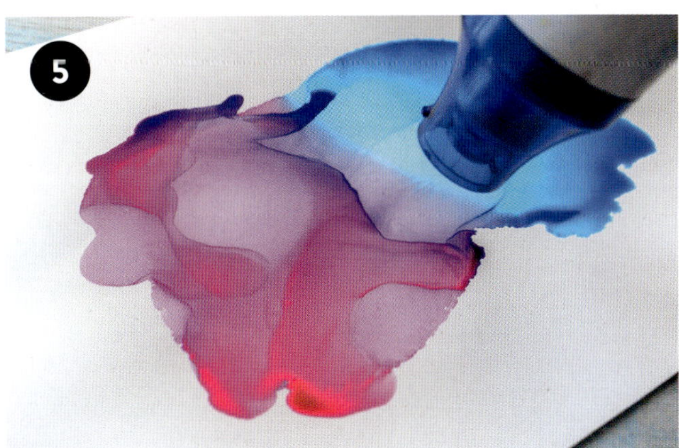

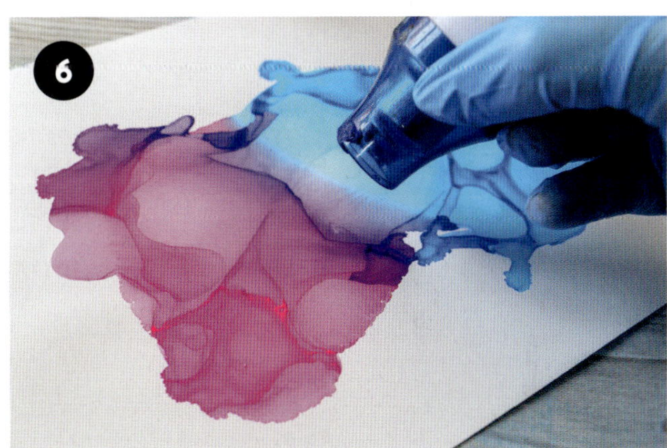

1 Wipe the surface with alcohol to prepare it. This causes the surface tension to disappear, allowing the ink to flow more easily.

2 The cloud formations have a paint edge. This is achieved by painting wet on dry. In other words, apply the diluted alcohol ink from the bottle onto the dry surface.

3 Add a good drop of isopropanol, depending on how much ink you put on and how intense it is. Drop it right in the centre and also around the edge if you wish.

4 Now use the hot-air blower to disperse the ink, holding the blower above the surface.

5 Direct the ink as desired, but make sure that you define the boundaries of the coloured areas by sending the alcohol ink from the edge of the cloud back to the centre.

6 Repeat step 5 until you have achieved your desired effect, making sure you always blow-dry from different directions.

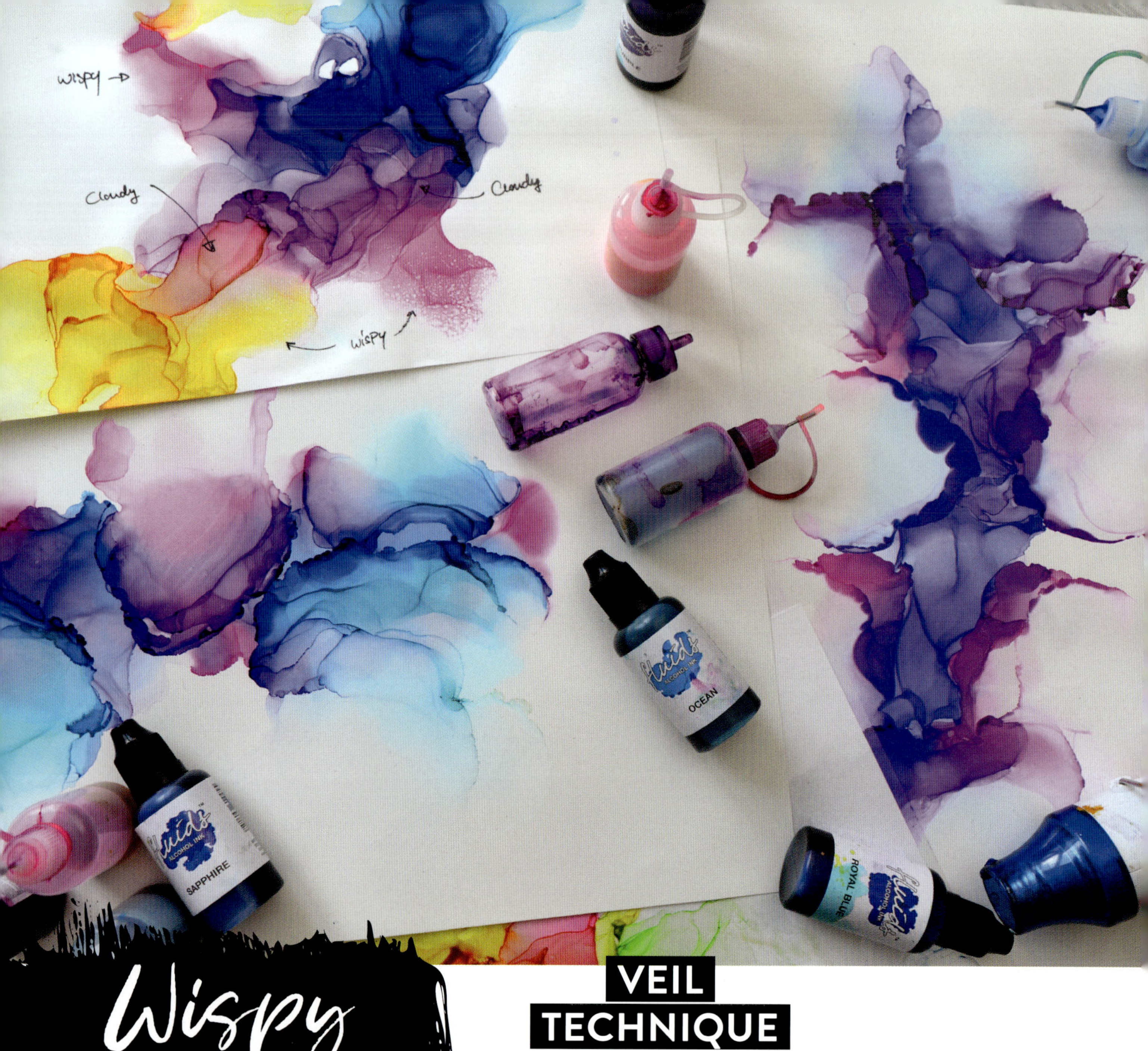

Wispy

VEIL TECHNIQUE

'Wispy' is a magic word and almost a discipline of its own. The aim is to create areas with fine colour gradients. The artwork is very characteristic of alcohol ink painting and is often finished with metallic effects. I'll explain how to do that in the Special Materials section. First of all, let me show you how to create a painting which can be called Wispy using just alcohol ink. Starting from a basic shape, there are two ways of creating Wispy areas.

YOU'LL NEED

– Small hot-air blower or airbrush
– Non-absorbent surface
– Alcohol ink
– Isopropanol (alcohol) in a pipette or applicator bottle

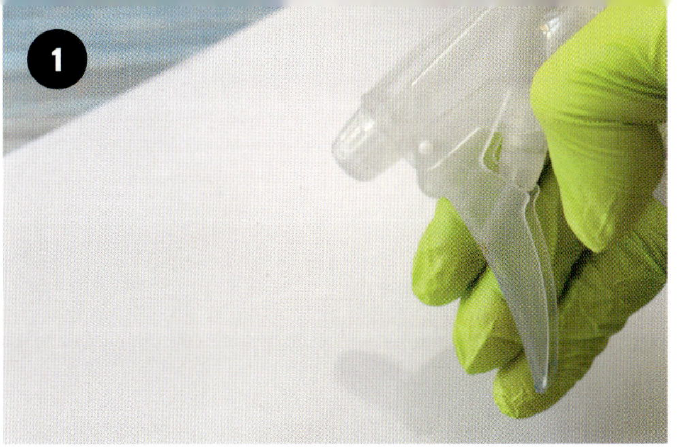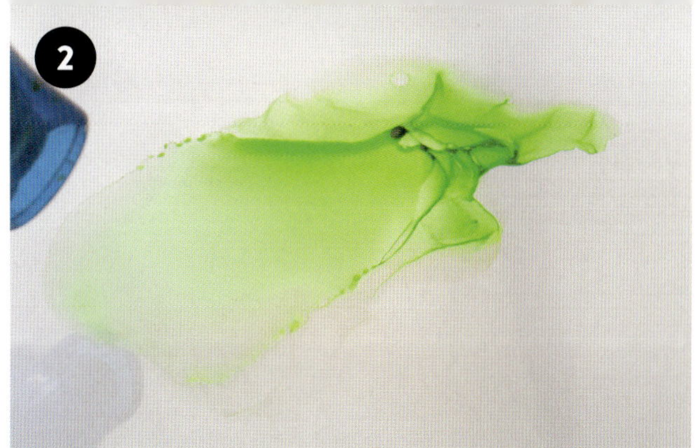

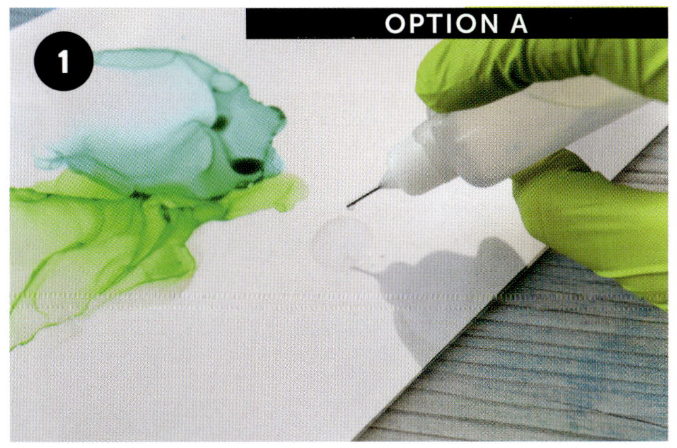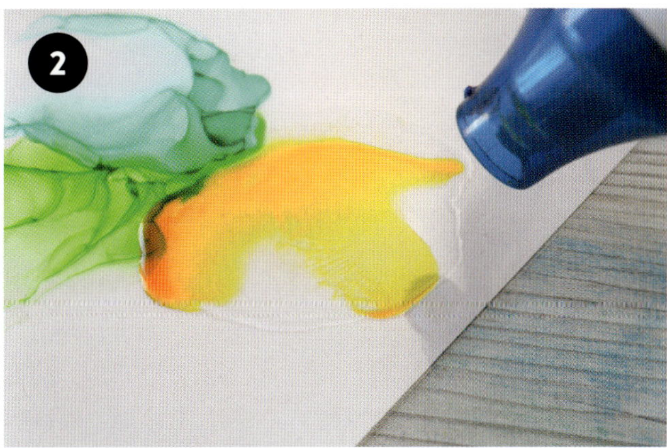

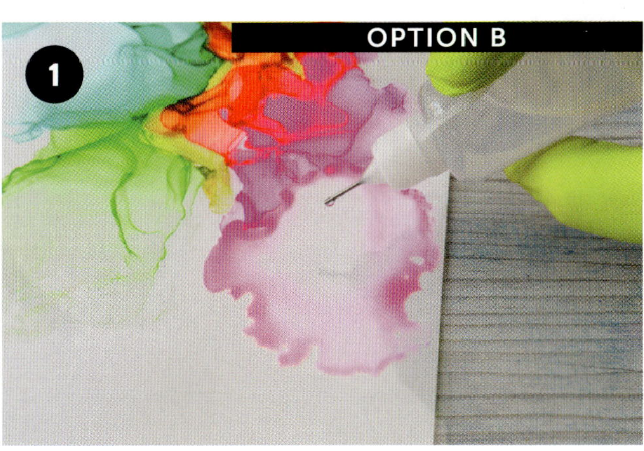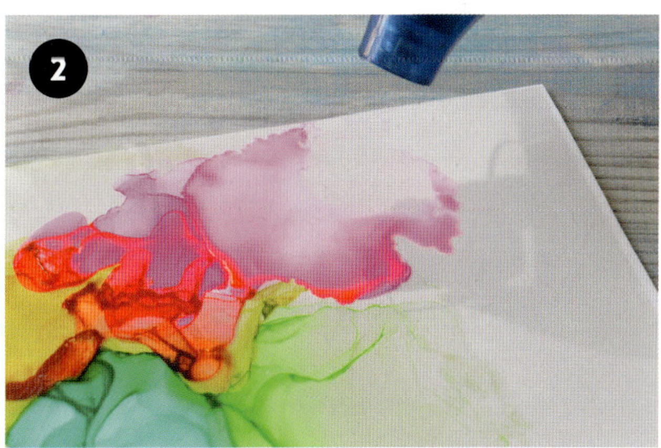

1 Evenly spray the surface with isopropanol. This film of alcohol makes it easier to achieve the Wispy effect. Then add your first drop of ink.

2 You must now act quickly: drive the ink apart with the hot-air blower. Then immediately send it inwards at the edges to prevent them from forming defined boundaries, resulting in the creation of a fine Wispy veil without an edge.

OPTION A

1 Partially prepare the area you want to paint with isopropanol. To do this, add a few drops of alcohol to the area and distribute it in a circular motion with your finger (remember to wear gloves!).

2 Now drip the alcohol ink on to the area that's still wet at the farthest point and drive it immediately in one direction with the hot-air blower. This creates a fine veil.

OPTION B

1 As described in step 1 of ‚Soak', apply neat alcohol to dry ink at the edge of your painting and wait.

2 When you see that everything is evenly covered and dissolved, blow the wet coloured area inwards towards the centre of your artwork. Adding further drops of alcohol at the outermost edge makes the Wispy veil become finer and finer.

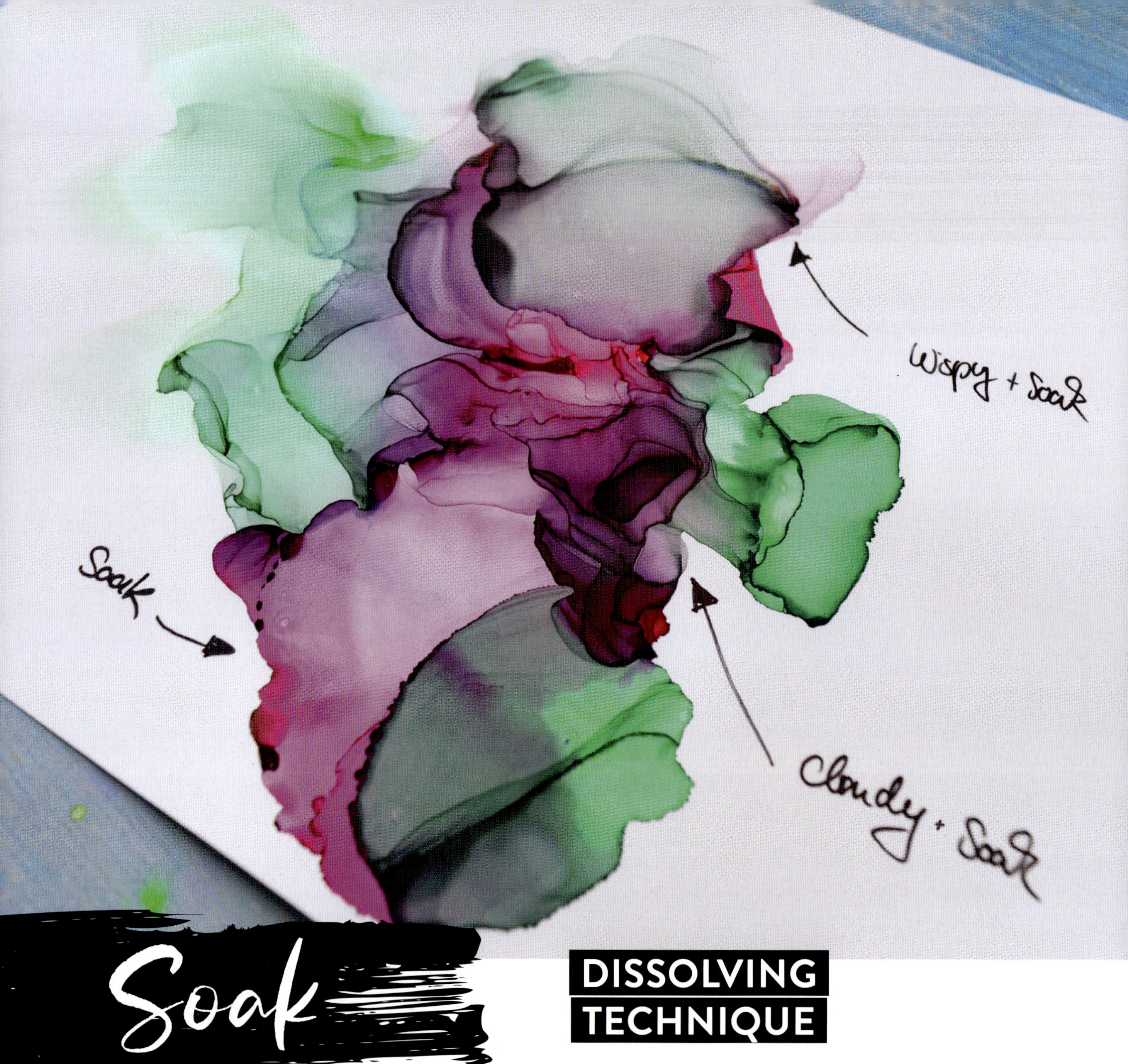

Soak

DISSOLVING TECHNIQUE

With this technique, you can re-dissolve areas of your painting using alcohol or diluted alcohol ink, letting the newly wet area take effect. Thus, in the first basic step you're painting passively by adding isopropanol to the painted, dry ink and just waiting. From here, you can slowly dry the redesigned area yourself or you can continue to work on it.

YOU'LL NEED

- Small hot-air blower or airbrush
- Non-absorbent surface
- Alcohol ink
- Isopropanol (alcohol) in a pipette or applicator bottle

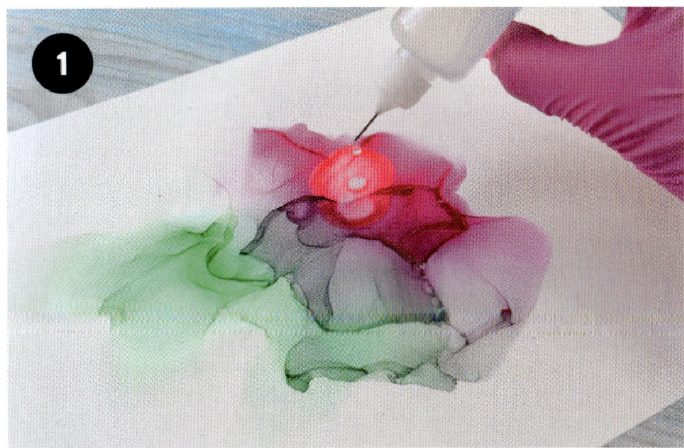
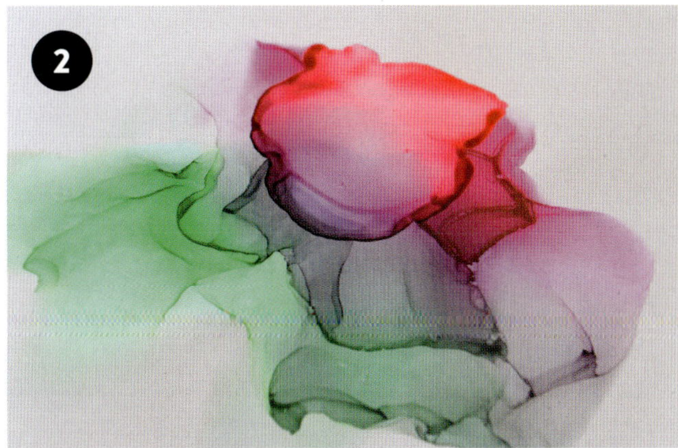
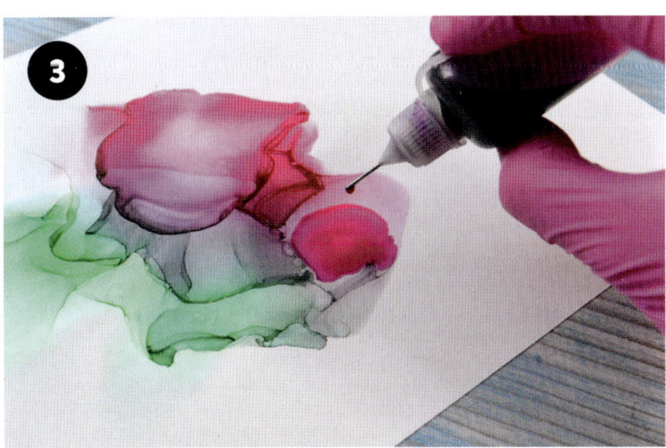
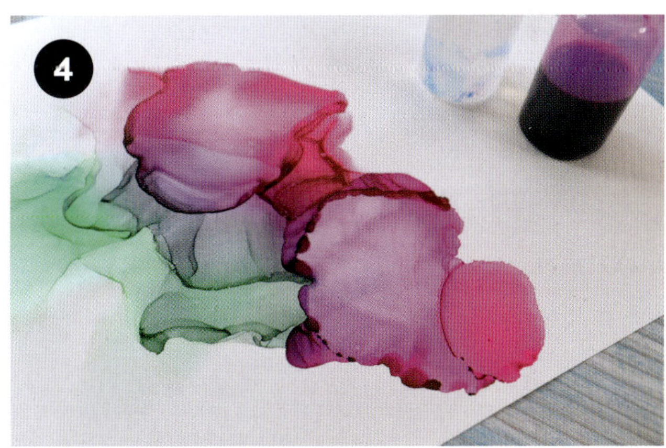

1 The initial shape here is Cloudy, painted on a wet surface. This creates gentle edges reminiscent of Wispy. Now use neat alcohol wherever you like and wait.

2 The colour will dissolve and form its own colour gradients and shapes.

3 For further effect, you can apply heavily-diluted alcohol ink using a pipette or applicator bottle.

4 The results of Soak are beautiful, soft colour gradients in clearly delineated shapes via these 'passively' painted areas - a strong element for abstract images and backgrounds.

If you want to know more about how to get the best out of alcohol ink, look at my online courses to learn lots of different techniques.

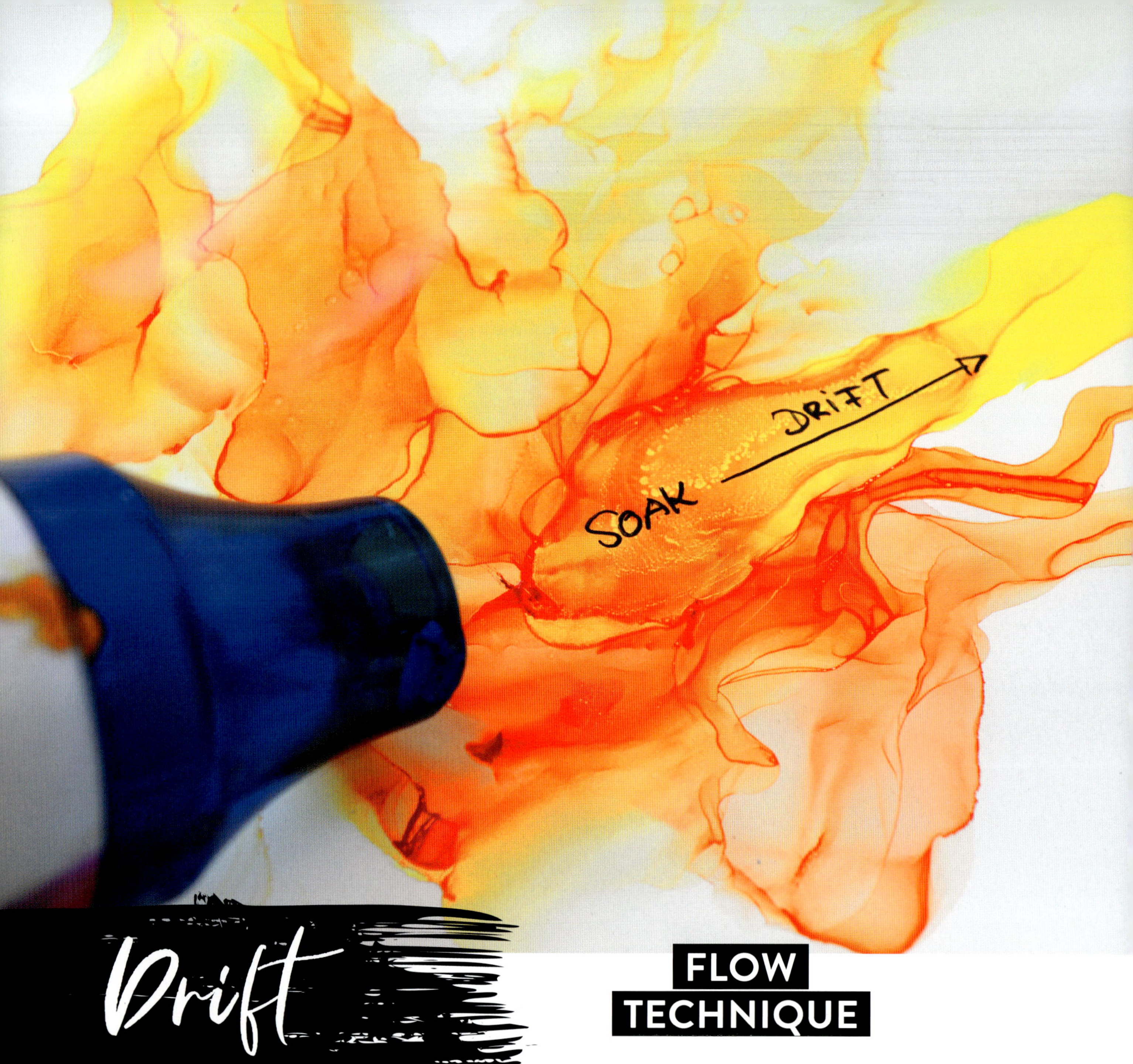

Drift

FLOW TECHNIQUE

With Drift, we want to achieve formations that are clearly recognisable as a flow. It's different to the other techniques in that it's blow-dried away from the painted area. With Drift, you can create trickle- and flame-like shapes. You'll use this technique later to paint flowers.

YOU'LL NEED

- Small hot-air blower or airbrush
- Non-absorbent surface
- Alcohol ink
- Isopropanol (alcohol) in a pipette or applicator bottle

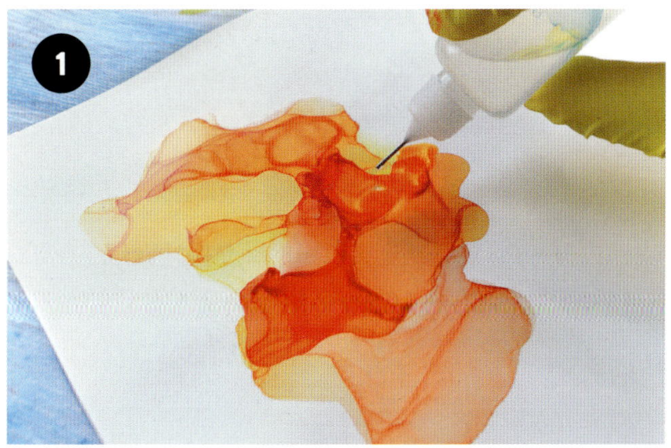

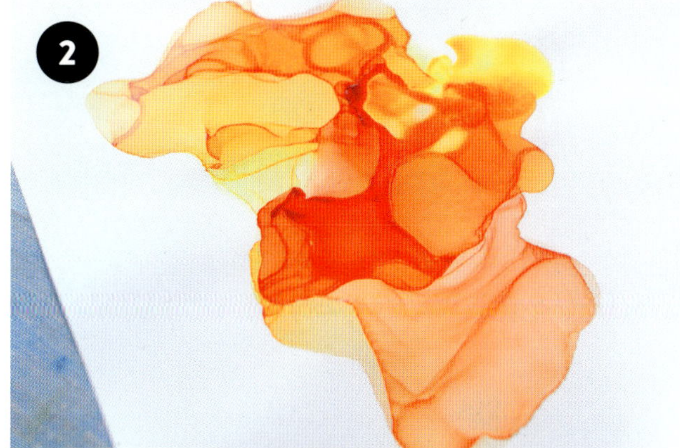

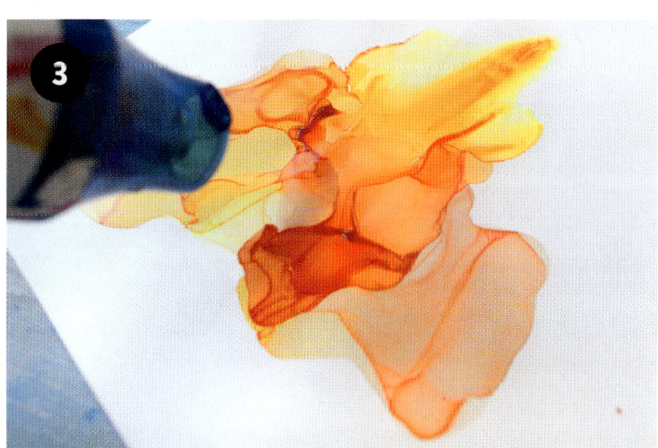

1 The starting shape is a dried Cloudy. Use Soak and apply neat alcohol ink to the painted area.

2 Wait and watch while the ink re-dissolves.

3 When the ink has dissolved, blow the liquid vigorously in one direction beyond the painting and on to the untreated area.

TRY THIS

A Don't do anything, just let the dissolved alcohol ink hit the untreated area of your surface. This results in runs like rays.

B Wipe the surface with alcohol beforehand to remove not only dust, but also the surface tension. This results in soft, controllable shapes with edges.

C Apply alcohol to the surrounding area too and leave it wet. The ink from the Soak and Drift areas distributes itself evenly and can even blend in quite softly, so that it's almost like Wispy without a hard edge.

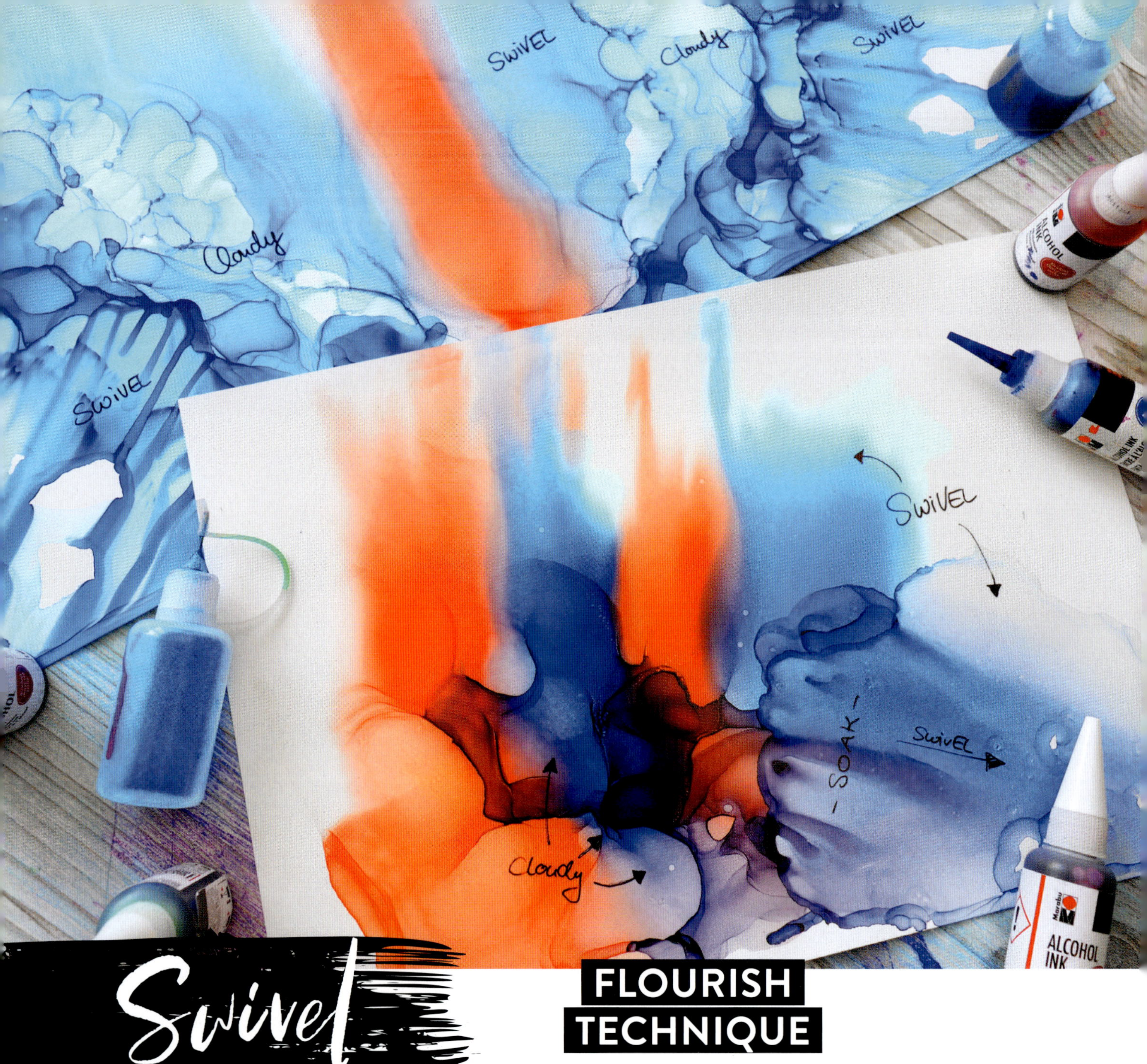

Swivel

FLOURISH TECHNIQUE

The 'Swivel' technique allows you to create softly faded backgrounds and is an exciting design element when combined with Cloudy, Wispy and Drops techniques. Swivel is the simplest shape to paint with alcohol ink and can be a great base for mixed media.

YOU'LL NEED

- Small hot-air blower or airbrush
- Non-absorbent surface
- Alcohol ink
- Isopropanol (alcohol) in a pipette or applicator bottle

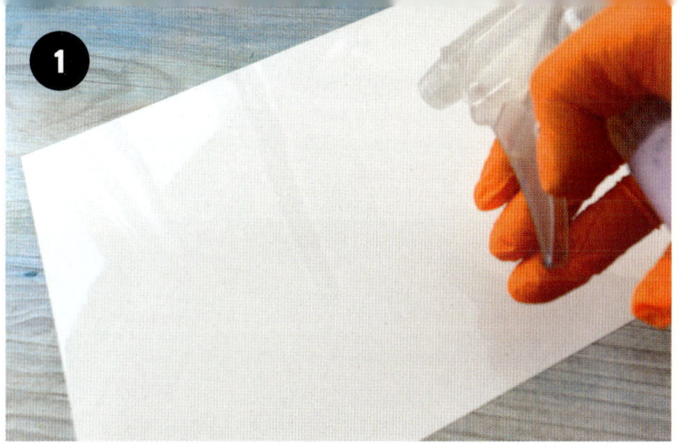

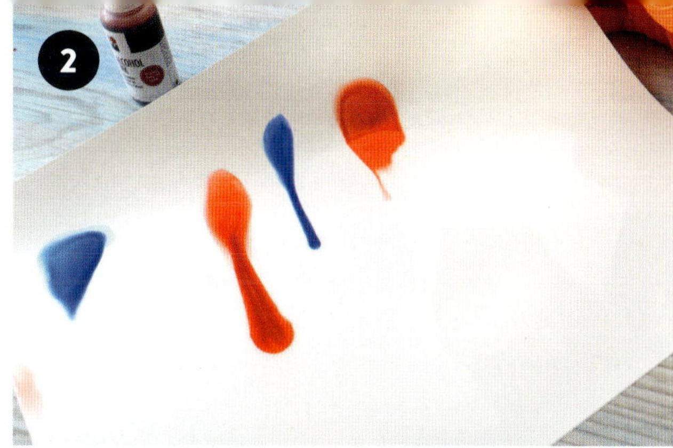

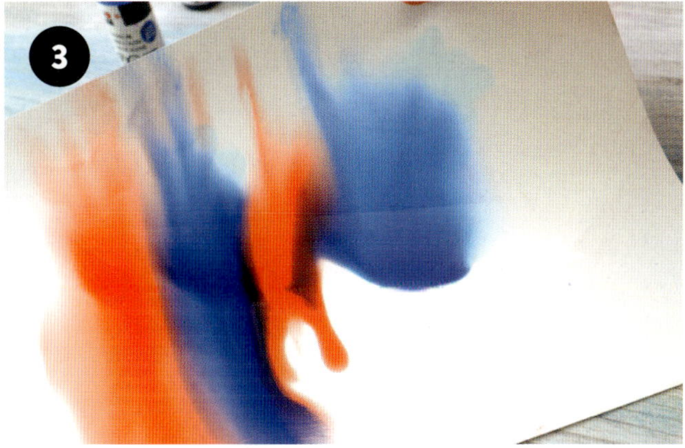

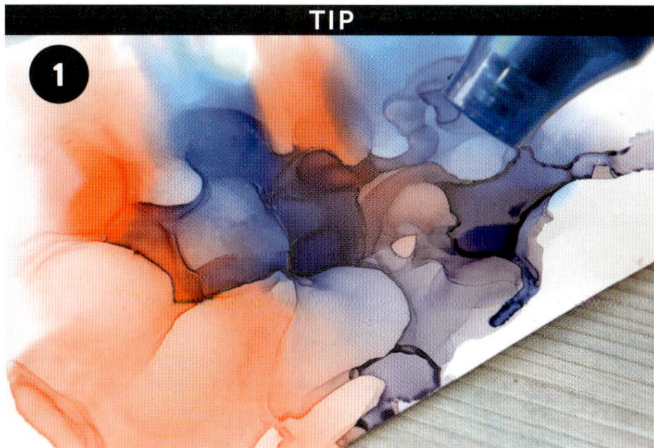

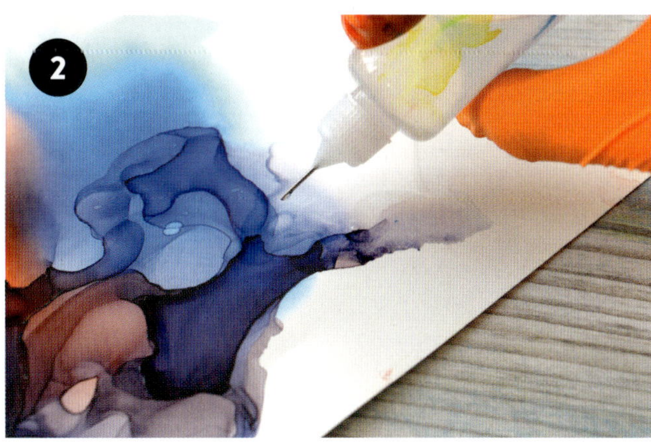

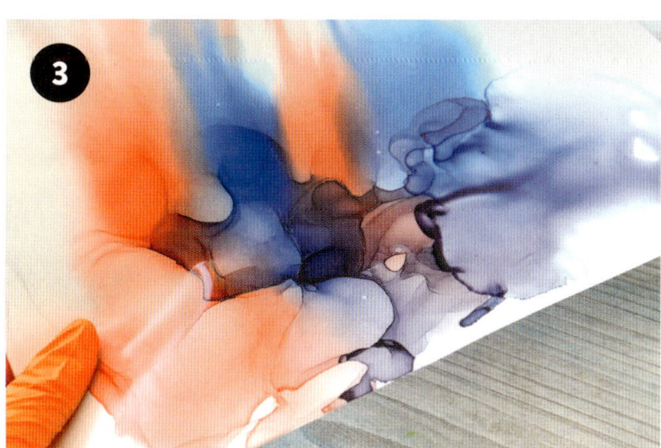

1 Spray your painting surface generously with isopropanol.

2 Apply neat alcohol ink either in precise areas or distributed evenly. You can create colour gradients with multiple colours.

3 Now hold the edges of your painting surface (here it's Yupo paper) and swivel it slowly to distribute the colour. When you are satisfied, place the painting back down on a flat surface and wait until it has dried.

1 Before the surface is dry, you can work on parts of it using the Cloudy or Wispy techniques. In the illustration, I applied the Cloudy technique to the surface while it was still wet.

2 As you can see, I applied Soak to another area and then used Swivel again.

3 The result is a colour gradient at the bottom right of the painting.

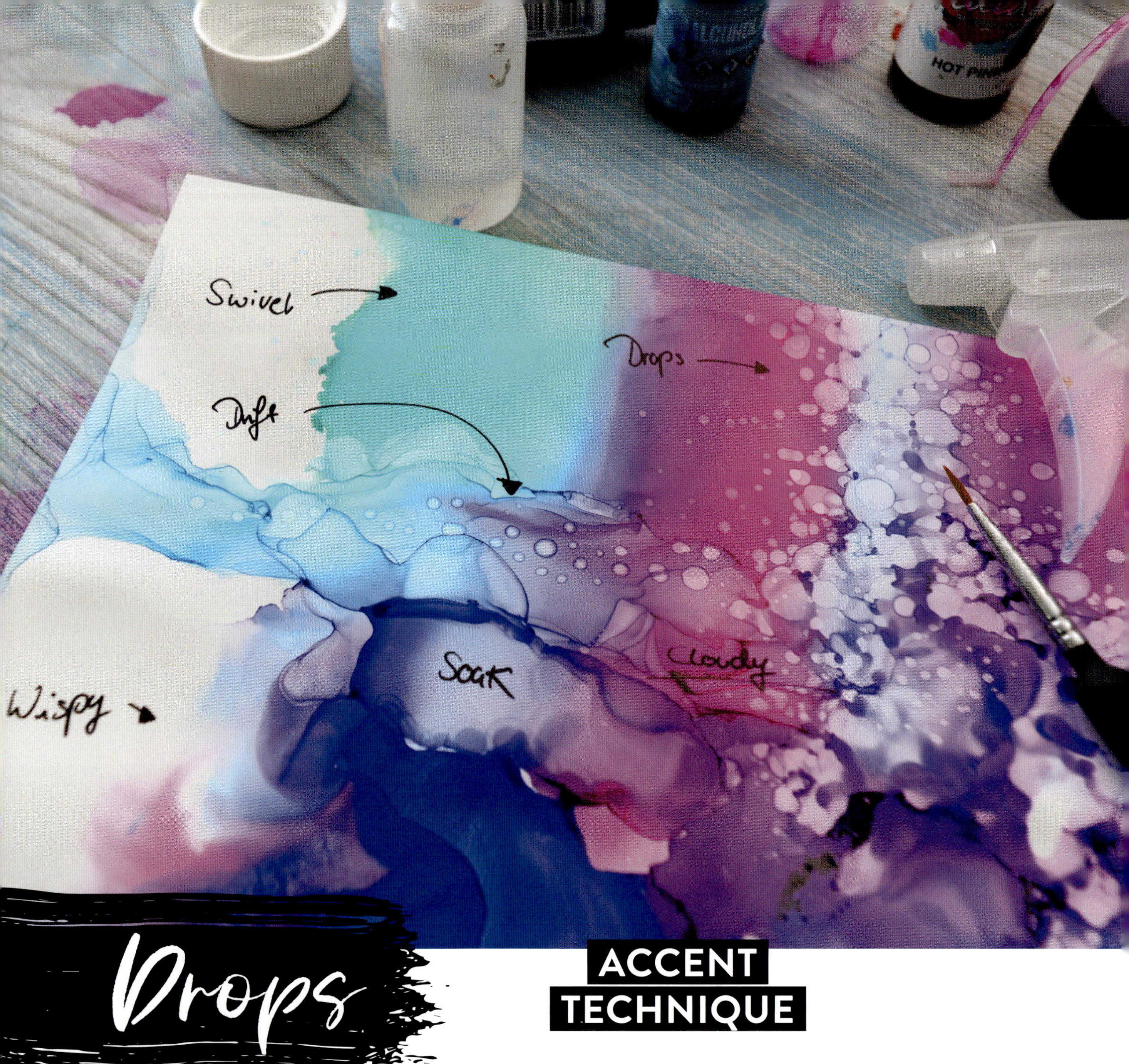

Drops

This is the perfect painting technique for putting accents in your design. 'Drops' are enchanting little details that breathe life into your artwork. You 'paint' them with isopropanol on the dry painting. The alcohol pushes the paint to the edge of the drop, and exposes the bright background.

YOU'LL NEED

- Small hot-air blower or airbrush
- Non-absorbent surface
- Alcohol ink
- Isopropanol (alcohol) in a pipette or applicator bottle

For Drops

- Fine tip paintbrushes and a bowl of isopropanol
- Isopropanol in a spray bottle

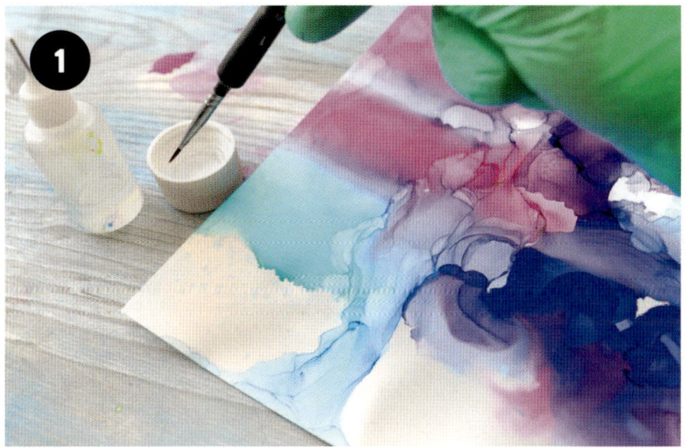

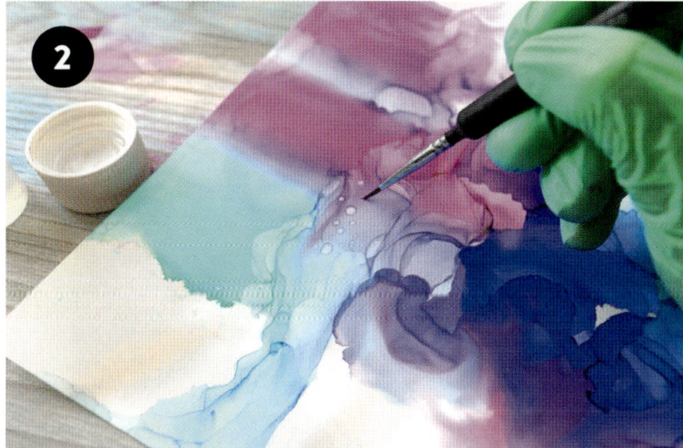

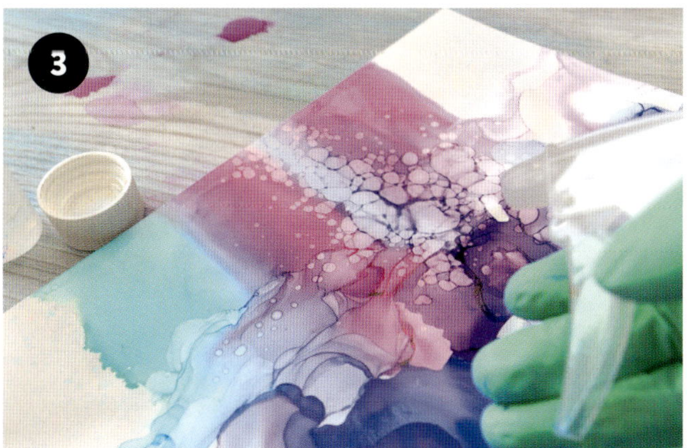

1 Begin with your (almost) finished and completely dry alcohol ink artwork.

2 Fill a small bowl with neat alcohol and pick up the alcohol with a small, fine tip paintbrush. You'll find the right quantity by trial and error. A lot of alcohol makes the drops big; less alcohol forms small spots.

3 Now tap the tip of the paintbrush very lightly and carefully on the painted area. Nothing more. You can now see the alcohol creating a dot for you. Your surface must be absolutely level for this to work well.

OPTION

You can also create lots of small drops in a dramatic cluster with a spray bottle. For this, spray your painting surface carefully or randomly with neat alcohol and leave to dry.

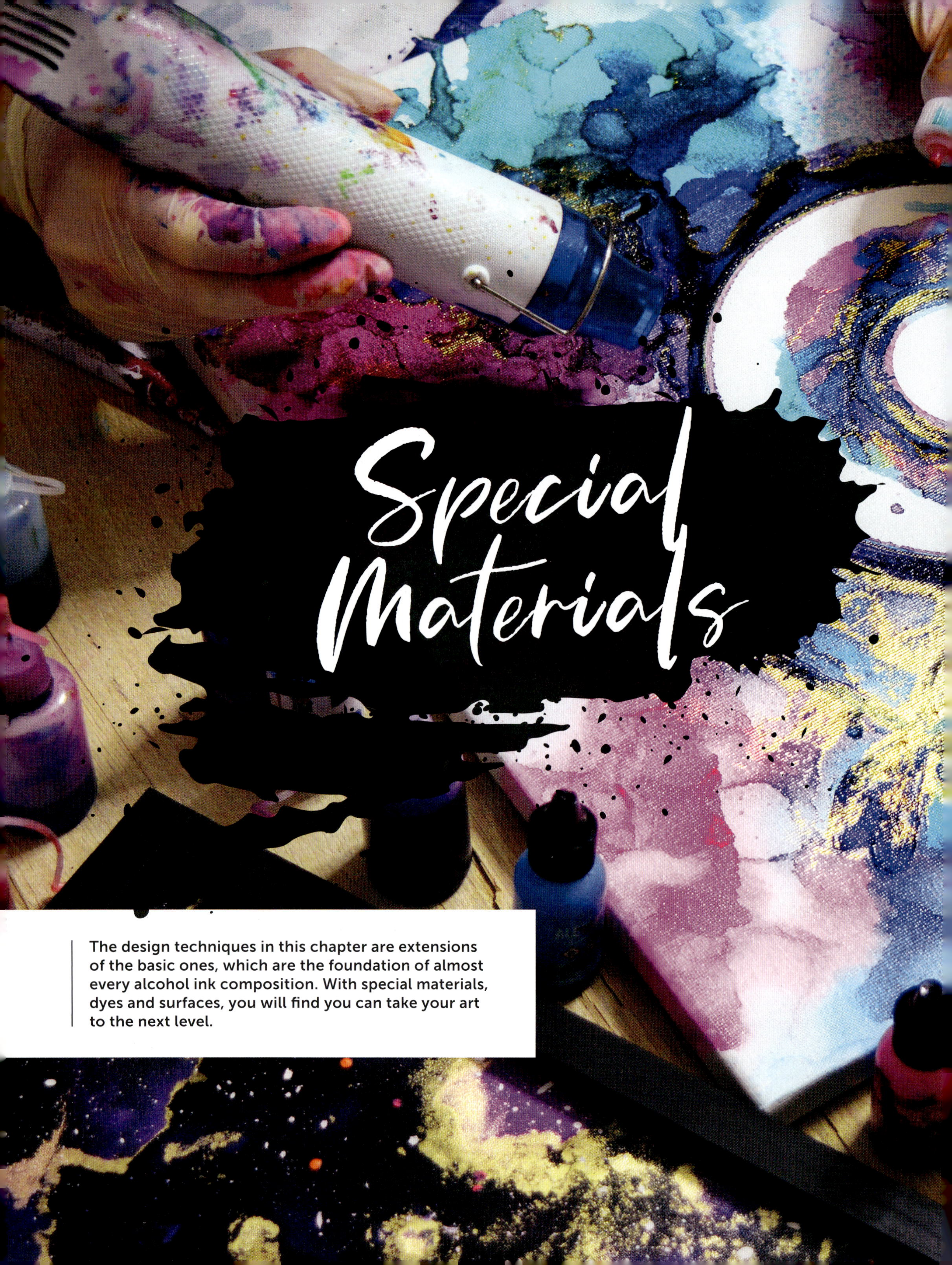

Special Materials

The design techniques in this chapter are extensions of the basic ones, which are the foundation of almost every alcohol ink composition. With special materials, dyes and surfaces, you will find you can take your art to the next level.

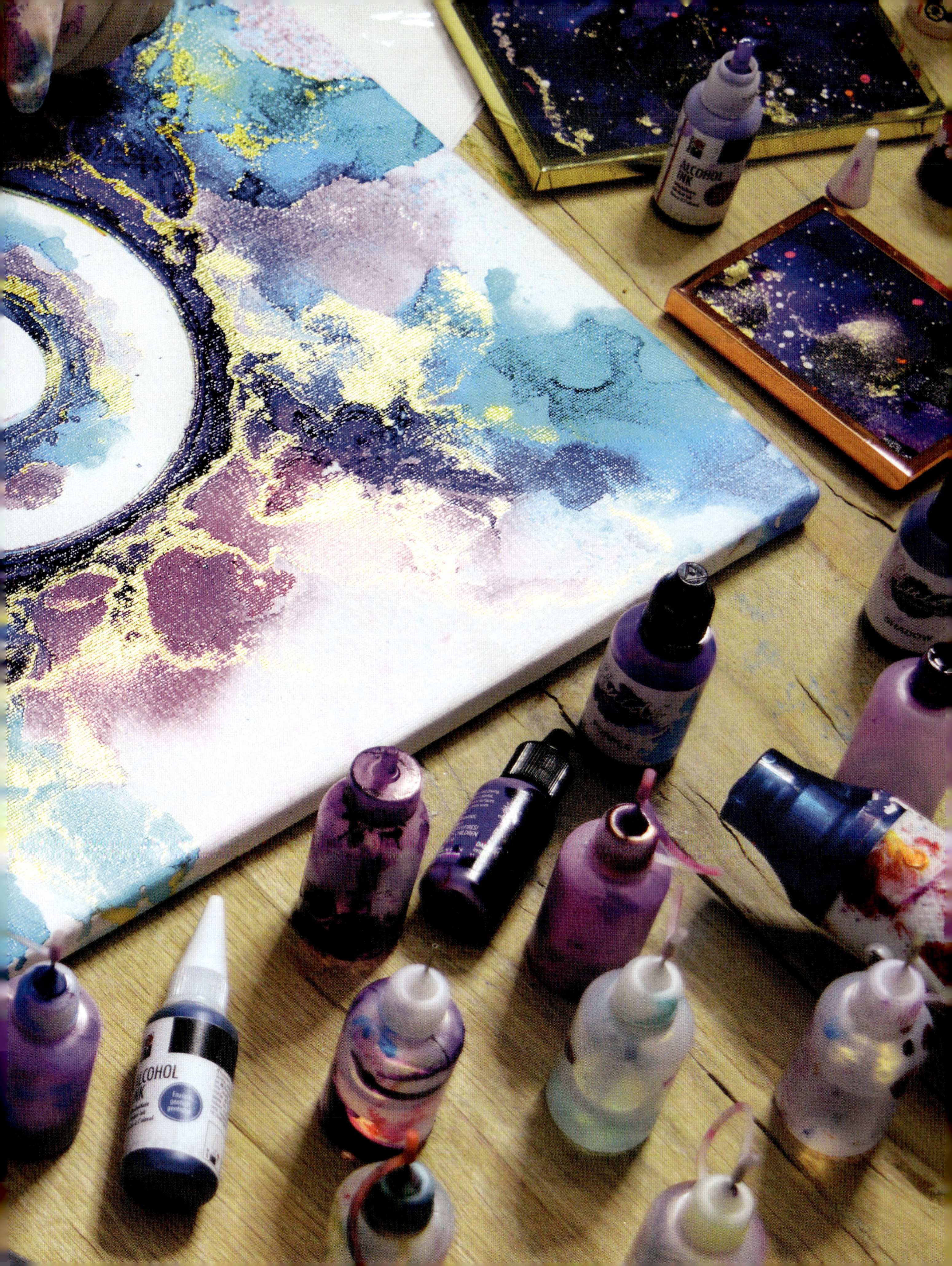

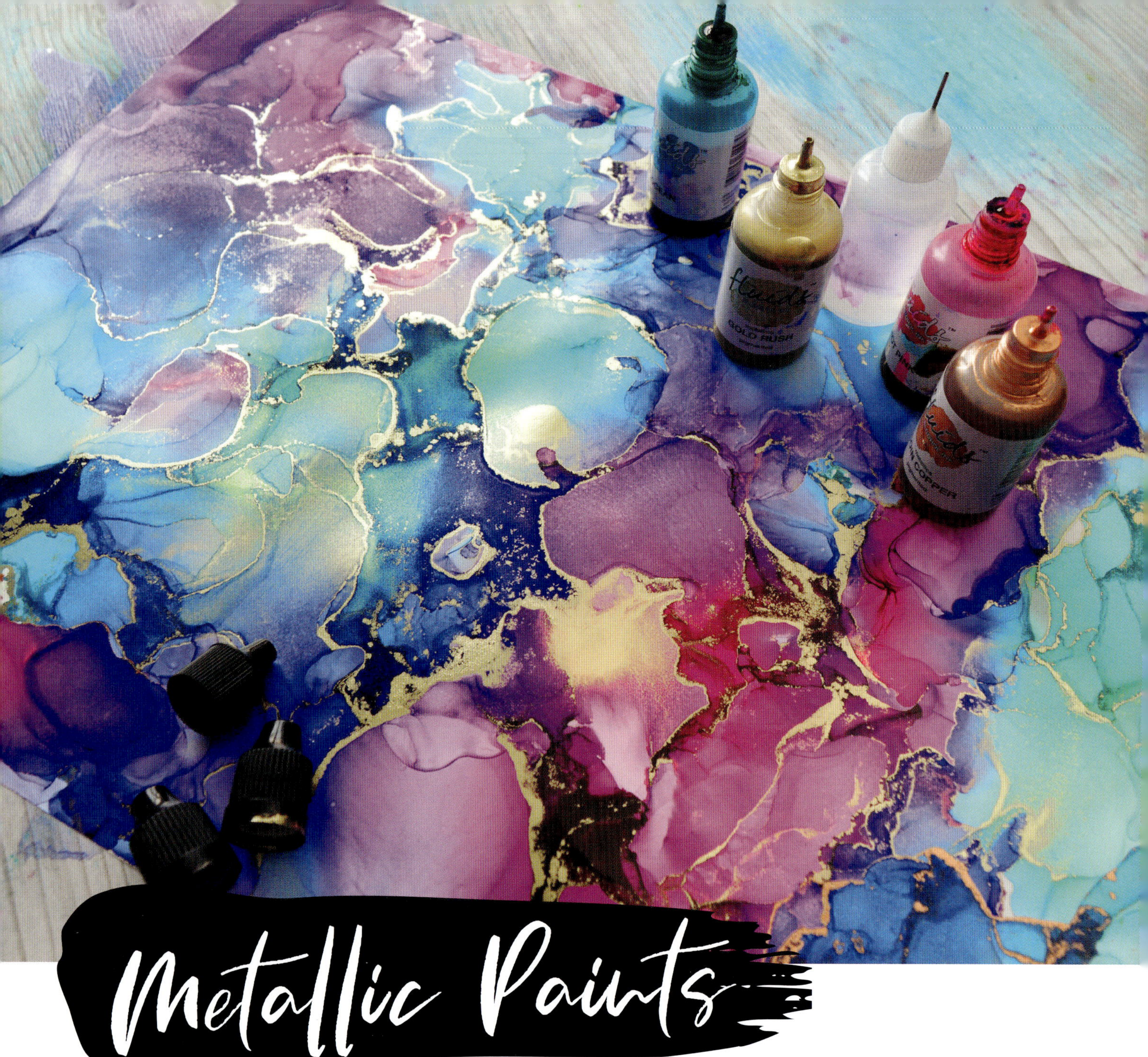

Metallic Paints

The Cloudy and Wispy techniques in particular can be beautifully refined with metallic paints. The effects that subsequently emerge are unparalleled. To achieve the shimmering veins of gold, you'll need the special metallic paints that are available as alcohol inks. Although you could still simulate the effect by painting the metallic veins with acrylics, it's just not the same.

YOU'LL NEED

- Small hot-air blower
- Non-absorbent surface
- Alcohol ink
- Metallic alcohol ink
- Isopropanol (alcohol) in a small bowl with a pipette or in an applicator bottle

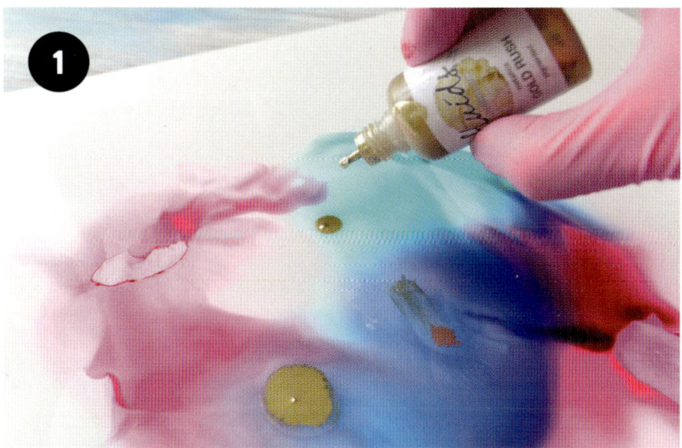

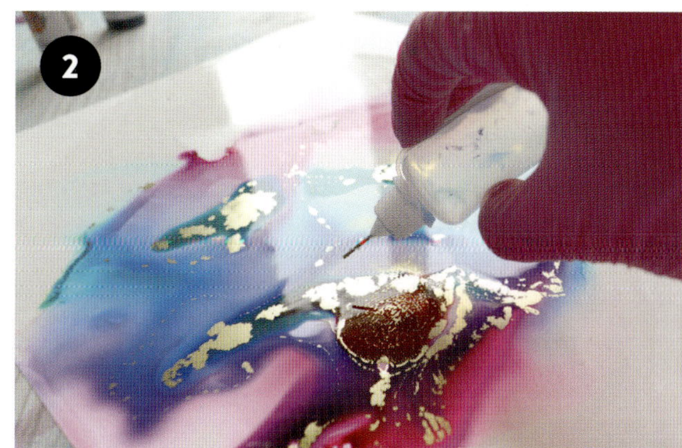

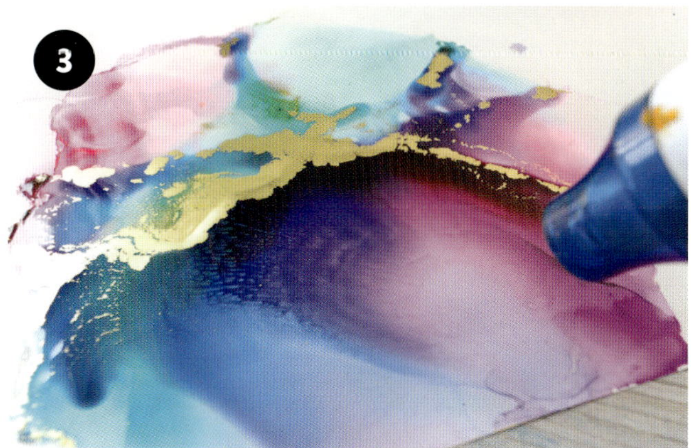

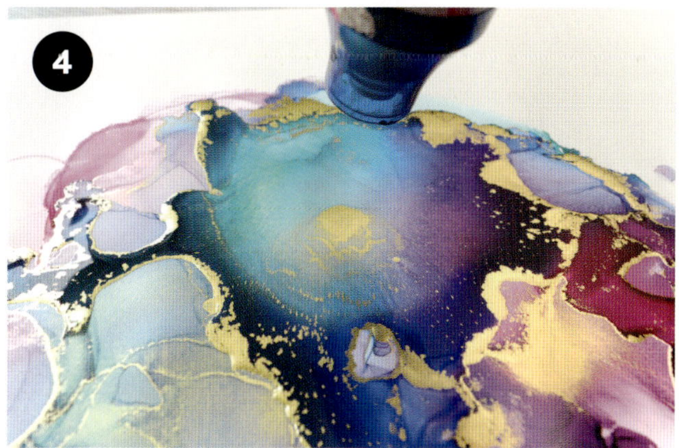

1 Have an applicator bottle ready with neat alcohol, or a bowl of alcohol and a pipette. Unscrew the lids of the alcohol inks. You need to be able to work quickly with everything. Start with a very wet surface as in the Cloudy technique, on to which you apply alcohol ink. You can roughly distribute the paint, but don't allow the liquids to dry. Now add one or two drops of gold alcohol ink on to a painted, wet area. The paint must be there first, then the metallic ink!

2 Now immediately drip neat alcohol on to the gold ink. Alternatively, immediately drip alcohol ink onto the painted area and follow straightaway with alcohol. This makes the gold particles drift apart and accumulate on the surface.

3 If you notice that there are too many particles on the surface, neat alcohol ink will help to pick up the pigments again. Even after you've started, this process can be repeated whilst the paint is still wet. (If necessary, stir once with your gloved finger.) Now you can start designing according to the basic techniques using the hot-air blower or airbrush.

4 With the hot-air blower, send the pigments quickly from different angles in different directions, as in the Cloudy technique. Let them collect a bit on the edge before sending them back in a different direction. This is how veins and islands are formed, creating a marbled effect.

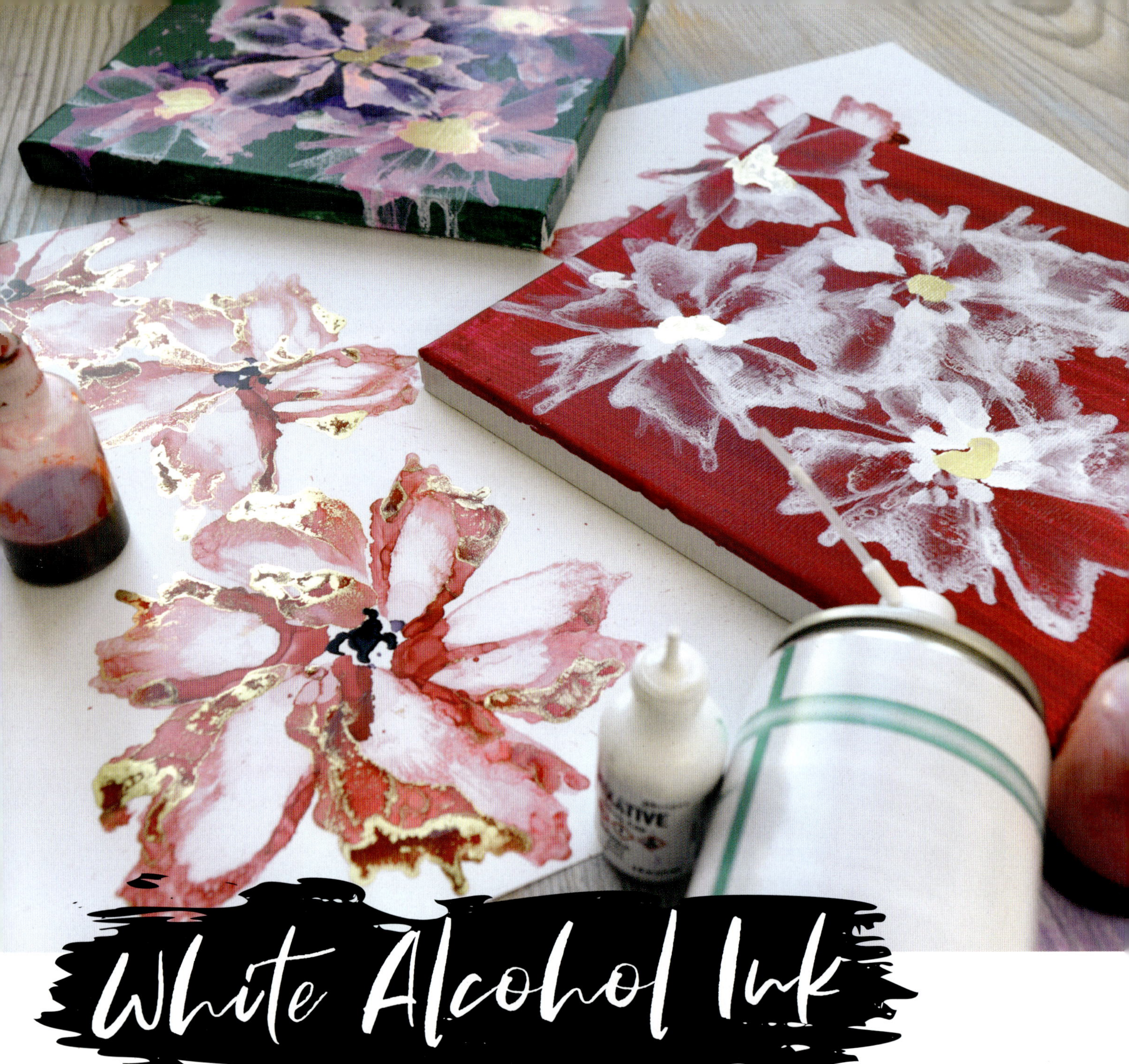

White Alcohol Ink

The colourful shades of alcohol inks can be supplemented with white, whose pigments behave slightly differently from those of the other coloured inks containing dye. You can mix white with the coloured alcohol inks or paint it on neat. I have given an example here of how you can paint with white to create my abstract flowers.

YOU'LL NEED

- Compressed air can with a small pipe
- Non-absorbent coloured surface
- White alcohol ink
- Gold metallic alcohol ink

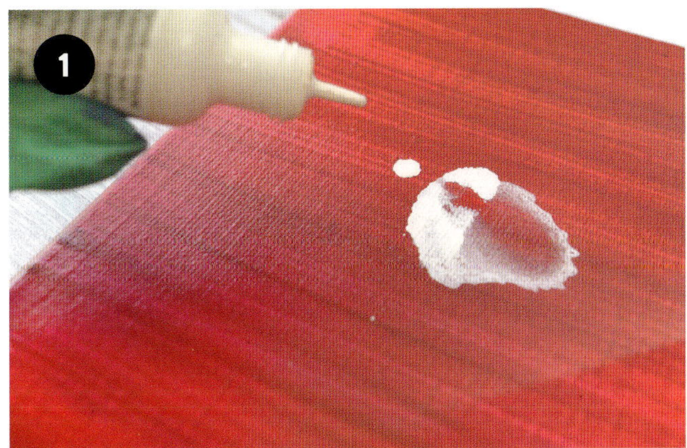

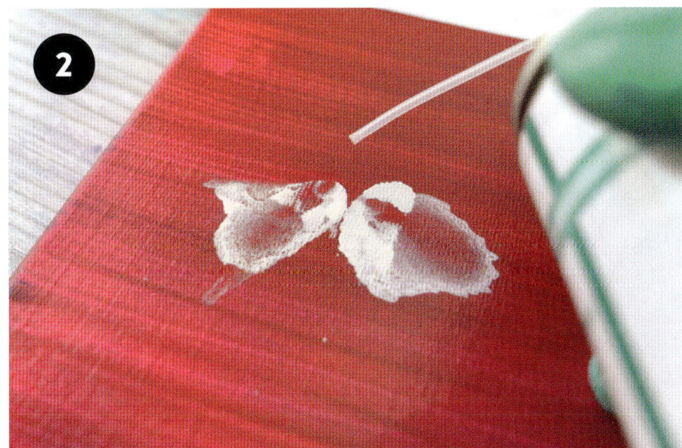

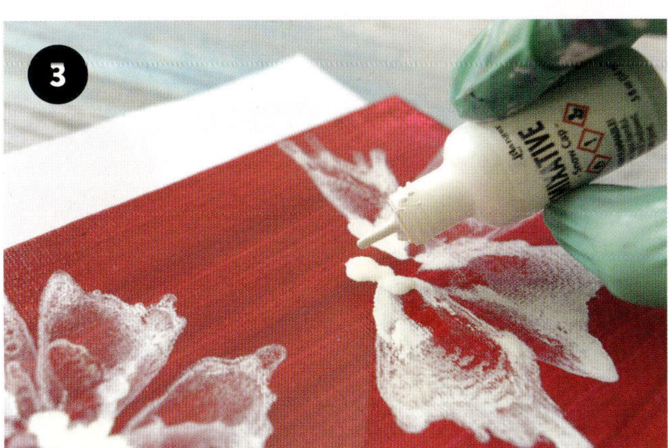

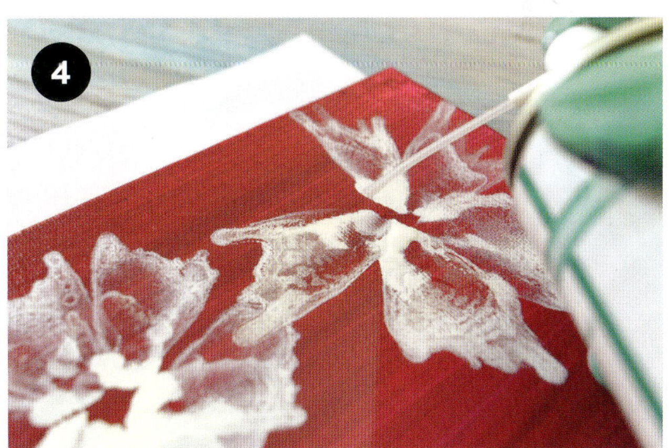

1 I painted a canvas all over with red acrylic paint and
let it dry completely. To create a petal, add one or
two drops of white.

2 With the compressed air can, spray quite close to
the drop. Other petals can be shaped, depending on
the angle. It's best to practise this on a separate
sheet. Holding the can flatter to the surface can
result in sharper shapes, while holding the can more
directly above the surface creates softer edges.

3 The next petal is created from another drop of
white ink placed next to it. Rotate your painting
surface to get the correct angle with the
compressed air can.

4 You can also create four or five petals directly
from a very large drop, but you have to work
quickly, because the white ink dries fast. To form
the centre of the flower, I have added blobs of
gold (see photo).

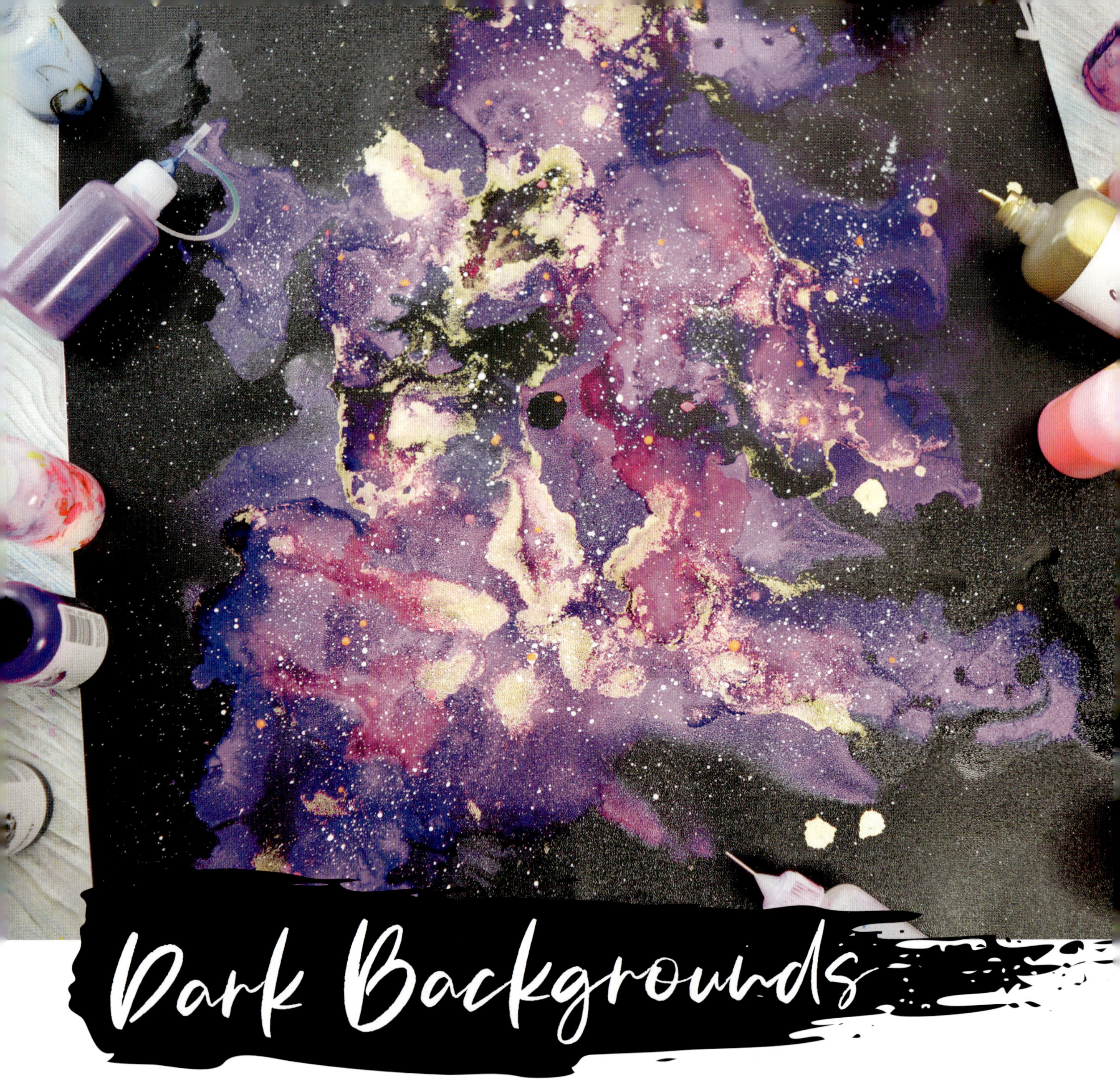

Dark Backgrounds

On dark and even black surfaces, you can paint with alcohol ink by mixing the inks with white, which gives them an opacity that shows up against the background. For this technique, fill an applicator bottle with coloured alcohol ink, such as pink, purple or violet, and add white. Experiment with different ratios. You don't need to add neat alcohol. If you don't want to mix the colours yourself, you can also buy opaque alcohol inks.

YOU'LL NEED

- Small hot-air blower
- Blackboard film
- Alcohol ink mixed with white (or pre-prepared opaque alcohol ink)
- Gold metallic alcohol ink
- Black alcohol ink
- Isopropanol (alcohol) in a bowl with pipette or in applicator bottle
- White acrylic paint; also orange and pink (optional)
- Pointed, fine tip paintbrushes

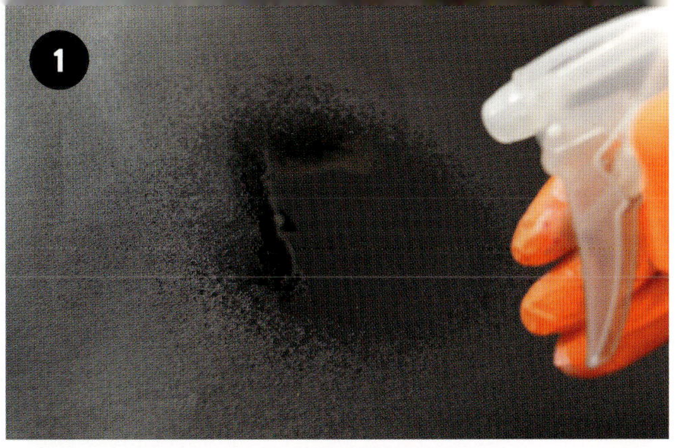

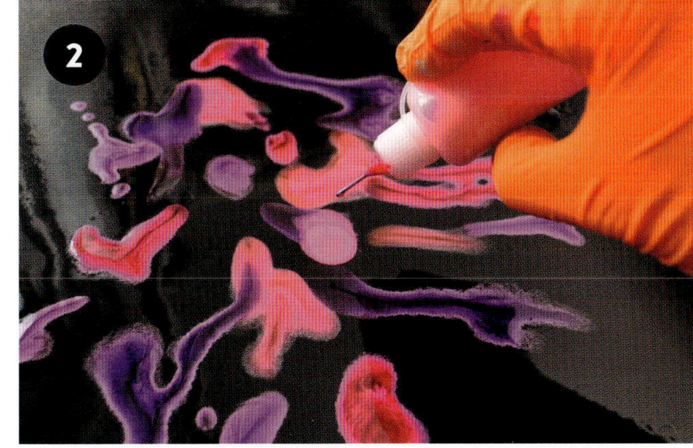

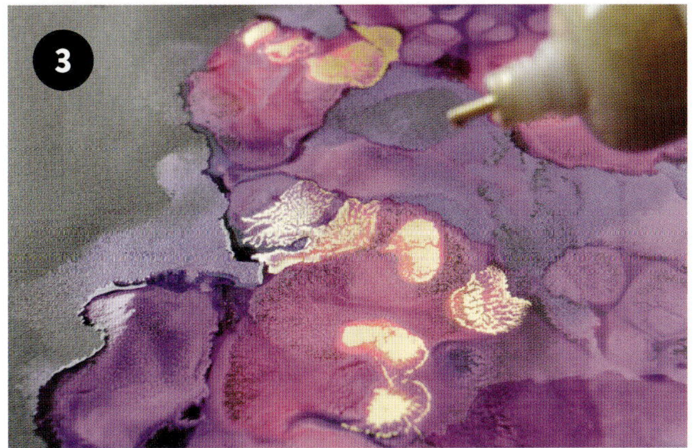

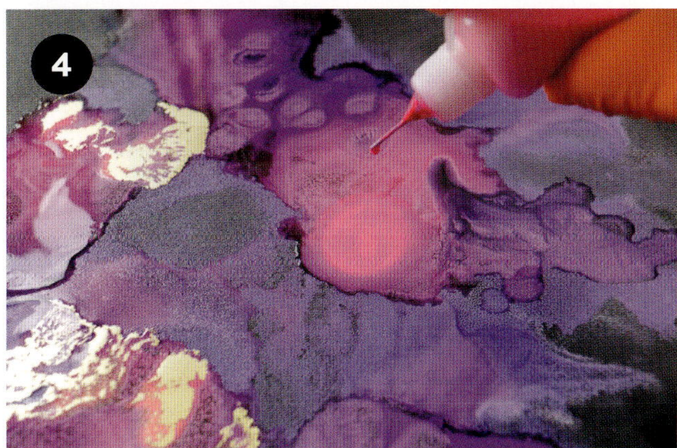

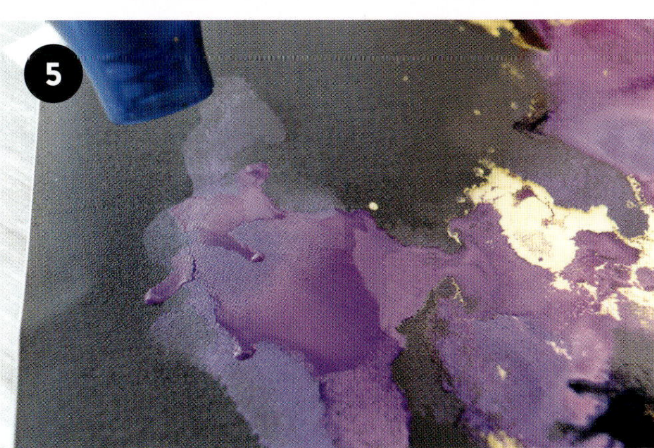

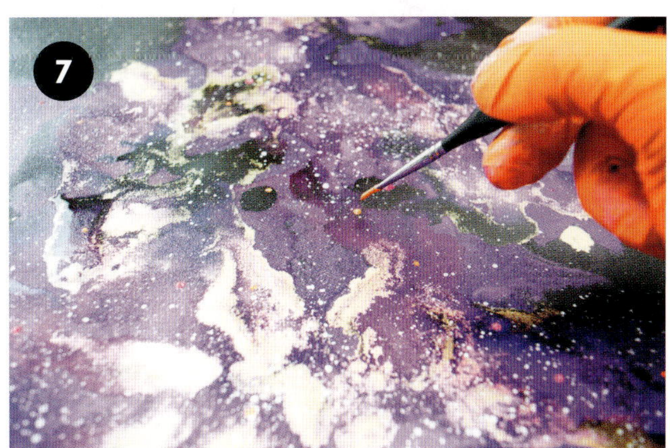

1 Spray the blackboard film generously with neat alcohol.

2 Apply the paint, using the Cloudy technique, and blow them to the outer edges, making them as Wispy as possible, with Cloudy effects in the middle. Don't let the inks dry.

3 While the area is still wet, add gold. Don't blow it dry, leave it to work without intervening – there shouldn't be any marbling effects.

4 You can break up the gold areas using alcohol ink by trickling neat pink or black on to them.

5 In other areas, you can continue to design with the mixed alcohol ink or add neat pink. Leave the centres alone, and actively blow-dry the outer areas by blow-drying, so that a haze is created.

6 When you're satisfied, let everything dry thoroughly and seal it with UV protector and clear varnish.

7 Finally, paint the stars with acrylic paints. Splatter white acrylic paint on to the surface with a paintbrush or a toothbrush, and paint the coloured stars with a fine tip paintbrush using pink and orange acrylic paint (optional).

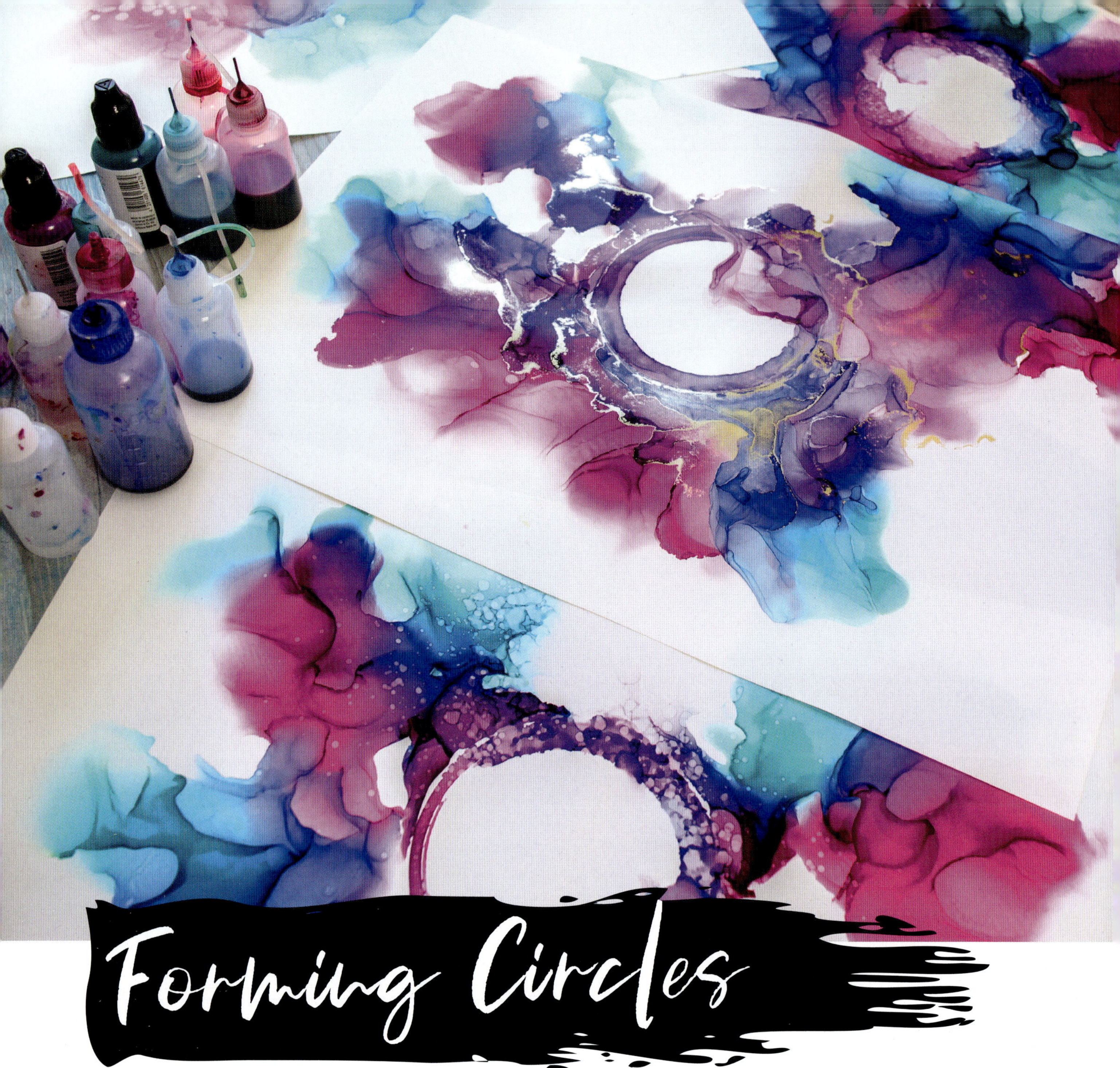

Forming Circles

There's a knack to working with alcohol ink in a controlled way, but you can easily achieve perfect circles by placing a circular object on your painting surface and letting the ink flow around it. The white spaces that emerge are great for framing lettering or small illustrations, or to create mystical, abstract openings.

YOU'LL NEED

– Small hot-air blower or airbrush
– Non-absorbent surface
– Alcohol ink
– Isopropanol (alcohol) in a pipette or applicator bottle
– Isopropanol in a spray bottle

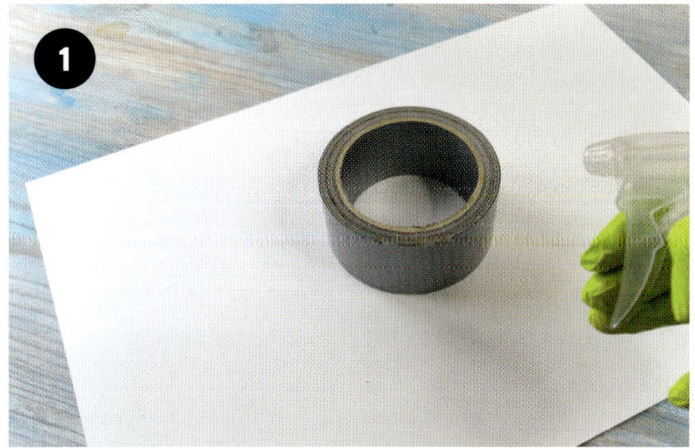

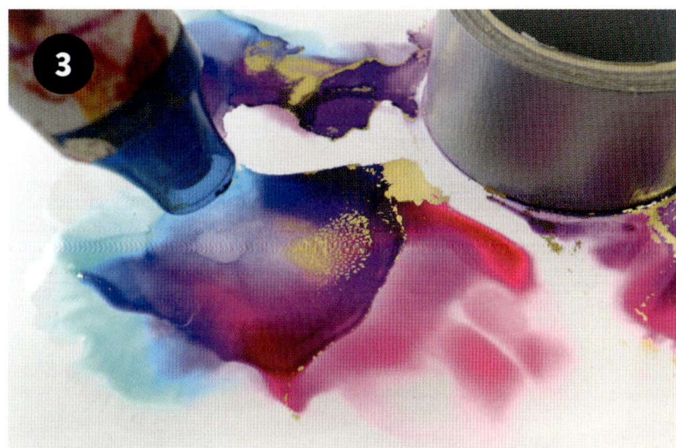

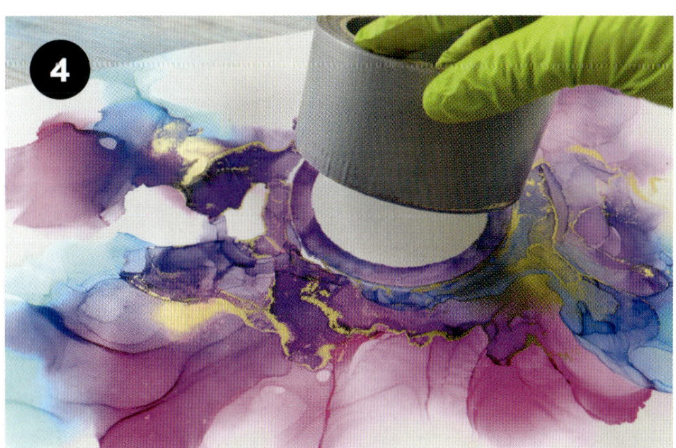

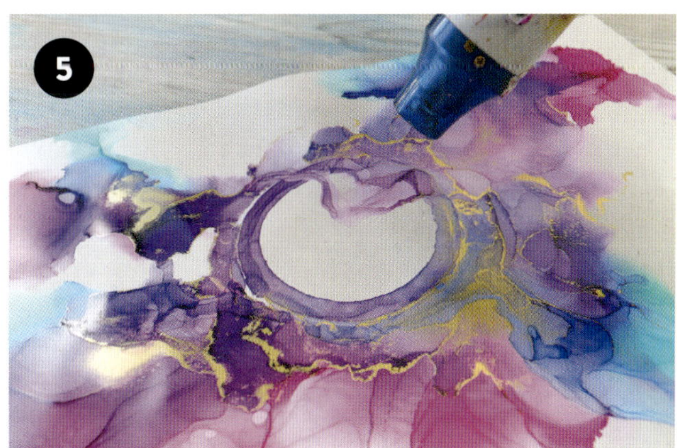

1 Place your round object on the painting surface.
I use a roll of duct tape or even a vase.

2 Spray the painting surface around it with alcohol.
Don't get any alcohol inside the circle.

3 Now apply alcohol ink and one or more basic
techniques around it, working inwards towards the
object. For simplicity, I've combined Cloudy shapes
with Wispy ones.

4 When the outer area is dry, you can remove your
round object from the painting surface and dry the
paint close to where it was.

5 From here, the ring can be further diluted, shaped
and reshaped.

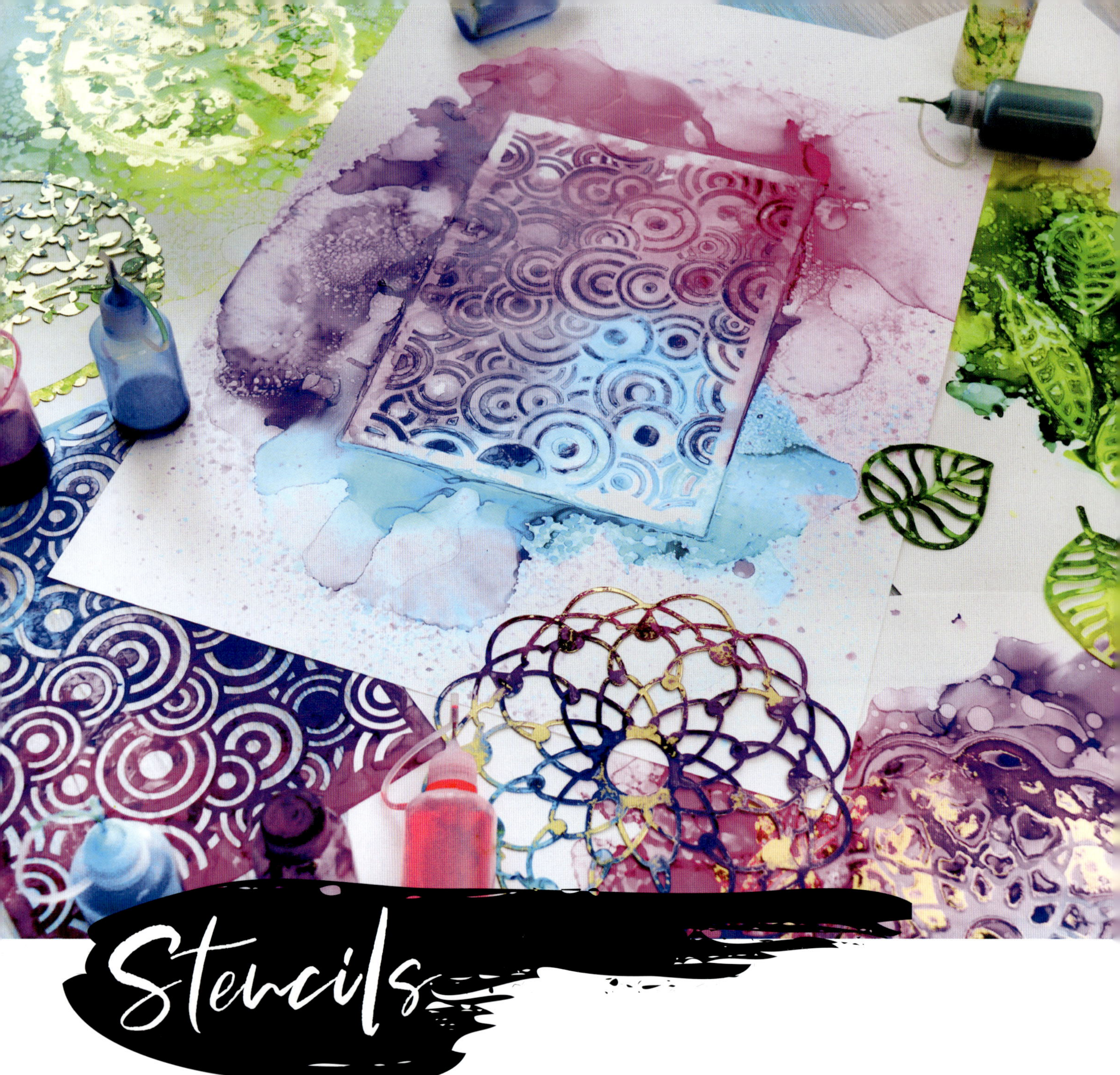

Stencils

Alcohol ink is well suited to creating shapes using stencils. However, the technique is slightly different from spraying or stippling paint, because the ink will usually manage to get into the areas that the stencil would normally mask. However, this creates images that have their own unique character. It's therefore important that you use stencils where the shape is designed with an outside edge to give a defined border.

YOU'LL NEED

- Small hot-air blower or airbrush
- Non-absorbent surface
- Alcohol ink
- Isopropanol (alcohol) in a pipette or applicator bottle
- Isopropanol (alcohol) in a spray bottle
- Self-adhesive laser-cut or punched stencils (or use temporary spray adhesive)

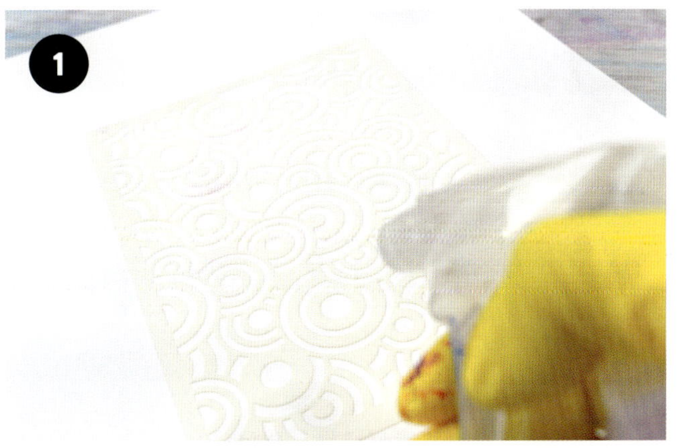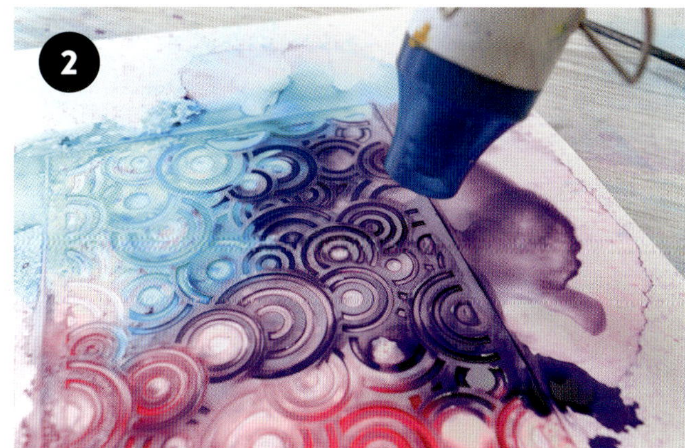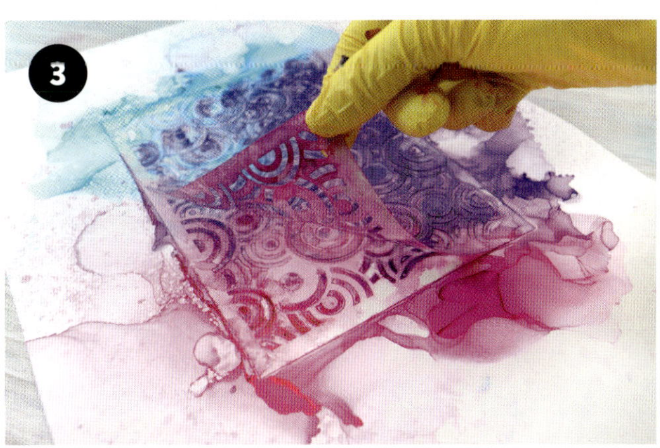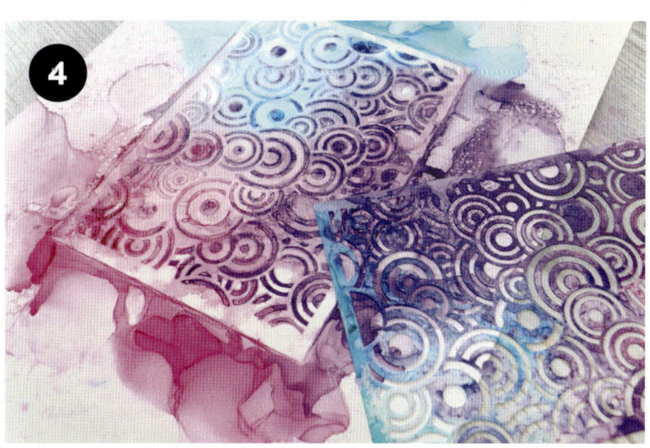

1 Use self-adhesive stencils, or spray them with spray glue as I did, to ensure they stick. The painting surface should be super smooth, so press down well. Now, following the basic techniques, spray everything with alcohol.

2 Next, sprinkle neat alcohol inks onto the stencil. Create your shapes with the hot-air blower, mixing the colours into one another.

3 When everything is dry, carefully remove the stencil and dry any wet areas under the stencil with the hot-air blower.

4 From this point, you can continue to design and dissolve the colours to create new shapes and effects, or leave it as it is.

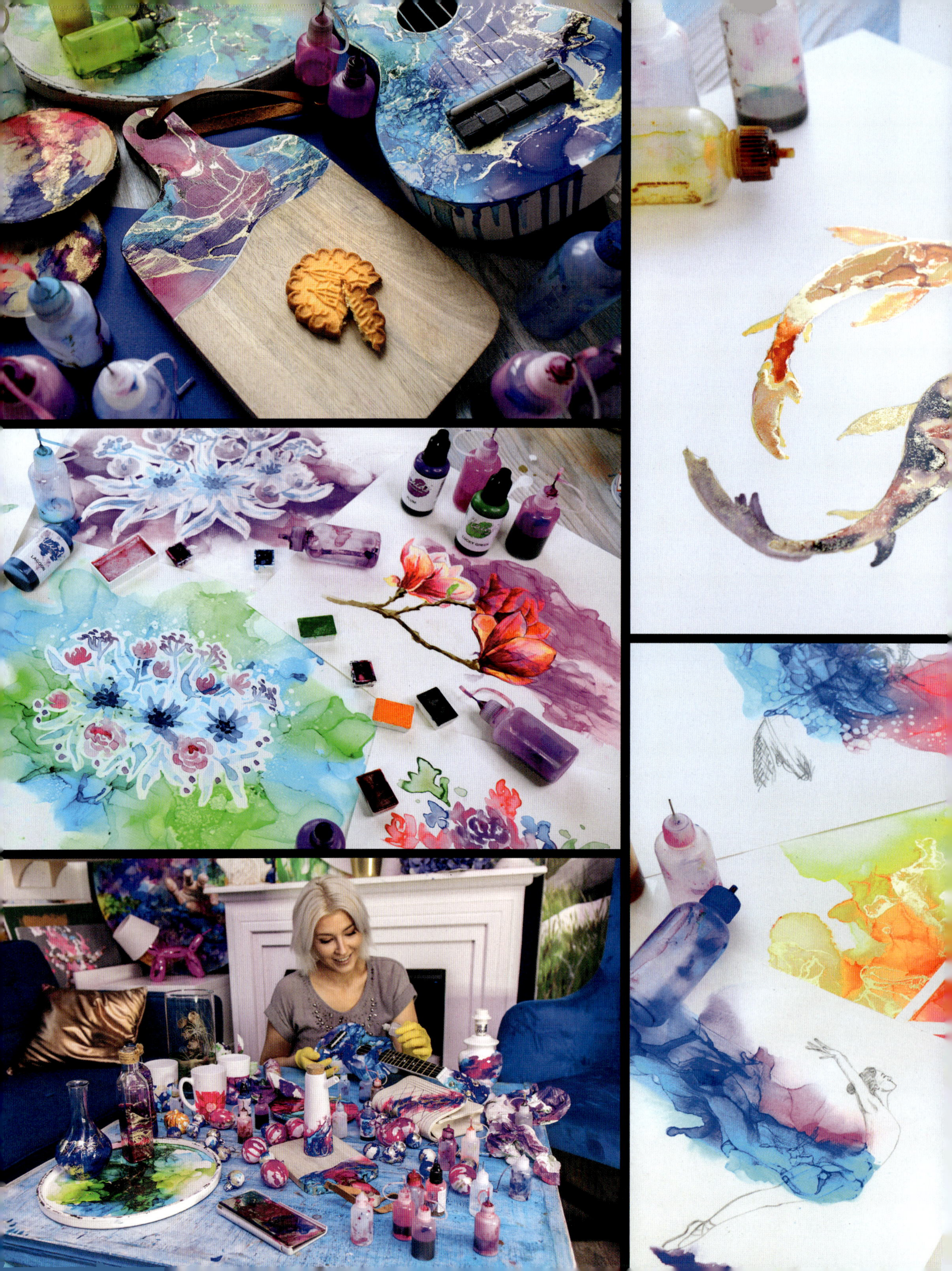

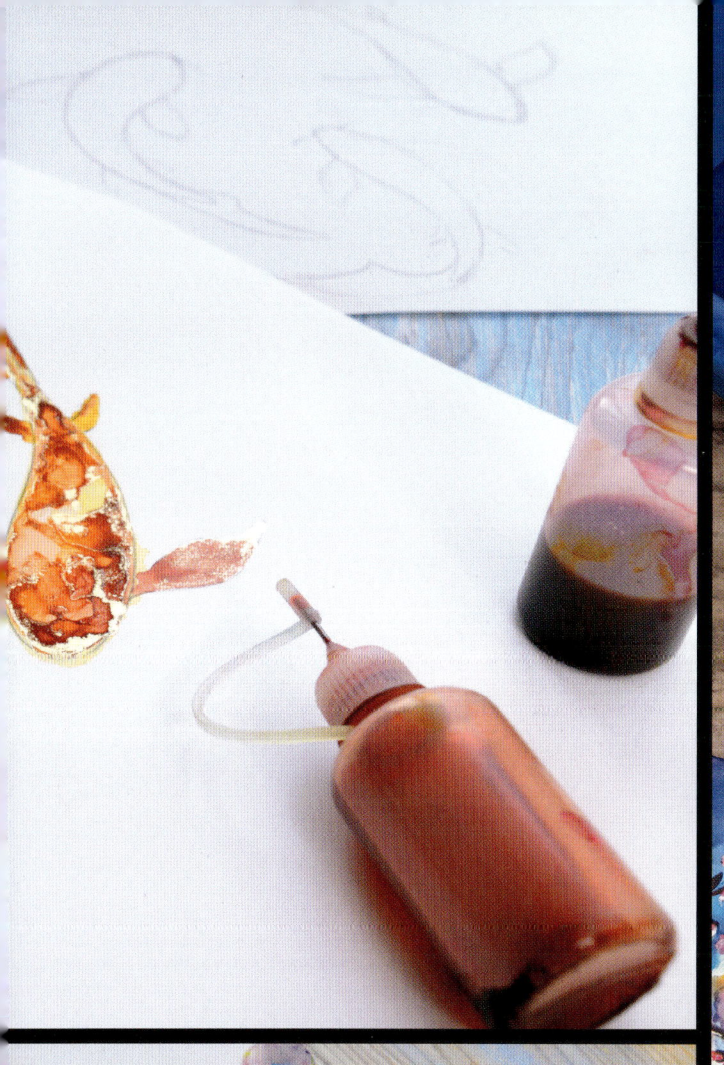

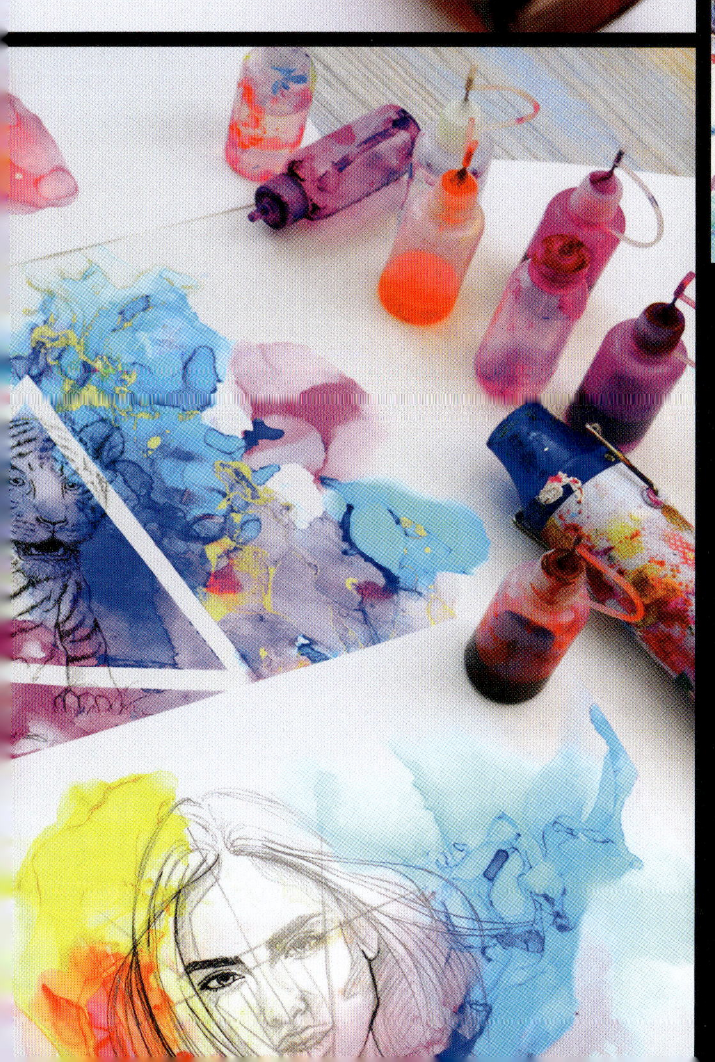

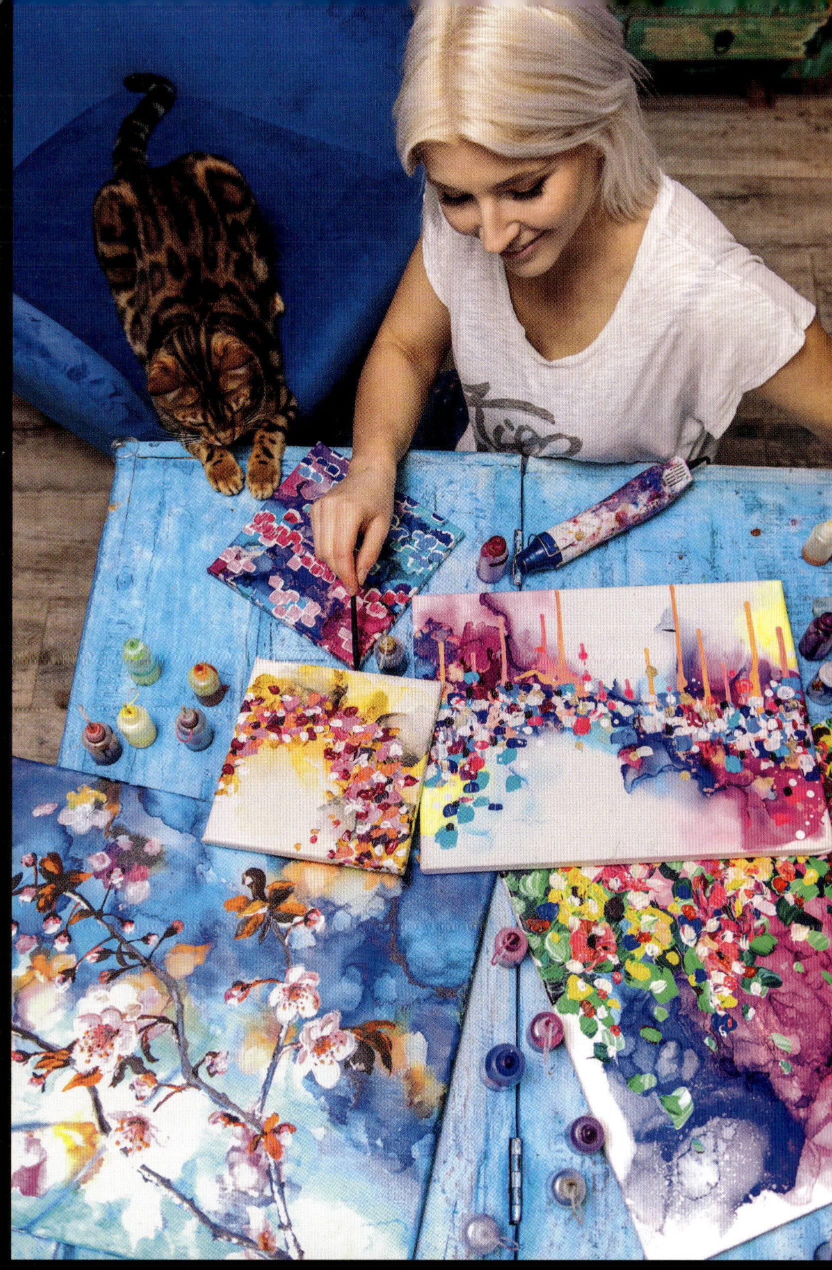

PROJECTS

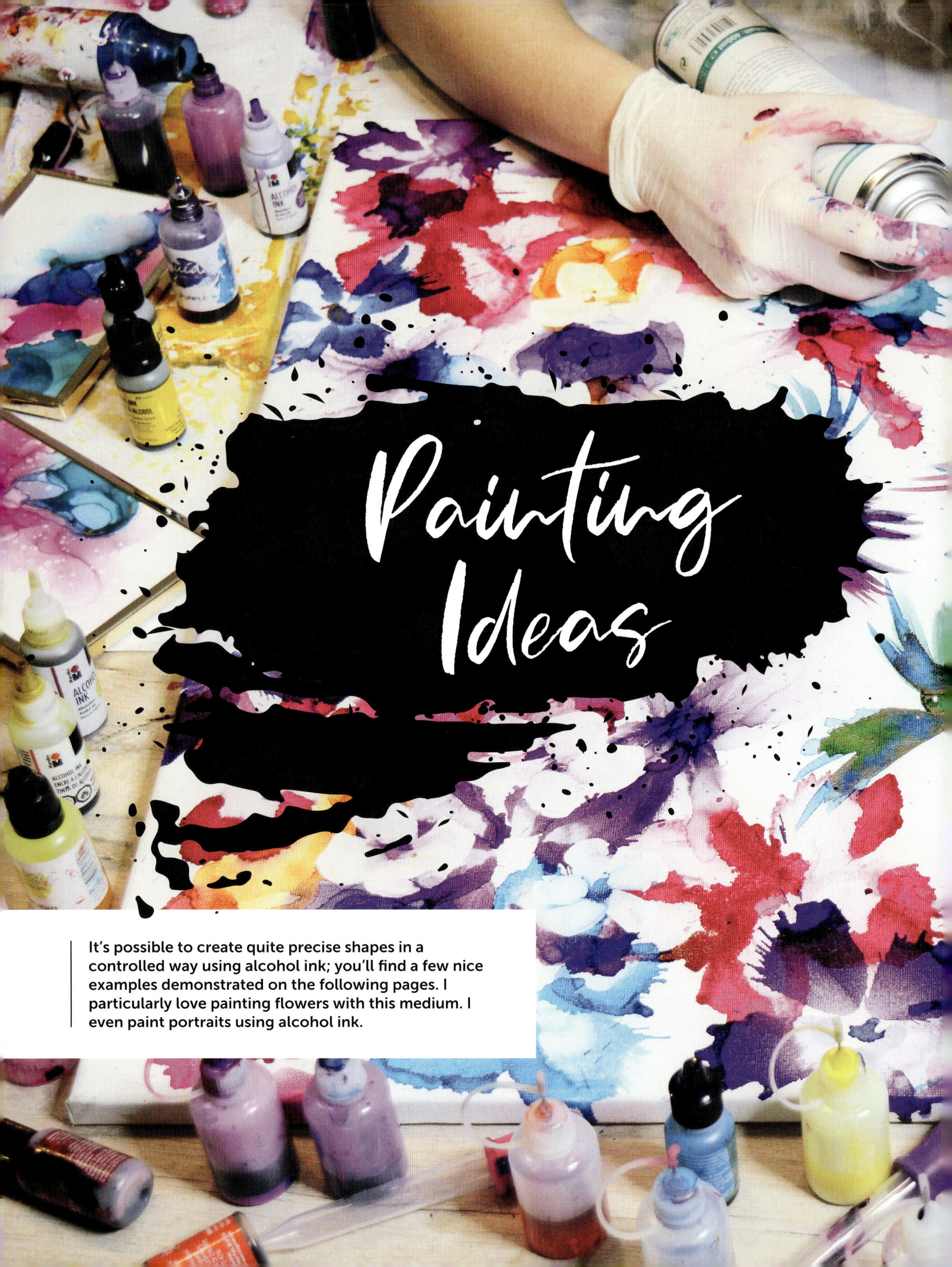

It's possible to create quite precise shapes in a controlled way using alcohol ink; you'll find a few nice examples demonstrated on the following pages. I particularly love painting flowers with this medium. I even paint portraits using alcohol ink.

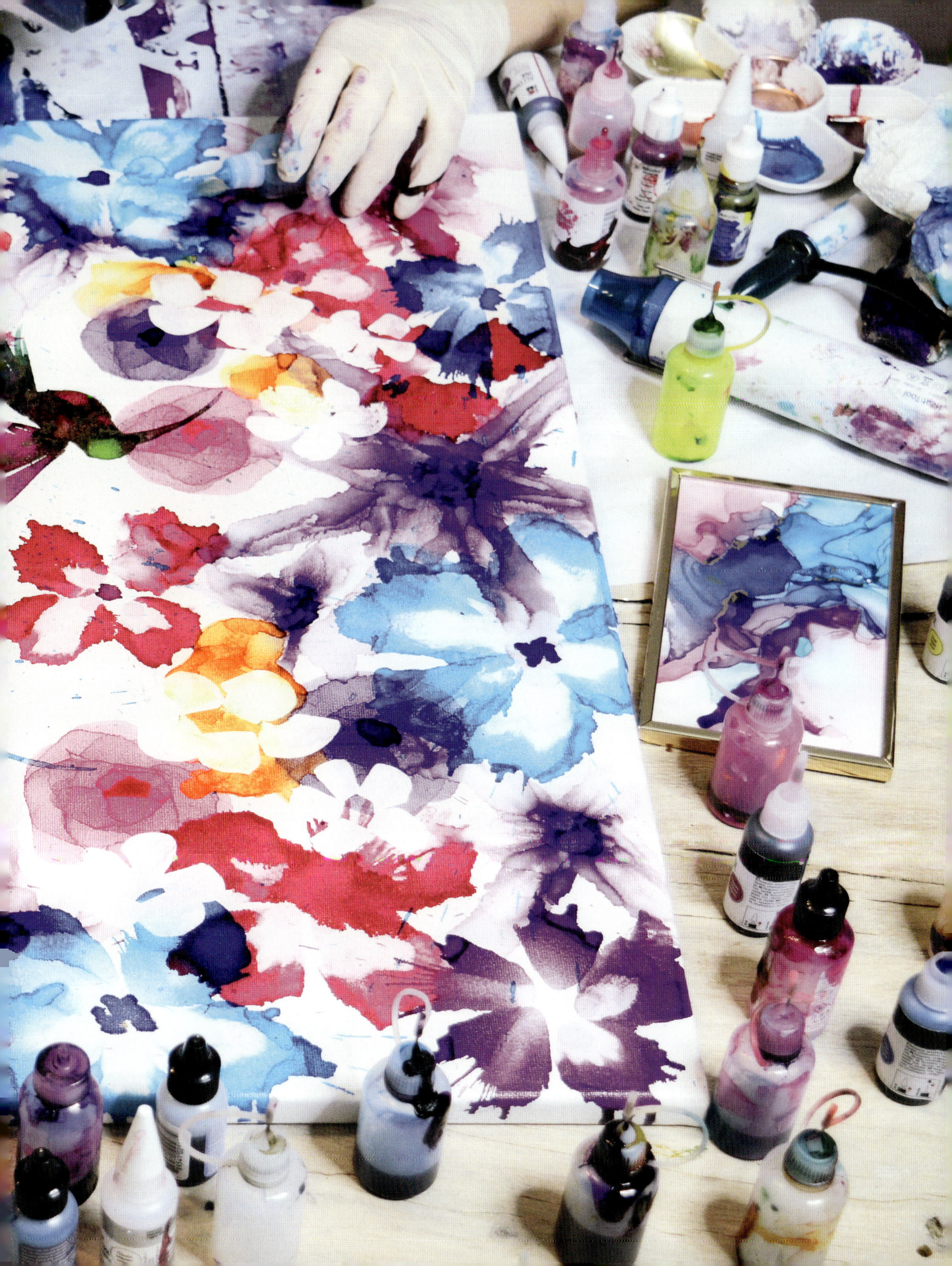

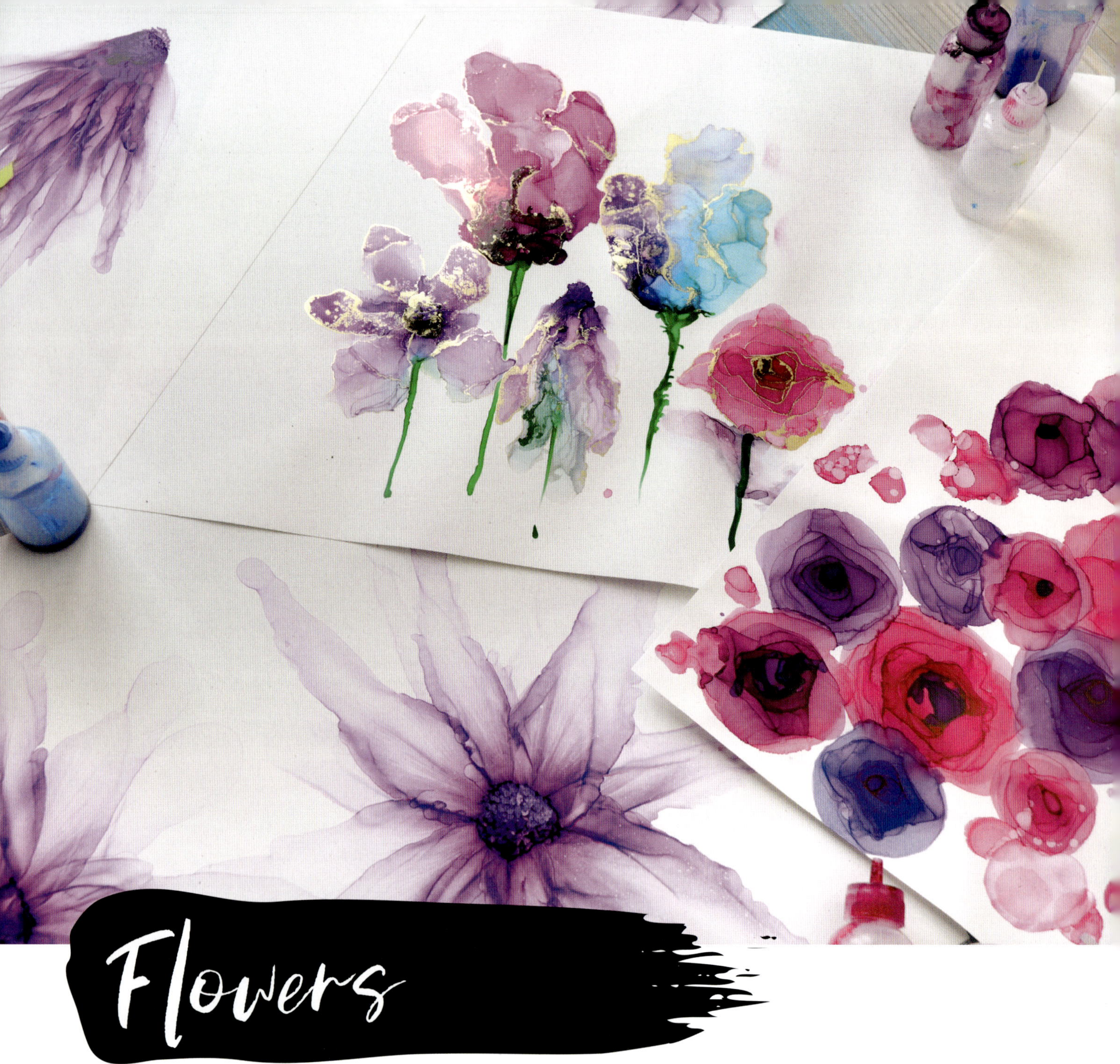

Flowers

Roses, daisies, echinacea and tulips can all be painted using alcohol ink and a bit of practise. These flowers always have a random, abstract feel, which will make each of your paintings unique. Gold can be used to create fabulous embellishments for petals. The flowery figures are formed using the basic techniques of Cloudy, Drift and Soak.

YOU'LL NEED

- Small hot-air blower and airbrush
- Non-absorbent surface
- Alcohol ink
- Isopropanol (alcohol) in a pipette or applicator bottle
- Isopropanol from a spray bottle

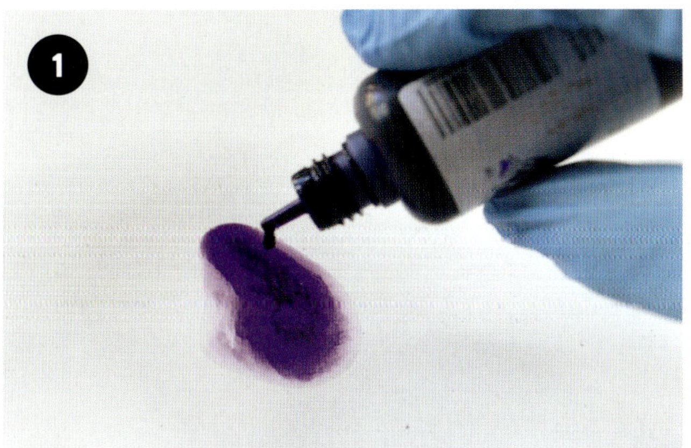

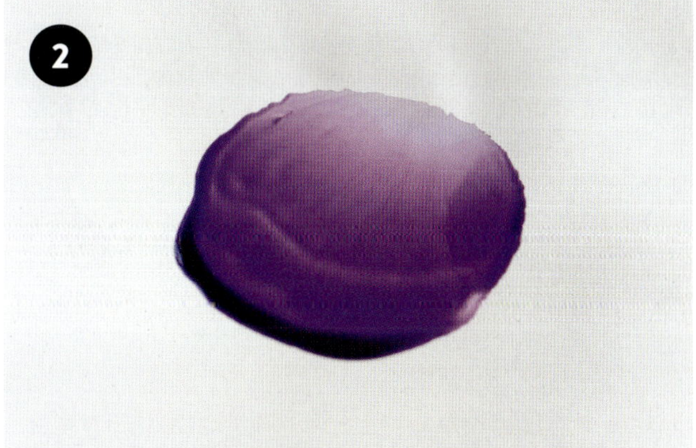

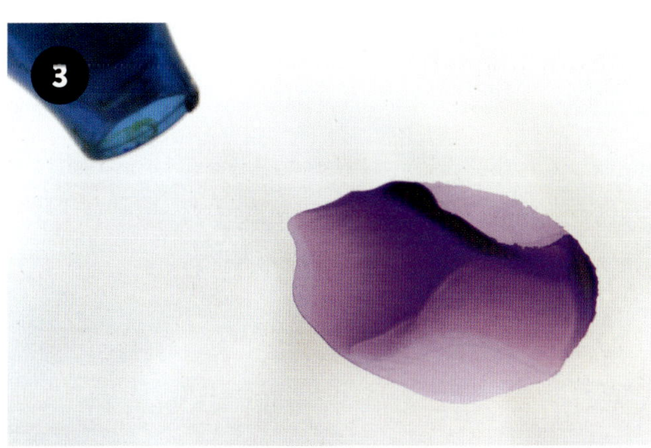

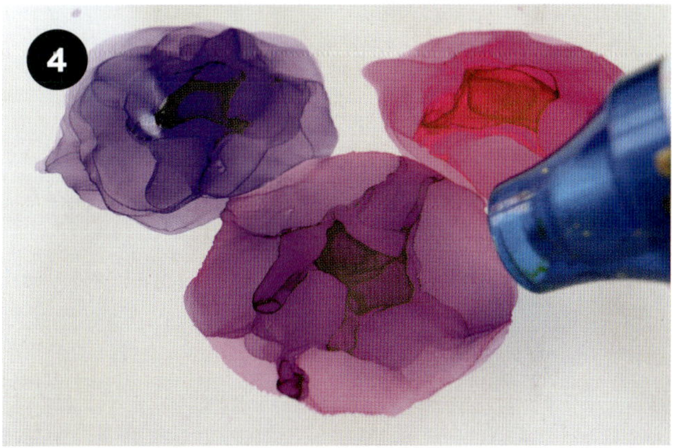

ROSES

1 Apply isopropanol and alcohol ink to a small area of your prepared surface.

2 Next, form a circle with the ink using your finger (but remember to put gloves on first!).

3 Now use the Cloudy technique to create the flower shape. Keep blowing the ink over the area from different angles in a controlled way.

4 To give the impression of multiple petals, dry an area at the edge. Then send the ink from the opposite direction a little bit more into this dried area, then immediately away from a different angle. This creates the thin line of more concentrated ink that marks the petal edge.

5 Keep going like this in different spots until you arrive in the middle. The dye will accumulate here and form the flower centre.

NOTE

Feeling inspired? Take a look at my online courses if you want to learn more.

PAINTING IDEAS

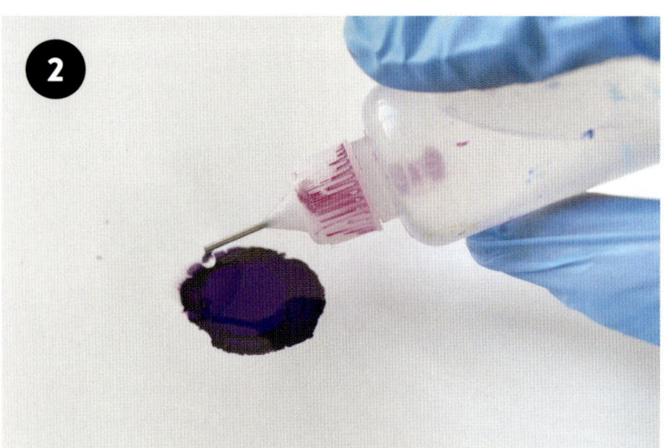

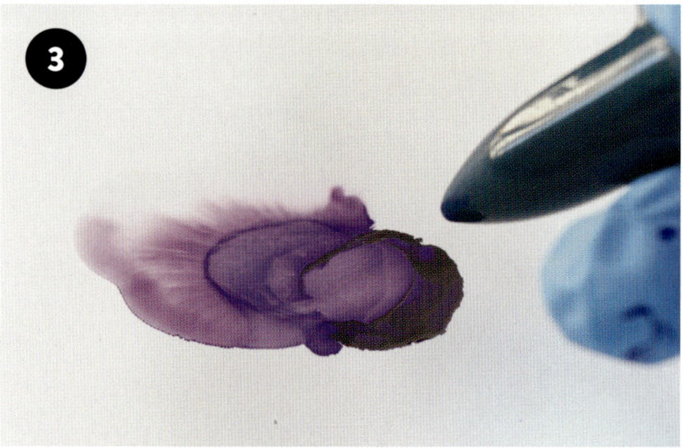

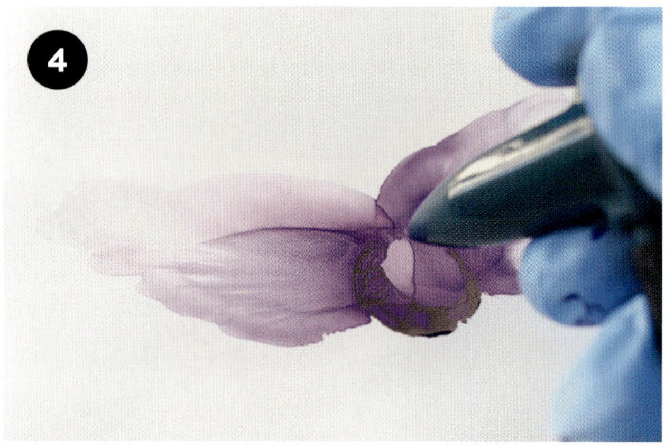

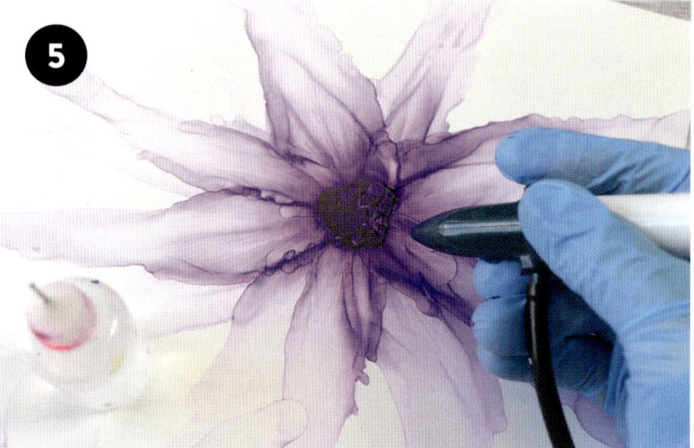

DAISIES

1 Put neat alcohol ink on to the surface. At the start, it's best to add a dark, intense colour. Let it dry.

2 **SOAK:** now apply a drop of neat alcohol to the edge, and briefly let it act. To facilitate the direction of flow for Drift, add a little more neat alcohol to the painting in that area.

3 Using the Drift technique, send the dissolved colour outwards using cold air from the airbrush or a small air blower.

4 The angle from which you blow has an effect on the resulting petal. For best results, relax as you shape the petals.

5 Keep going around like this until you have created the desired number of petals, and they form a complete flower around the centre. Speckle the centre of the flower using white ink.

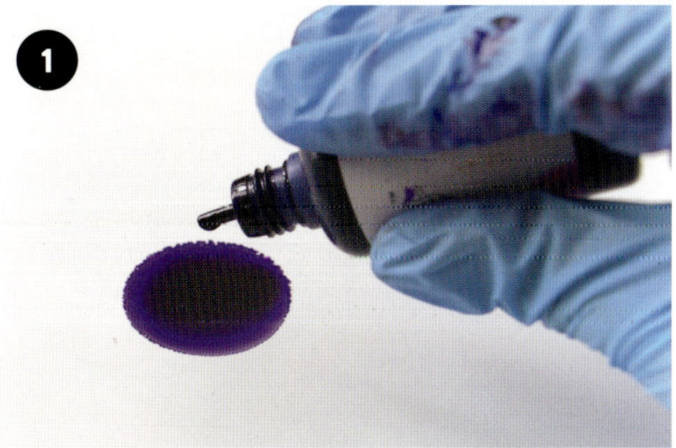

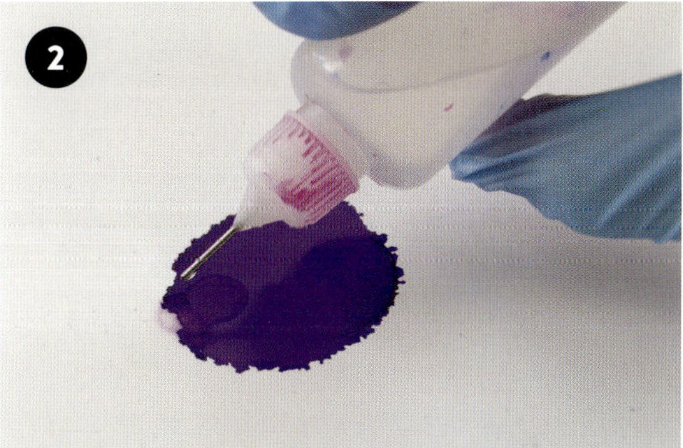

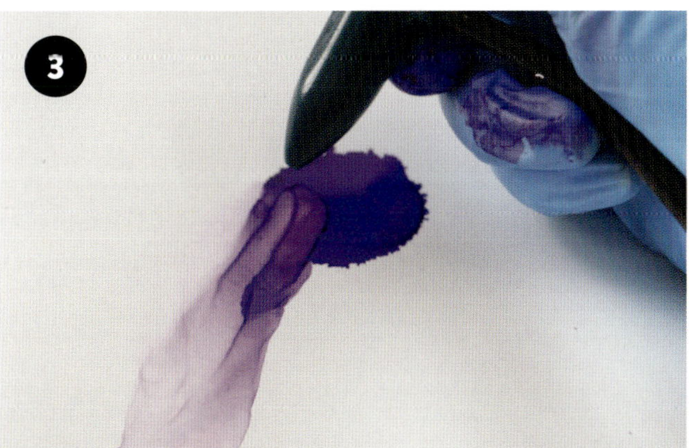

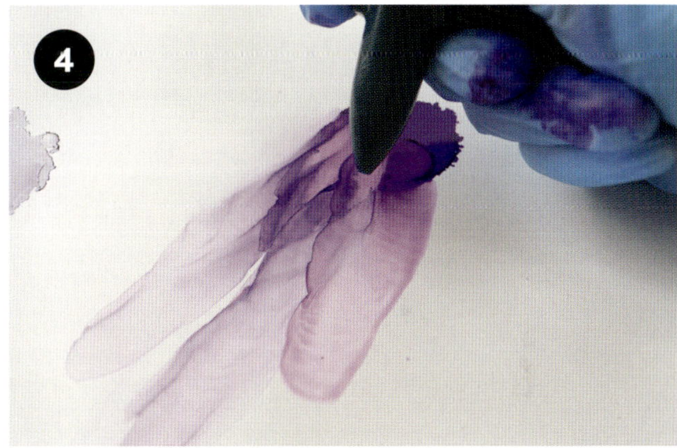

ECHINACEA

1 Drop neat alcohol ink on to the surface and let the little circle dry. The stem (see the middle flower on the finished picture) is made using green alcohol ink – draw a line directly from the bottle.

2 Use the Soak technique to to dissolve the ink using a neat drop of alcohol at the edge and …

3 … blow dry downwards using the Drift technique.

4 Repeat at the base of the petals in a fan shape. Use the same technique as for the daisy, but only blow at one edge so that the petals fan out in one direction only, and use Drift to make the petals more pointed.

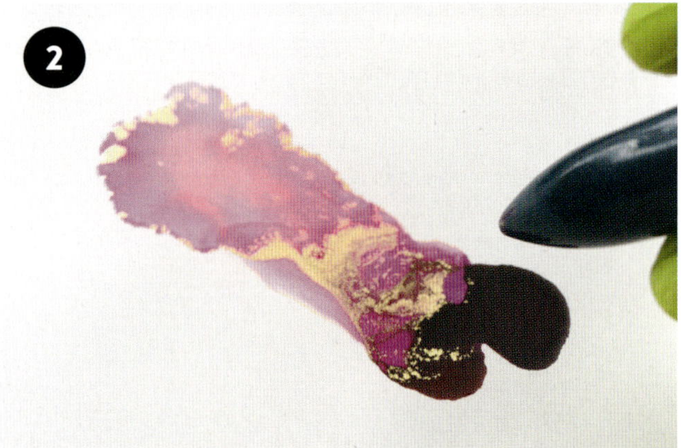

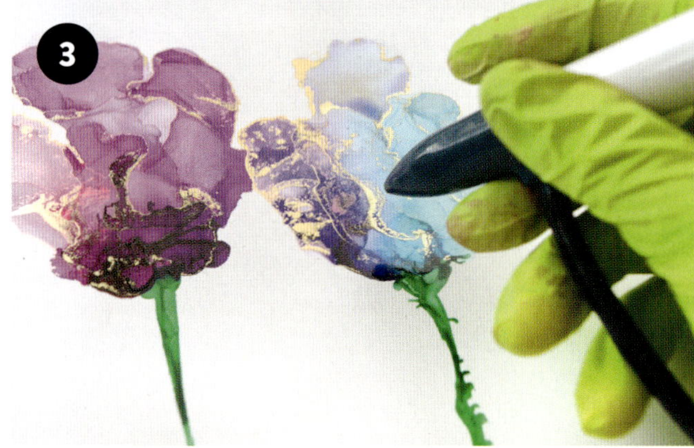

TULIPS

1 Apply two neat drops of alcohol ink in different colours, side by side. Let them dry.

2 Using Soak, allow a larger drop of neat alcohol to act. Then carefully blow outwards from a wide angle using the Drift technique.

3 Repeat three times on the top edge. Do the two outer petals, then the inner one. Allow each to dry before working on the next. This increases the likelihood of achieving a layering effect similar to watercolour. Add metallic ink for added shimmer using the technique described in the Metallic Paints section.

4 Add the stems with green alcohol ink, simply painting them in with a brush.

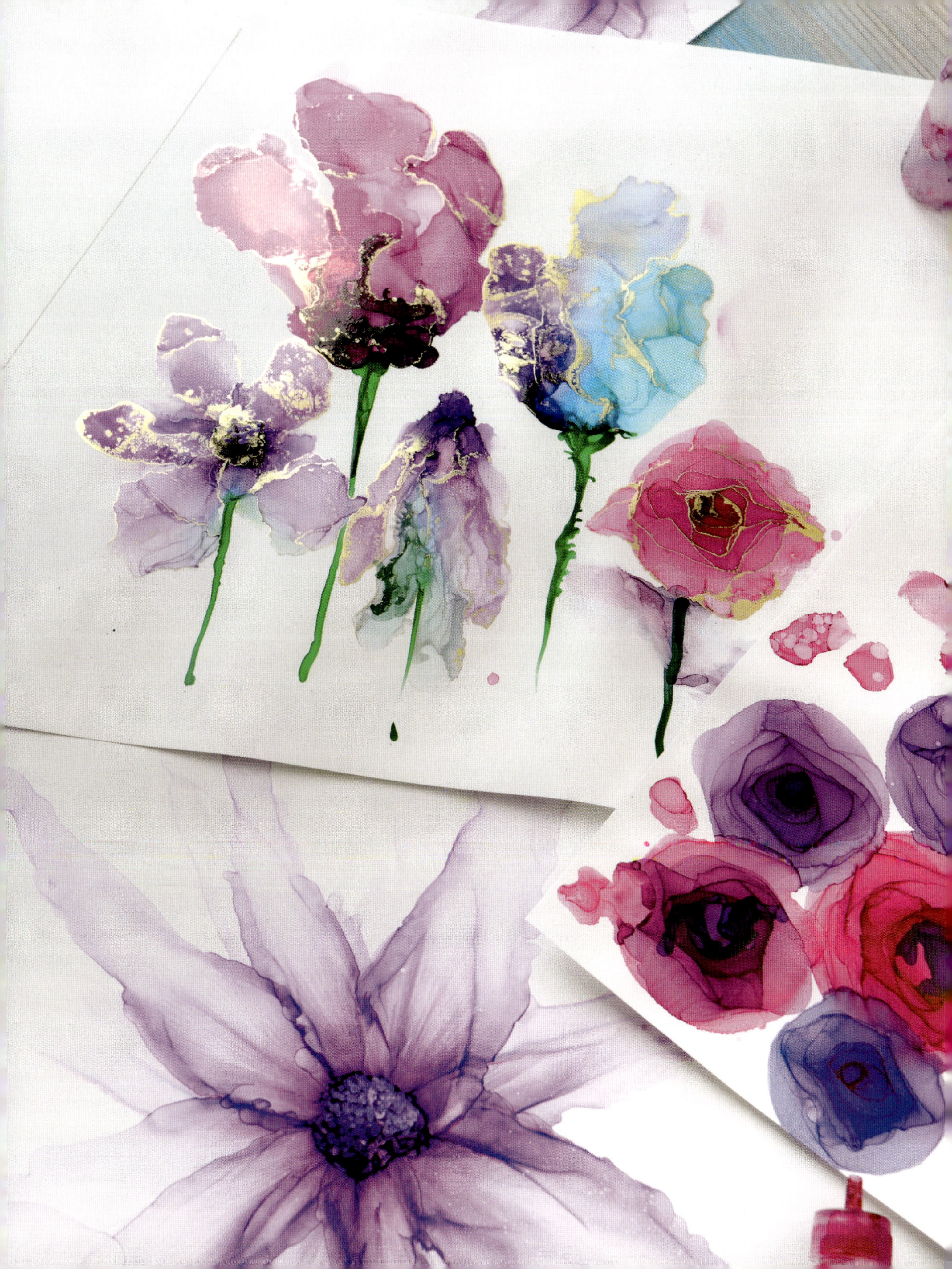

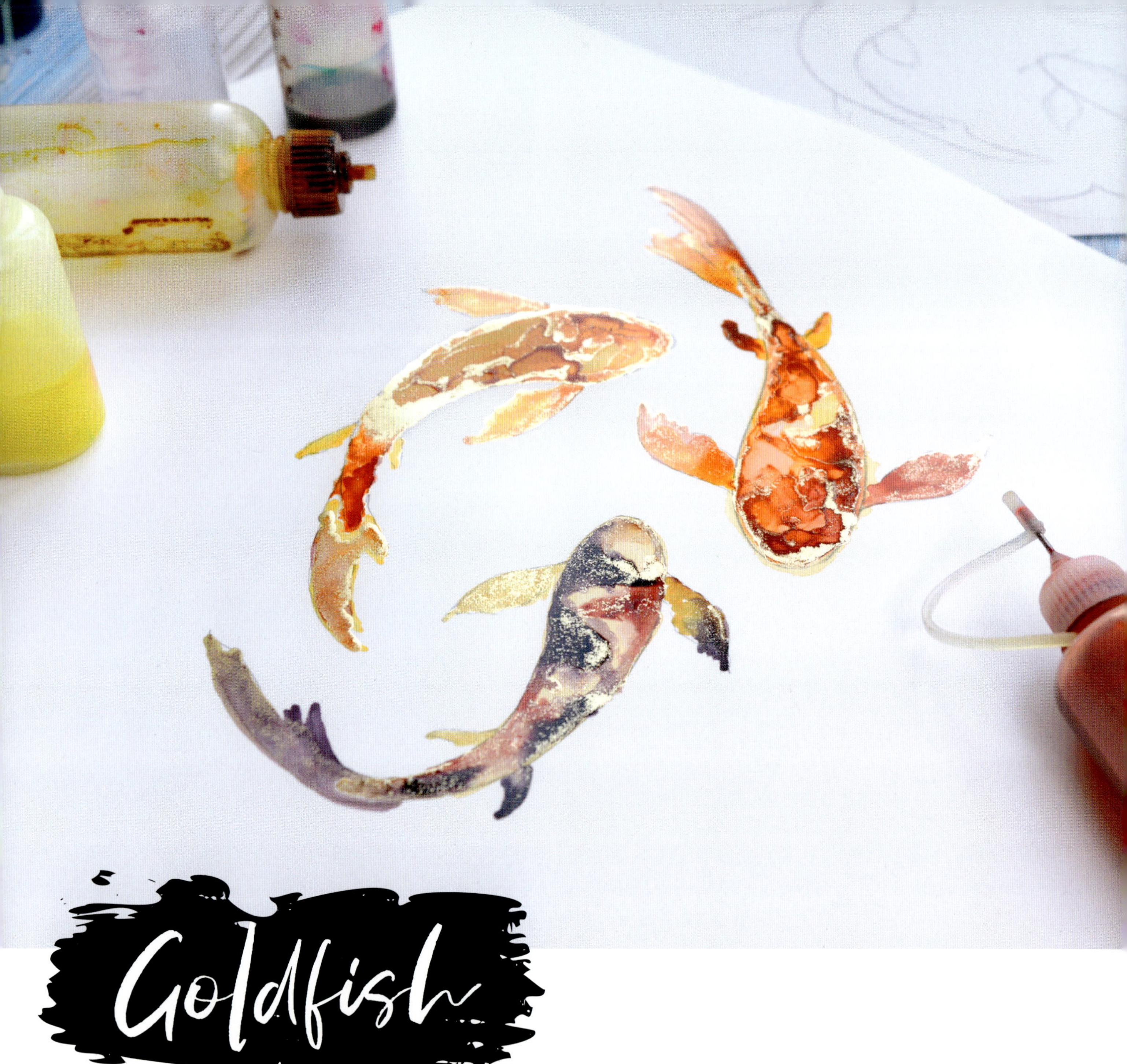

Goldfish

All sorts of objects, and even portraits, take on their own individual style with alcohol ink. To depict an item, animal or person, you'll need paintbrushes and a confidence with distributing the ink carefully. In the following example, I'll show you how I painted these iridescent goldfish.

YOU'LL NEED

- Small hot-air blower or airbrush
- Non-absorbent surface
- Alcohol inks
- Metallic alcohol ink
- Artist's palette
- H grade pencil
- Pointed, fine tip paintbrushes
- A small amount of isopropanol (alcohol) in a bowl

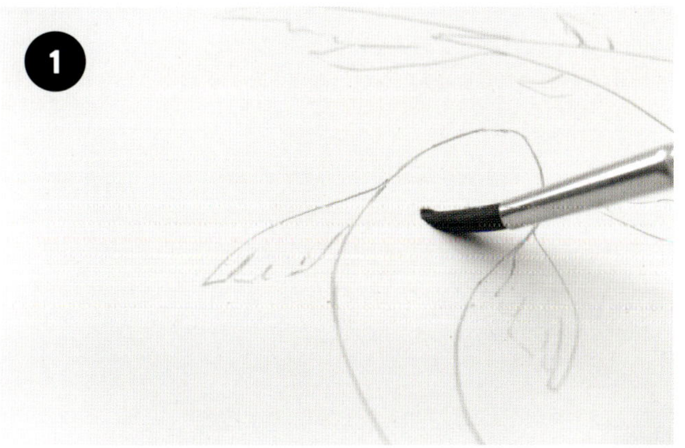

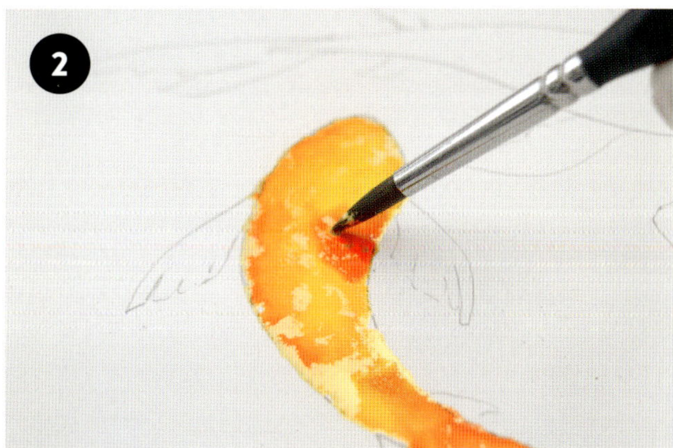

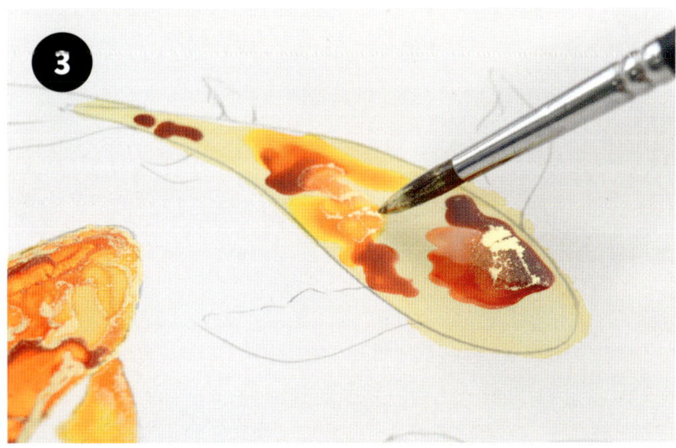

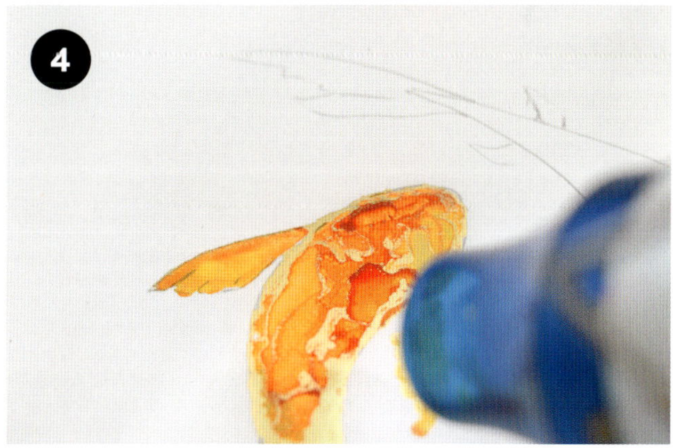

1 Draw your motif with light strokes using a hard pencil, so that the lines are distinct but barely visible. Now, with a paintbrush and neat alcohol, wet the area that is to be painted.

2 Put the alcohol inks in a palette and pick up the colours with a paintbrush, applying them in turn to the wet area as shown.

3 While the alcohol inks are still wet, create accents using the metallic ink.

4 Now create your design with the hot-air blower. Repeat the steps as needed.

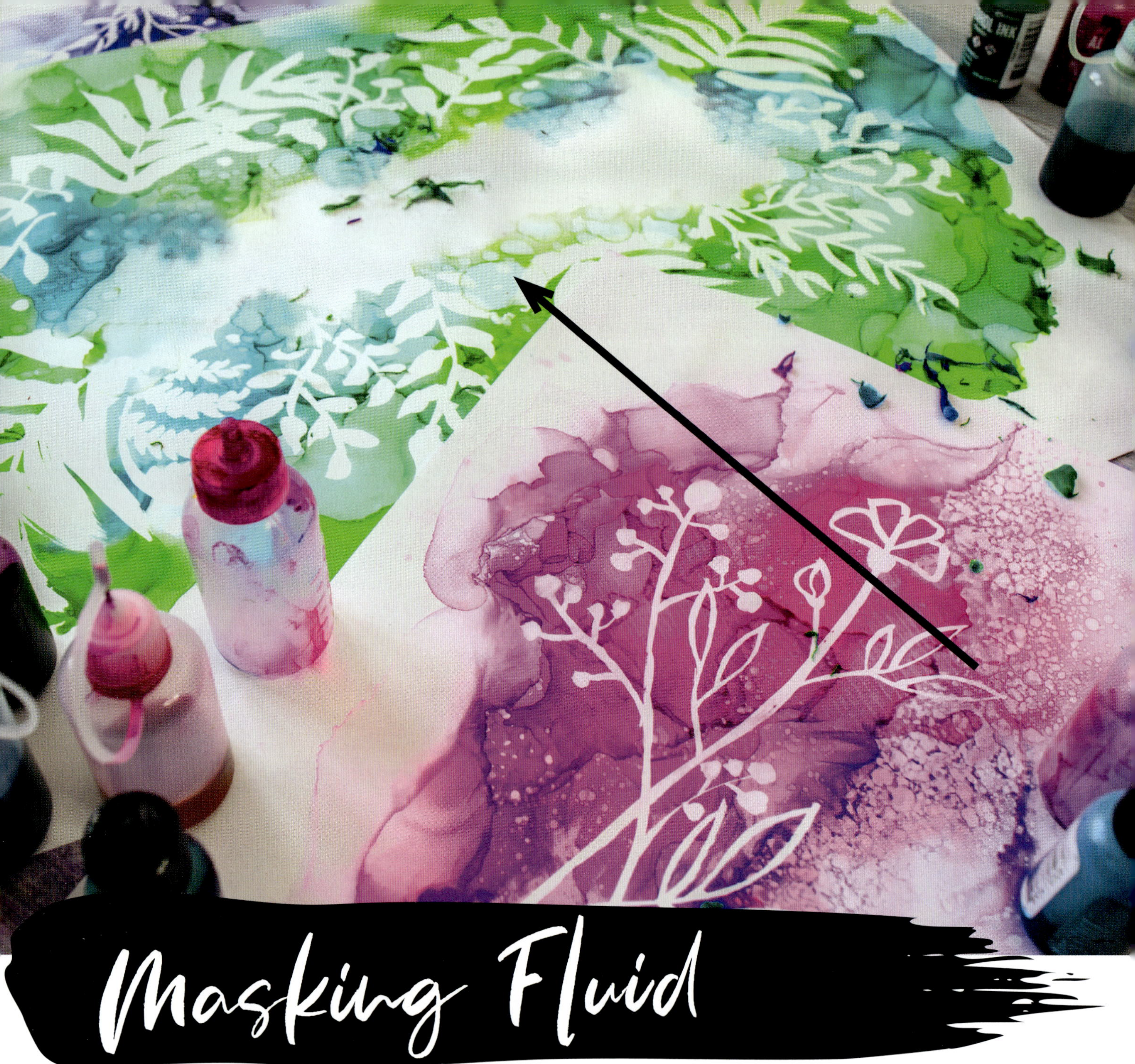

Masking Fluid

When painting an entire surface with alcohol ink, the results are really impactful when some areas are left blank. To achieve this effect, you'll need to use masking fluid or liquid frisket. They're both essentially the same and the application is super easy. In the examples I've stuck with masking fluid as we're making fluid art.

YOU'LL NEED

- Small hot-air blower or airbrush
- Non-absorbent surface
- Alcohol inks and isopropanol (alcohol) in a spray bottle
- Masking fluid

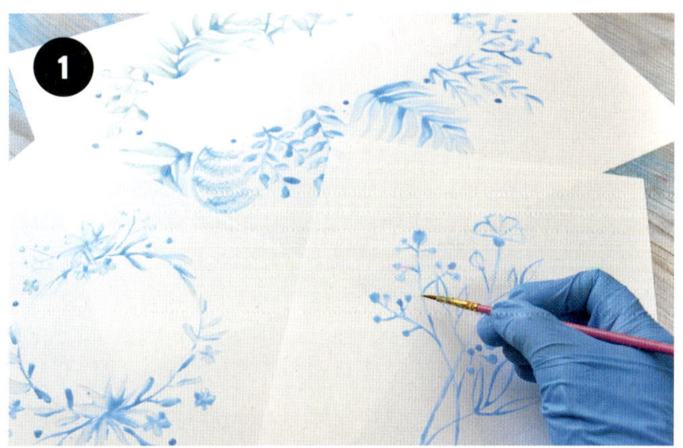

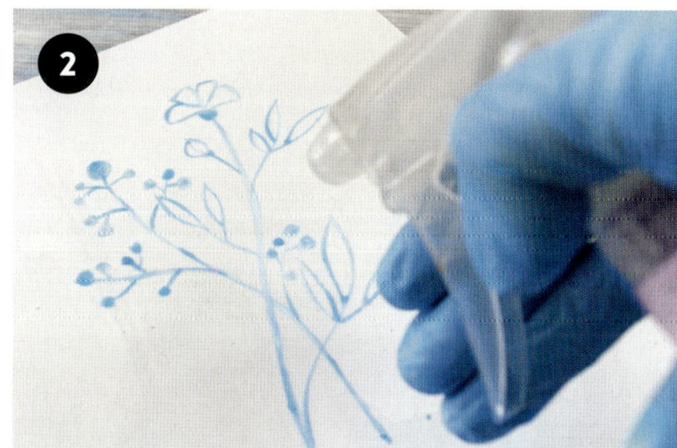

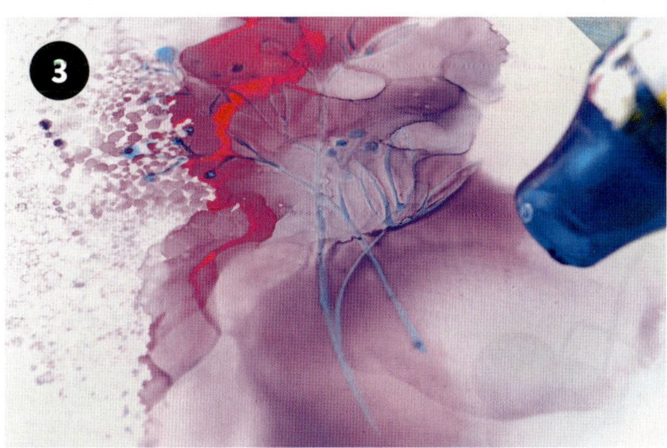

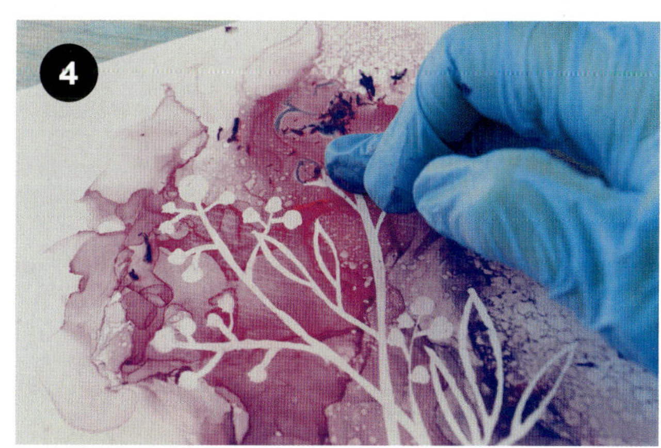

1 Masking fluid is available in an applicator pen or in a bottle. I used the latter with a paintbrush here and painted my floral illustrations as I would with acrylic paint. Allow the fluid to dry.

2 Next, wet the entire surface thoroughly with isopropanol from a spray bottle.

3 Now apply an alcohol ink of your choice and use one or more of the basic techniques to move the ink around.

4 When everything is completely dry, you can rub away the masked areas.

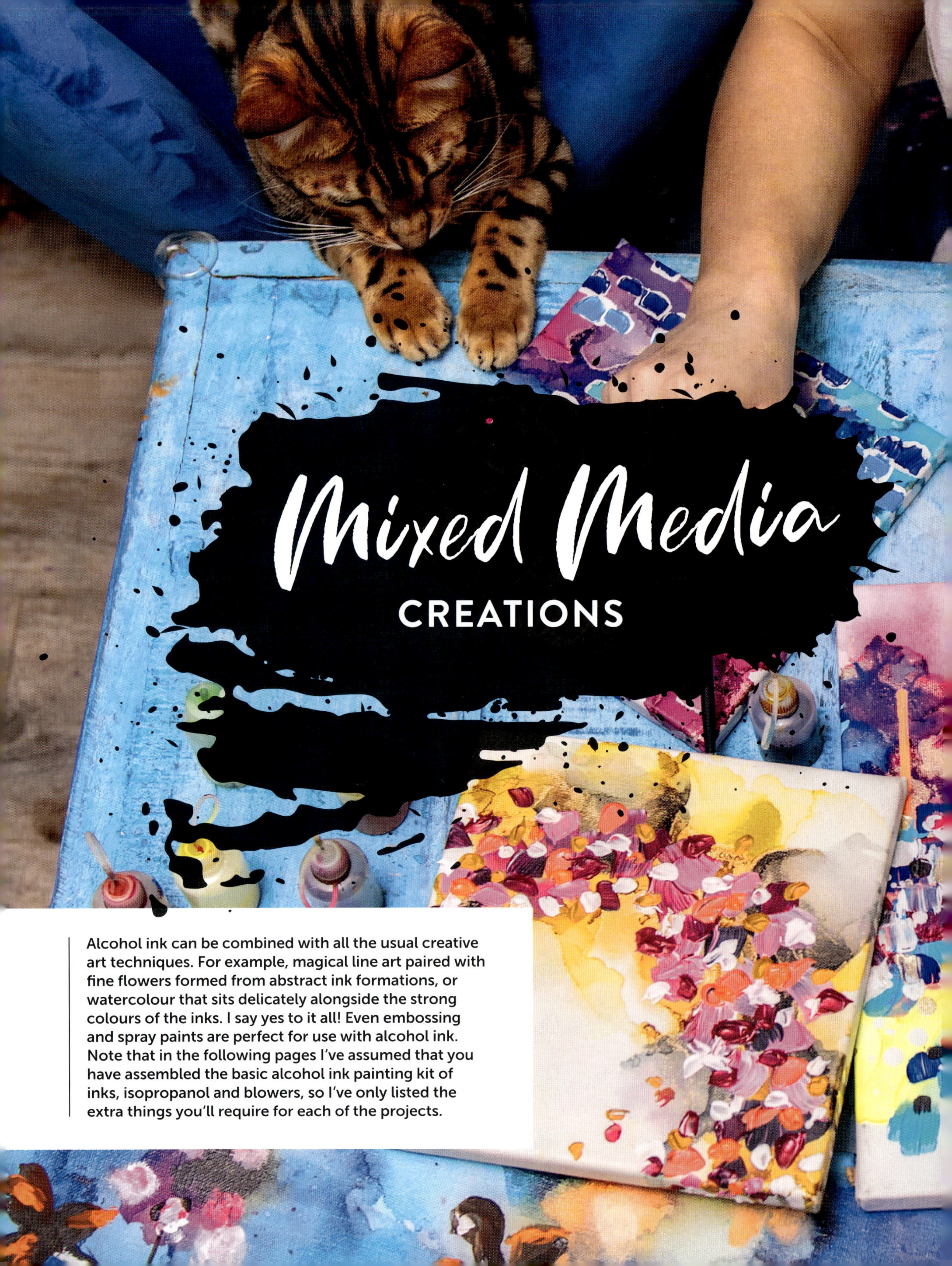

Mixed Media
CREATIONS

Alcohol ink can be combined with all the usual creative art techniques. For example, magical line art paired with fine flowers formed from abstract ink formations, or watercolour that sits delicately alongside the strong colours of the inks. I say yes to it all! Even embossing and spray paints are perfect for use with alcohol ink. Note that in the following pages I've assumed that you have assembled the basic alcohol ink painting kit of inks, isopropanol and blowers, so I've only listed the extra things you'll require for each of the projects.

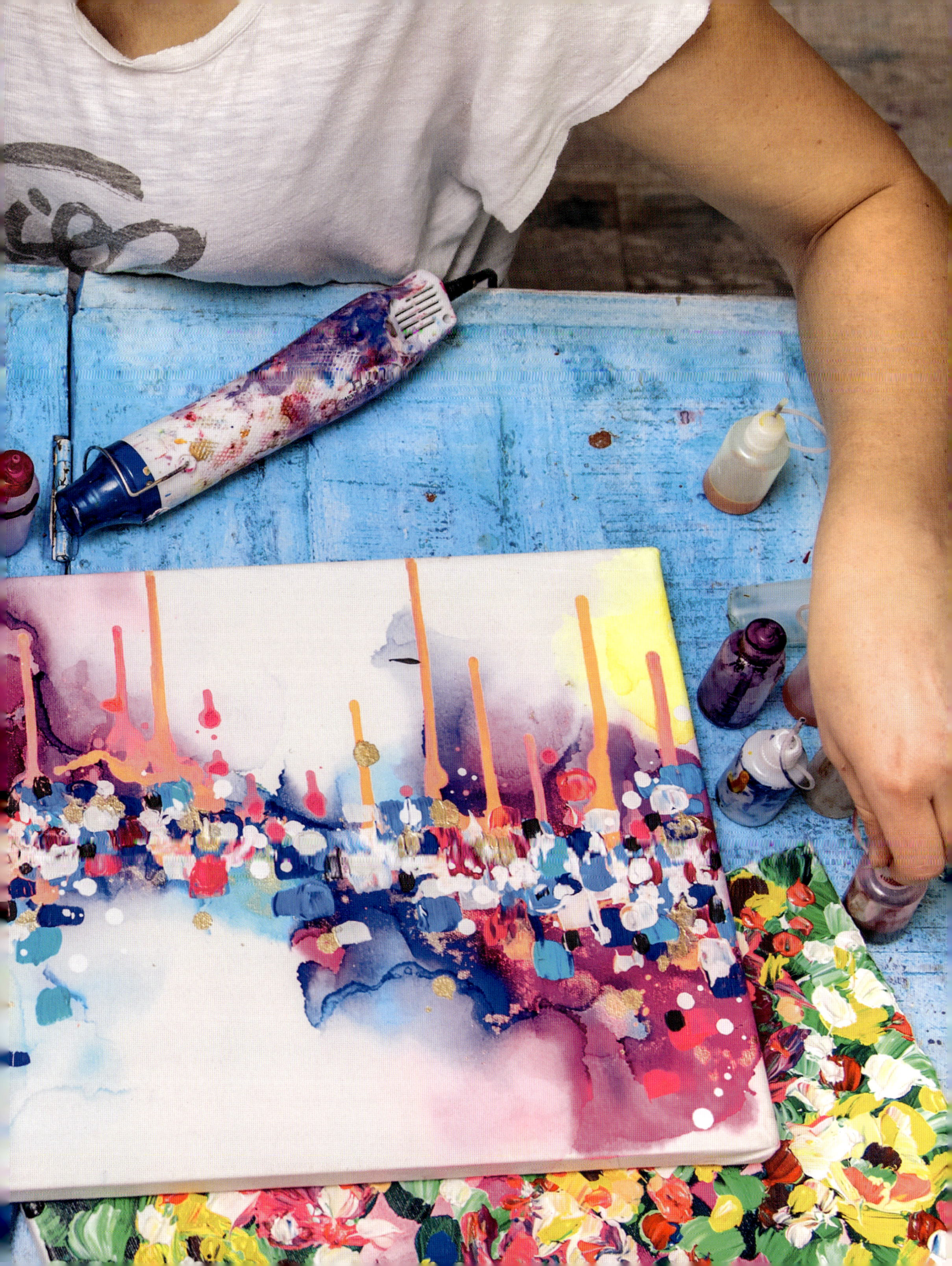

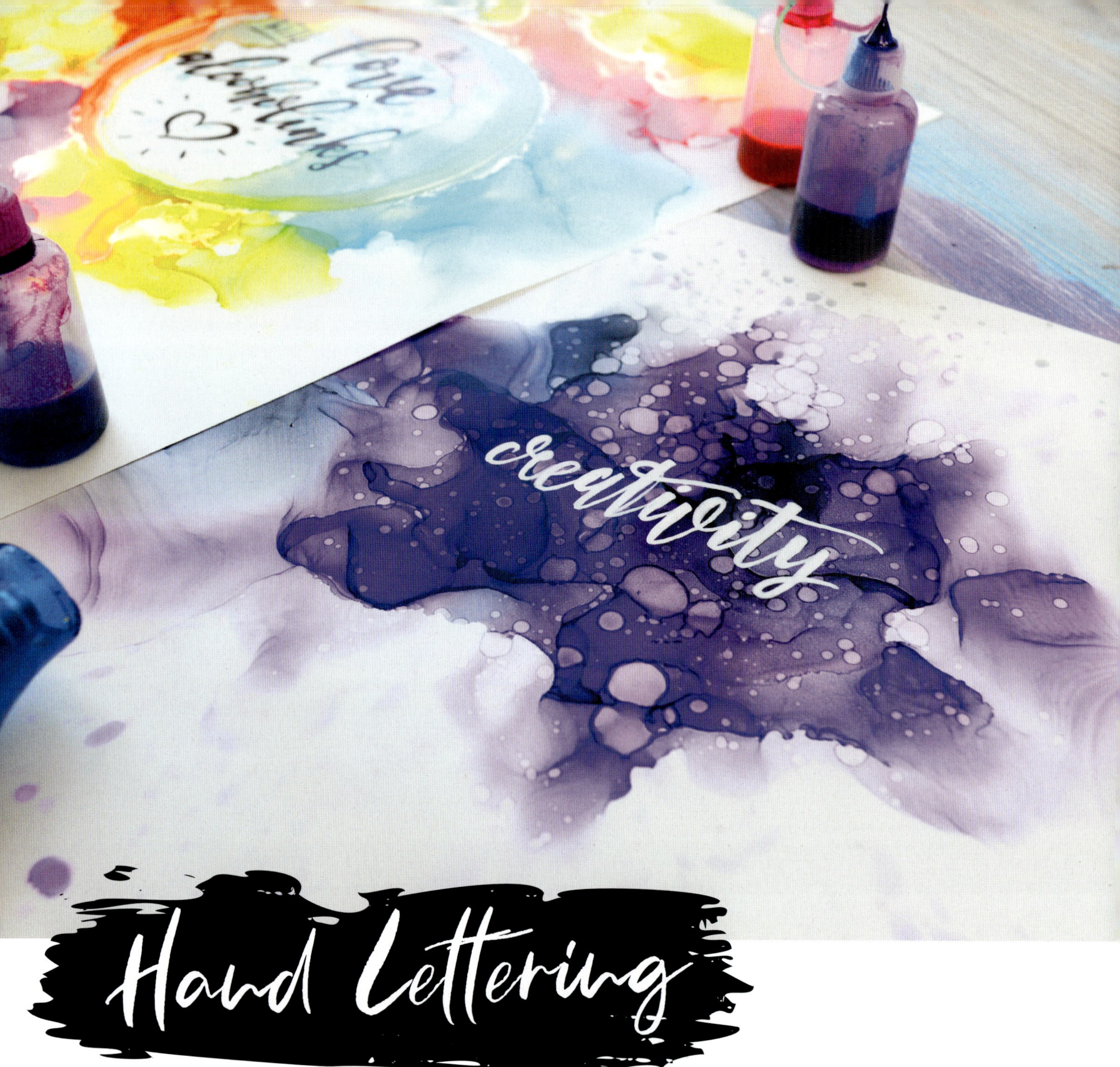

Hand Lettering

Artwork created using alcohol ink makes a great background for hand lettering. If you're looking for something that emphasises your lettering, this technique is definitely for you.

YOU'LL NEED

- UV clear varnish (matt or gloss)
- Fineliner pen
- Acrylic paints and fine tip paintbrushes

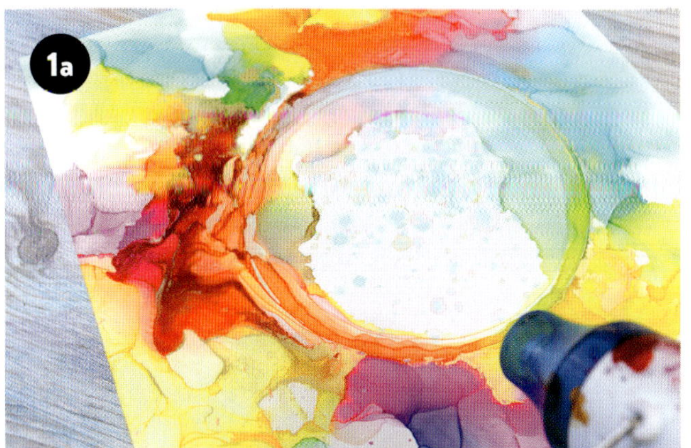

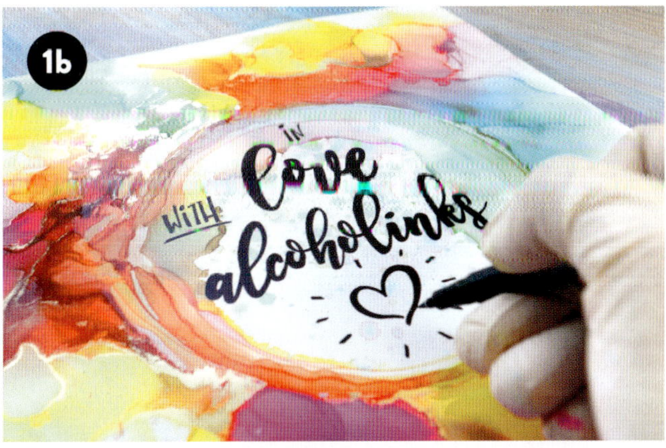

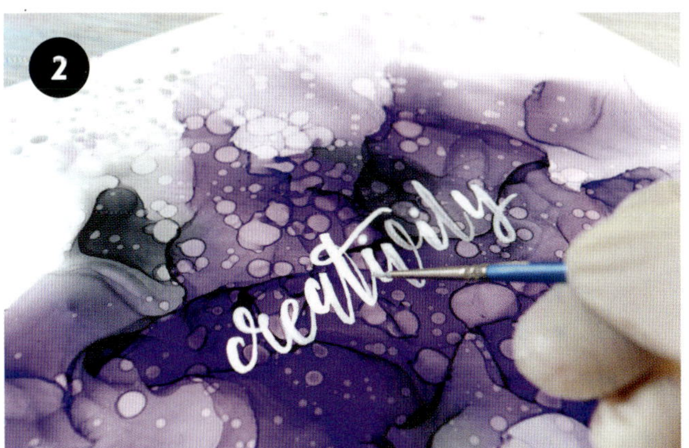

GOOD TO KNOW

If you write or paint on alcohol ink with other
paints – for example, acrylic – you should first
seal the alcohol ink layer with clear varnish.
This prevents the paint from drawing the dye
upwards and altering the acrylic. For example,
if you paint straight over red alcohol ink with
white acrylic paint, the red ink may turn the the
acrylic paint pink.

1 In this example, I've used the Forming Circles
technique to create the background art. When using
markers to write on alcohol ink, it's important to
note that they can quickly smudge on Yupo paper.
It's therefore necessary to use quick-drying pens
and/or write neatly, taking care to avoid your hand
touching the paper and smudging the ink as you
write. Then seal with spray varnish. Then seal with
spray varnish.

2 Here I have used the Cloudy and Drops techniques
to create a moody purple backdrop. This dark colour
can be written on using white acrylic paint and a fine
tip paintbrush. You may need to paint more than one
layer of the lettering to make it really opaque.

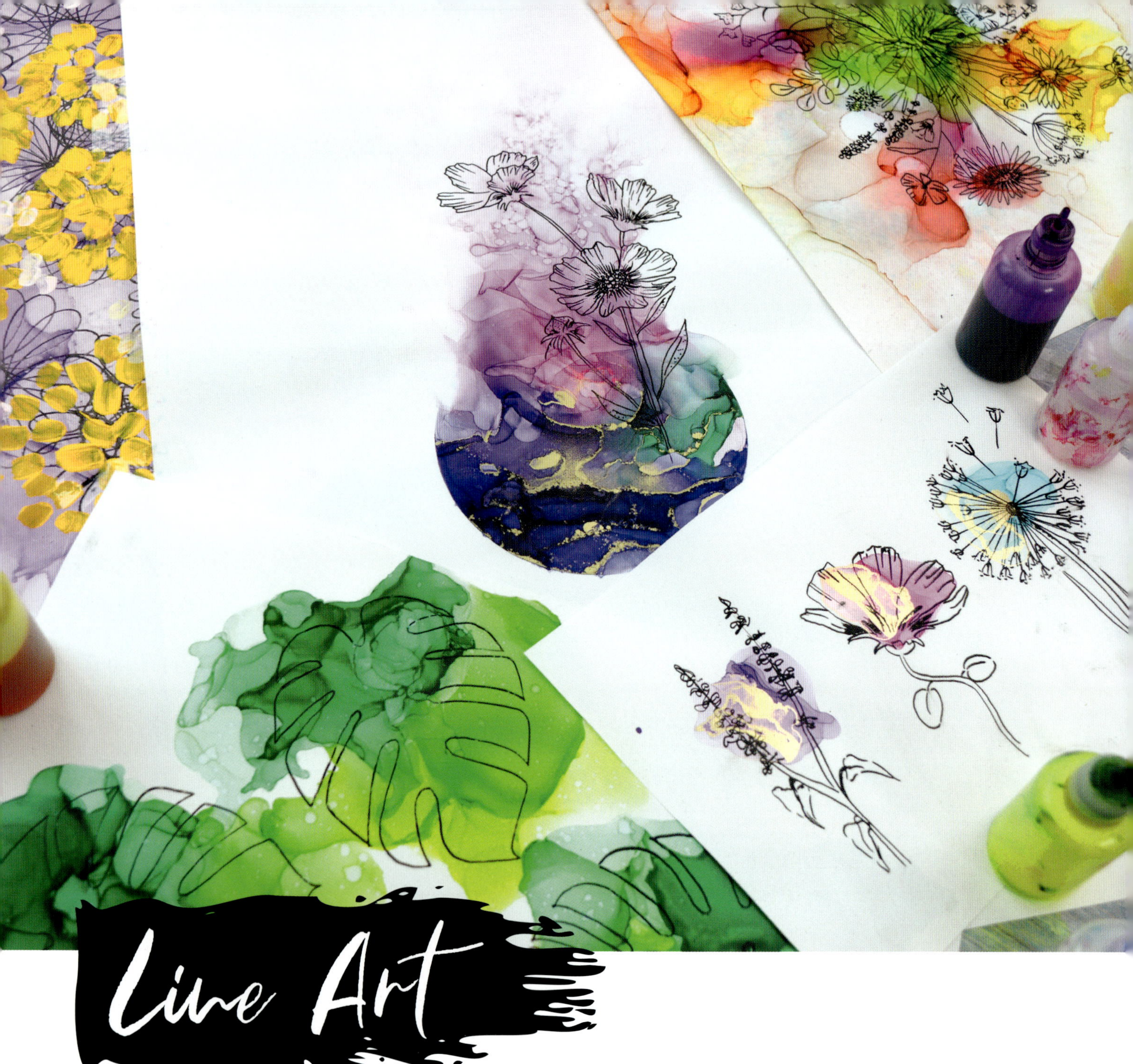

Line Art

The contrast of abstractly coloured painted shapes with fine line drawings is beautiful! Line art and alcohol ink are a dream pair, be it for floral illustrations or other subjects. Here, I've used clear film to create a crisp shape with alcohol inks before adding the line art.

YOU'LL NEED

– Fineliner/permanent marker
– Self-adhesive film
– UV clear varnish (matt or gloss)
– Masking tape

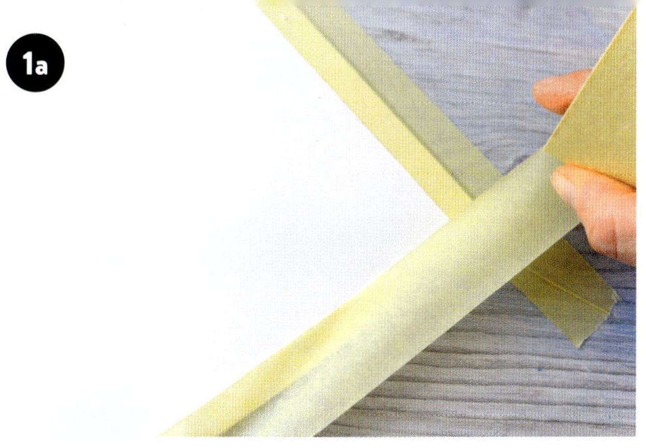

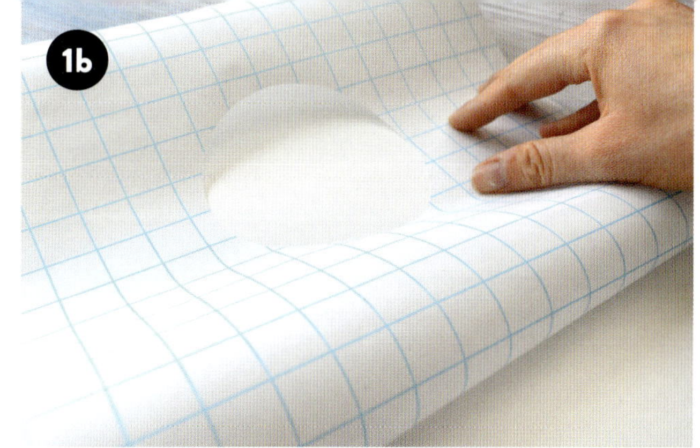

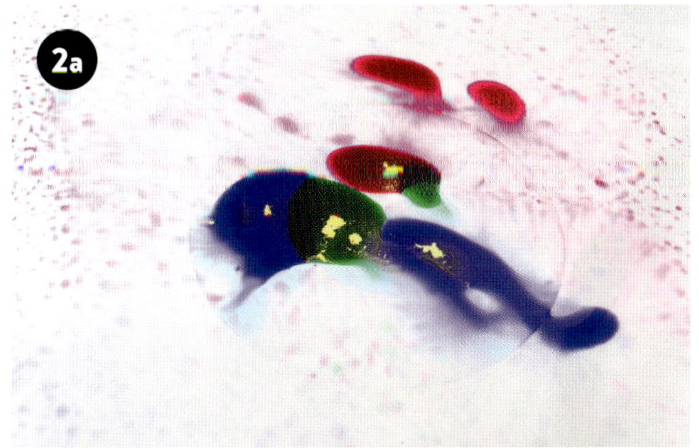

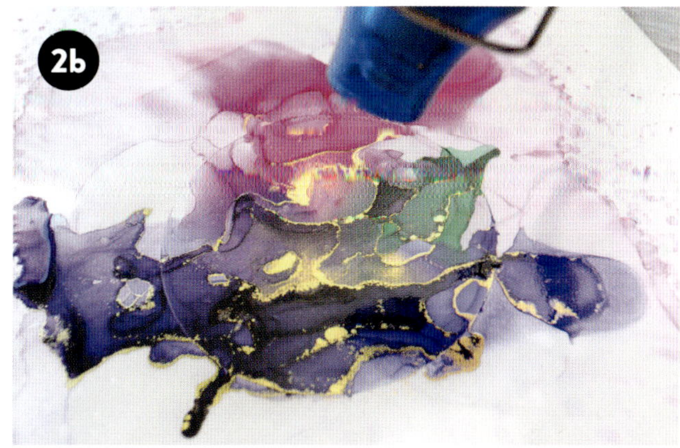

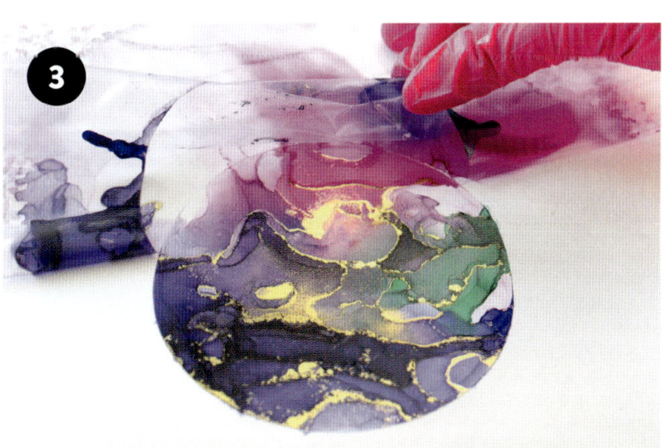

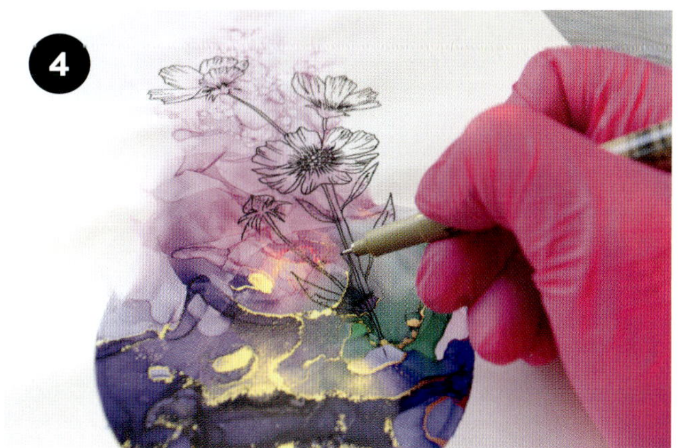

1   Fix the Yupo paper to your table top with masking tape to help you separate the film and the paper more easily later. The two materials are made for each other, as the film is relatively easy to loosen. Cut out a circle from the self-adhesive film, discard the circle of film, and glue the remaining film to the Yupo paper.

2   Once you have done this, you can use all the painting techniques as usual. In this example, I use the Cloudy technique with the Metallic technique, and Drift for the upwards paint flare.

3   After everything has dried thoroughly, carefully remove the film from the paper.

4   Your painting is now perfectly round and the ideal background for line art. I drew the flowers with fineliner directly on to the alcohol ink and then sealed them with matt UV clear varnish.

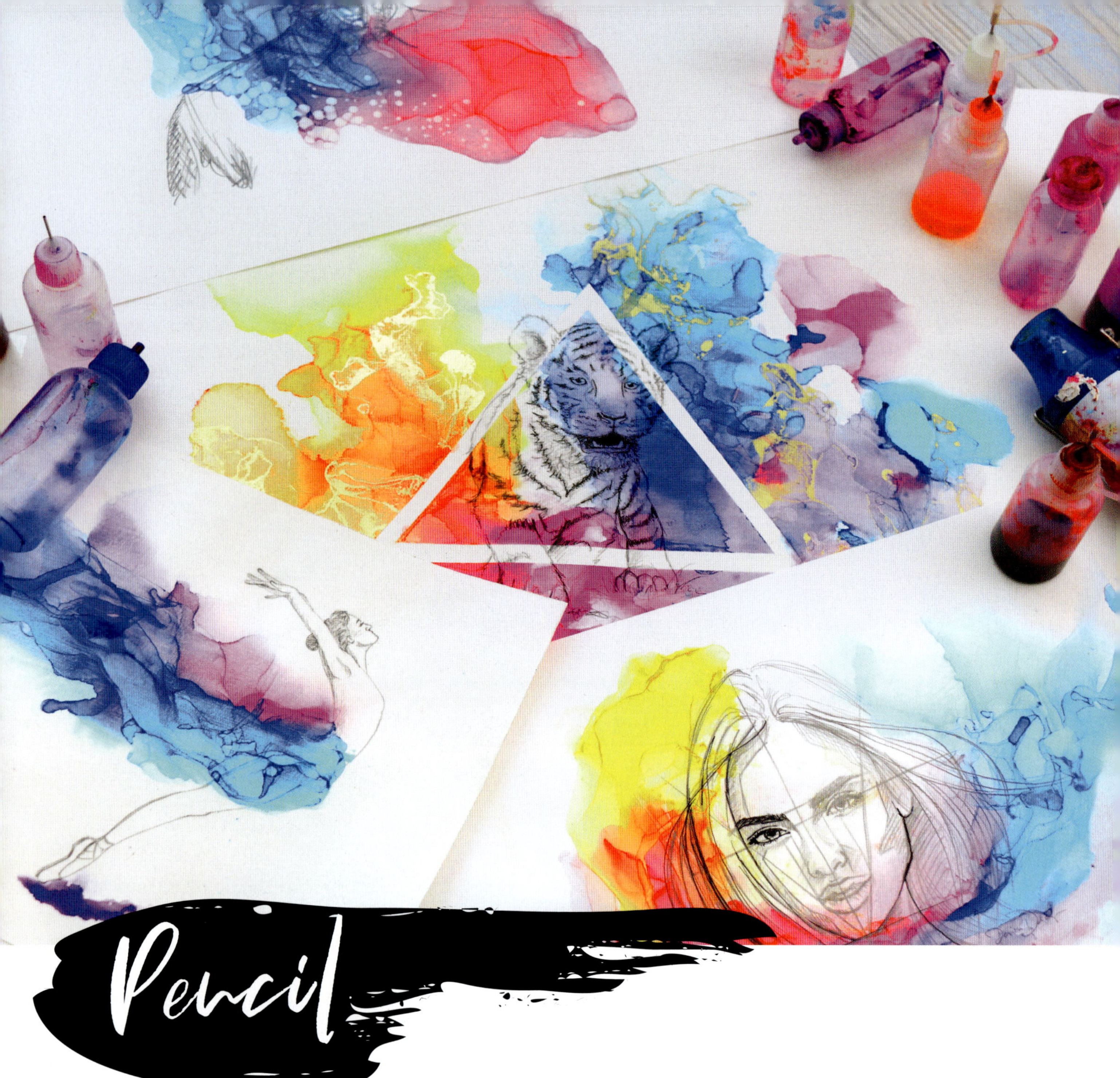

Drawings with pencil can be coloured in beautifully with alcohol ink. With hard pencils, you don't even have to seal the picture. Artwork created in this way has a unique look. Finally, something new! You can draw on Yupo paper and then colour it in directly using alcohol ink, or use normal paper and seal it first. I'll show you here how the latter works.

YOU'LL NEED

– Heavyweight mixed-media paper,
  at least 200gsm
– H2, HB and B pencils
– UV clear varnish (matt)
– Acrylic binder
– Masking tape
– Self-adhesive film (optional)
– Fineliner pen

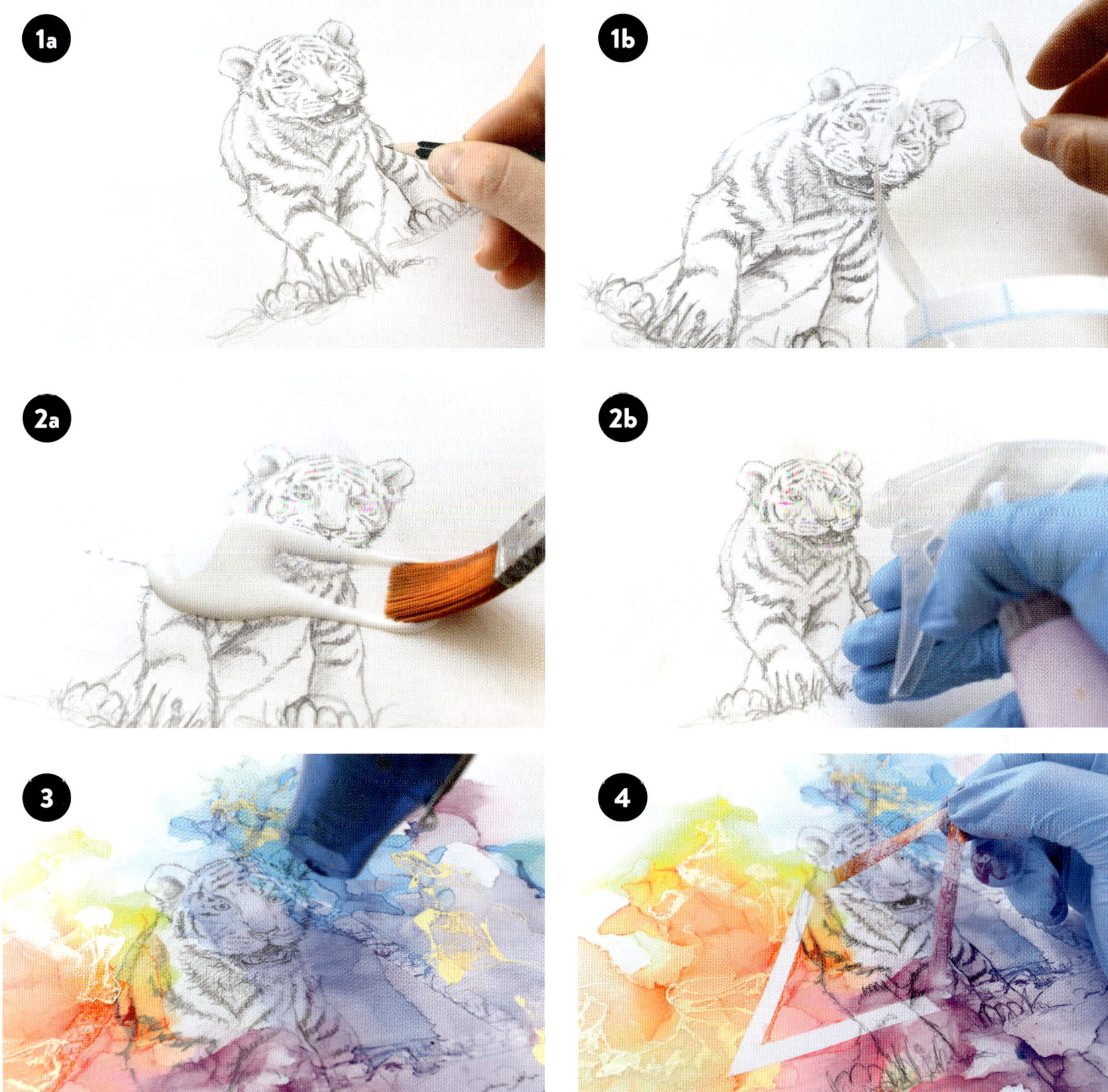

1 Attach the paper to your surface with tape. This will stop it becoming wavy due to the moisture in the acrylic binder in the next step. I drew the tiger using an H2 pencil, used an HB pencil to give depth and a B pencil for accents. I sealed the drawing with UV clear varnish. For a graphic effect, I glued on a triangle of self-adhesive film.

2 Before using the alcohol ink, the paper must be sealed with a clear acrylic binder. Don't forget that the pencil drawing must be sealed with clear var nish first to avoid it smudging when applying the acrylic. Apply the acrylic binder with a wide, fine-hair paintbrush, painting vertically and horizontally. Apply two coats, letting each layer dry thoroughly. This takes just a few minutes with a hot-air blower, or one to two hours without one, depending on the room temperature.

3 For the pattern, I selected the Cloudy and Wispy techniques combined with the Metallic technique. The alcohol ink needs to be more transparent than usual when used with pencil drawings. You can thin it in applicator bottles.

4 Once the alcohol ink was dry, I removed the triangle of self-adhesive film and emphasised the tiger again in some places using a fineliner pen. Watercolour and acrylic are also ideal for combining with this technique due to the suitability of the paper.

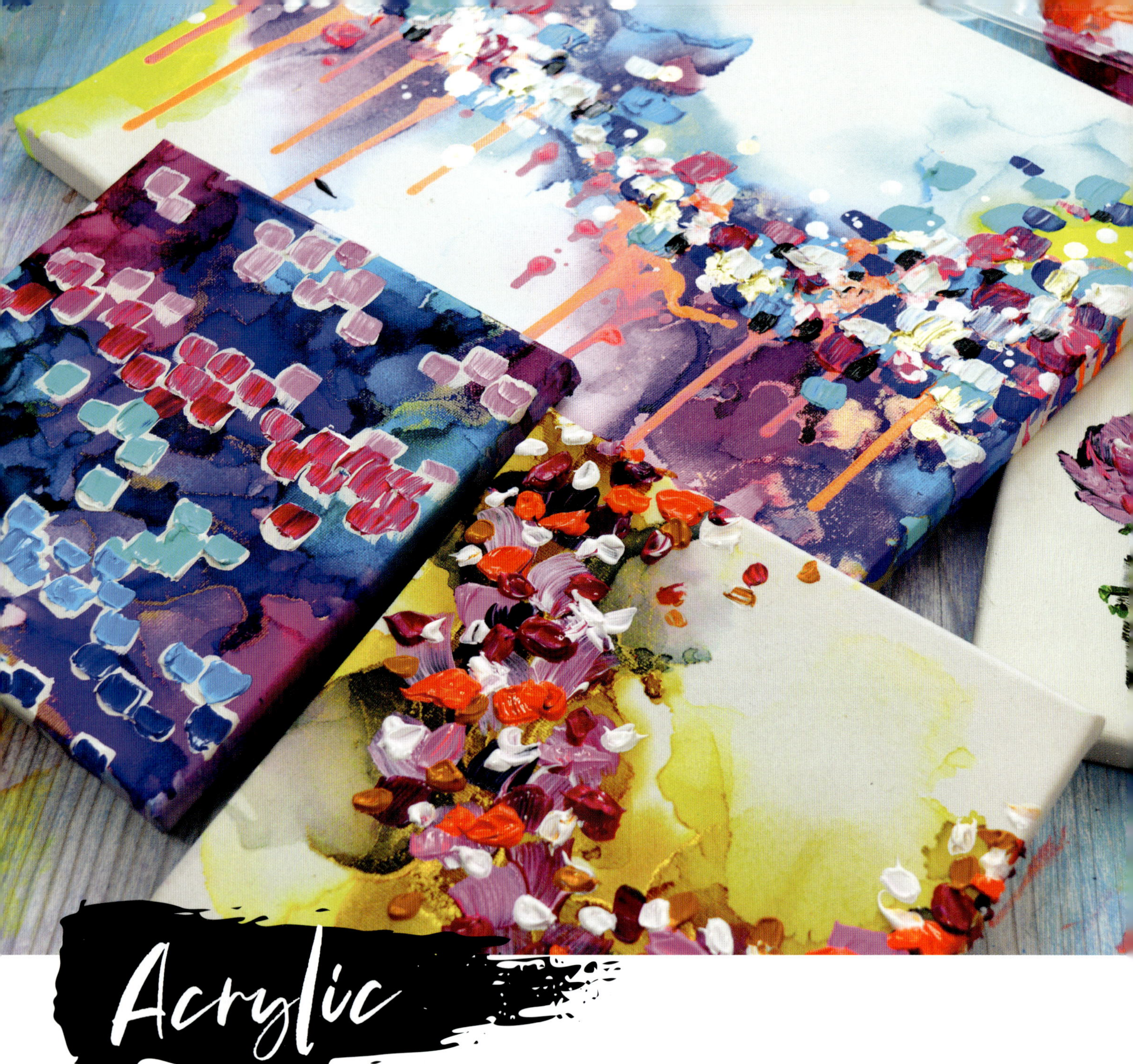

Acrylic

Painting using alcohol ink and acrylic is one of my favourite combinations. Of course, elaborate portraits in one or the other are great, but it's so simple and magical to combine acrylic and alcohol ink to create abstract images. These can be anything from graphic or cubist, through to impressionistic or floral – anything is possible.

YOU'LL NEED

– Canvas on a stretcher frame
– Acrylic binder
– UV clear varnish (matt or gloss)
– Paint roller
– Acrylic paints
– Paintbrushes

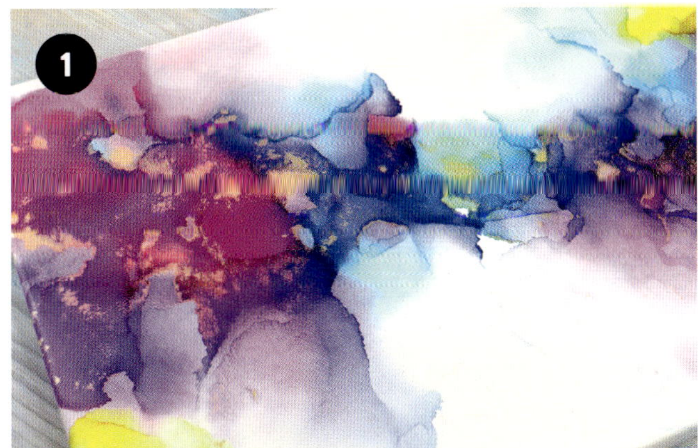

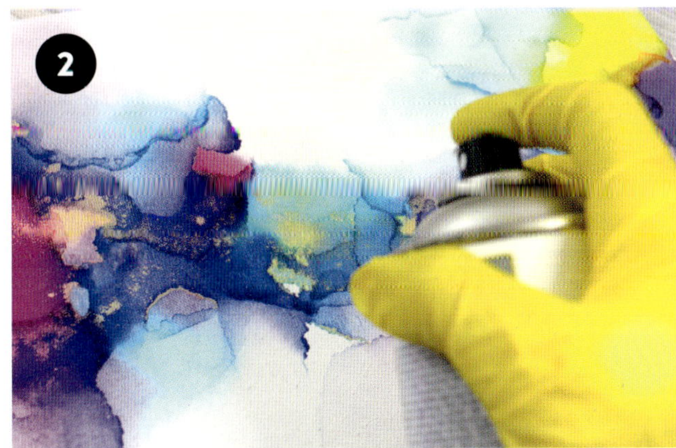

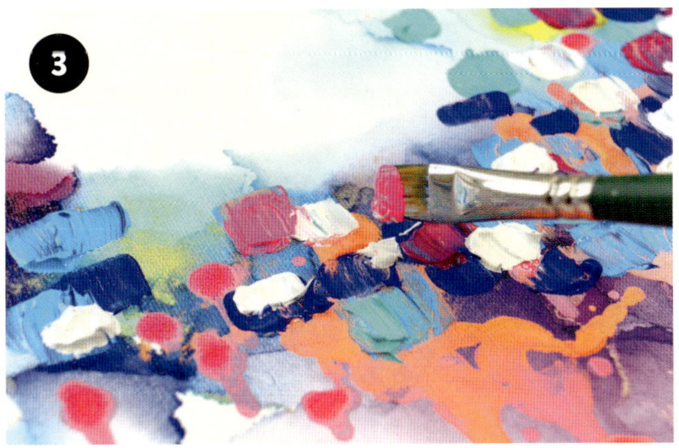

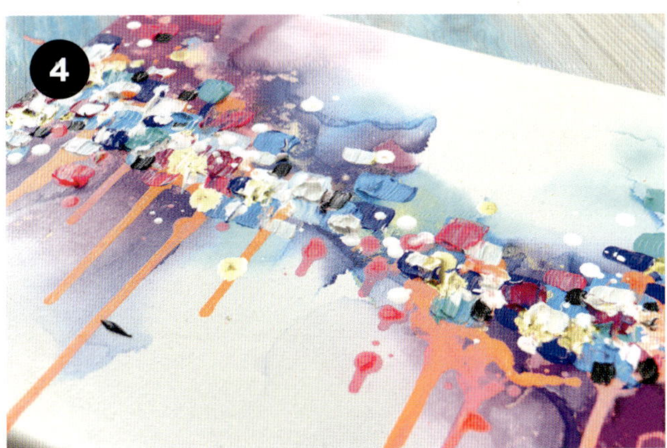

1 When combining with acrylic paints, the difference is obviously the canvas, which you need to seal with clear acrylic binder before you begin to paint. Use a fine roller to prevent brush marks from marring your work later. Apply one or two coats and dry thoroughly for a few hours.

2 The texture of the canvas changes how you paint with alcohol ink. The flow properties of the painting techniques are slowed down, so I use more isopropanol on canvas. That's something that comes with practice – just try it out. In this example, you'll see a combination of the Cloudy, Wispy, Soak, Metallic and Drops techniques.

3 To be able to paint on the alcohol ink, you must seal it with clear varnish after it has dried. I use a combination of UV protective varnish and a layer of matt or gloss clear varnish. This prevents the acrylic paint from drawing the dye out of the ink. When the paint layer is dry, you can start with the acrylic painting.

4 In the photos, you'll see some design ideas. You can paint directly onto this acrylic layer with more alcohol ink. This creates interesting effects – there are no limits to your creativity here!

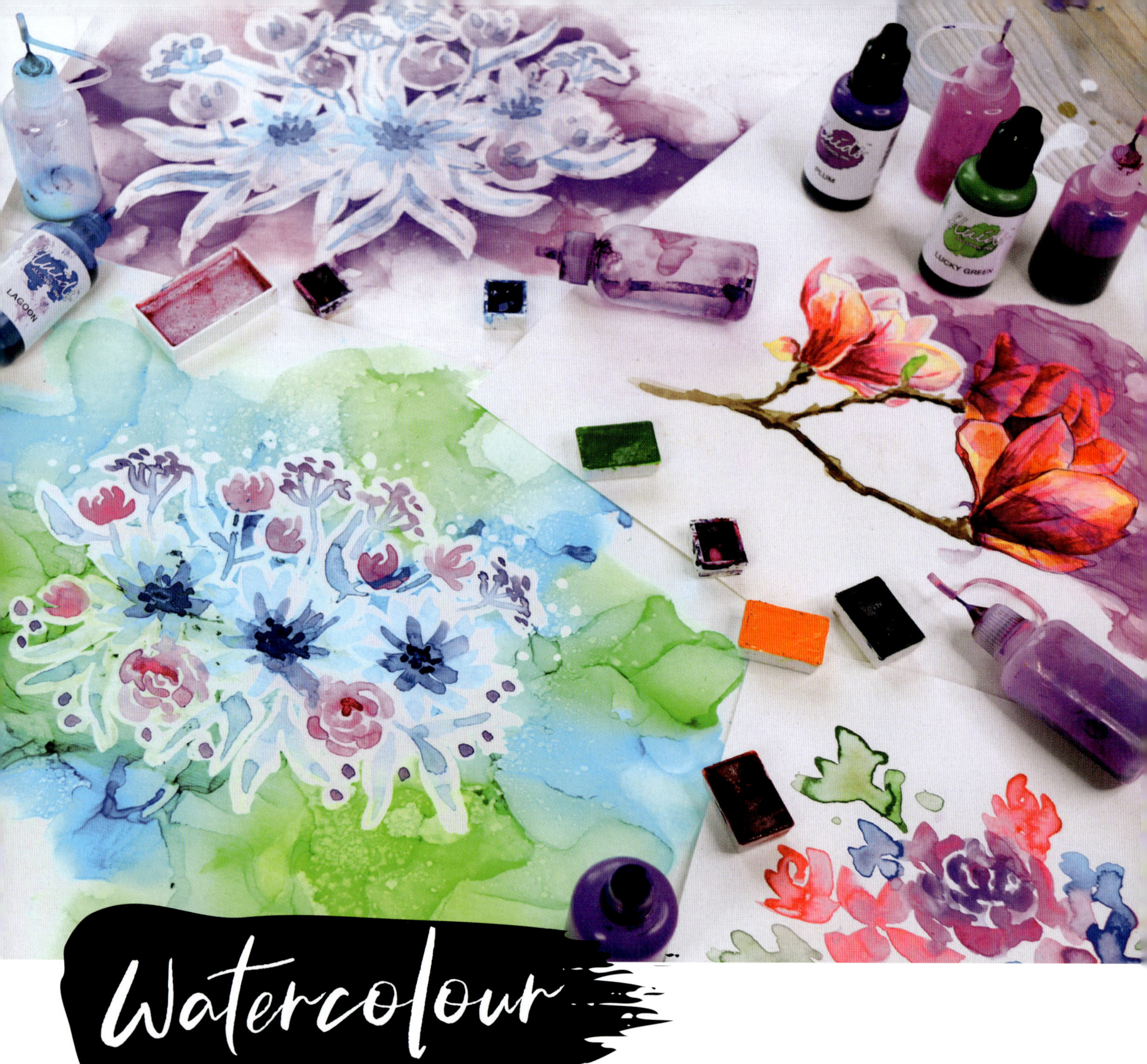

Watercolour

Watercolours, such as aquarelle or gouache, are not as intensely coloured as alcohol ink. Nevertheless, both can be combined for unique effects. Again, paint on normal paper and seal it before using the alcohol ink.

YOU'LL NEED

- Watercolour paints
- Paintbrushes
- Watercolour or mixed media paper
- Masking fluid
- UV clear varnish (matt)
- Acrylic binder
- Wide fine-hair paintbrush and small paint roller
- Masking tape

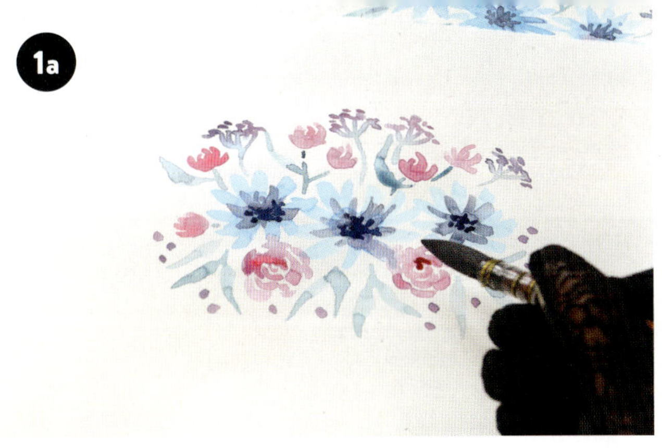

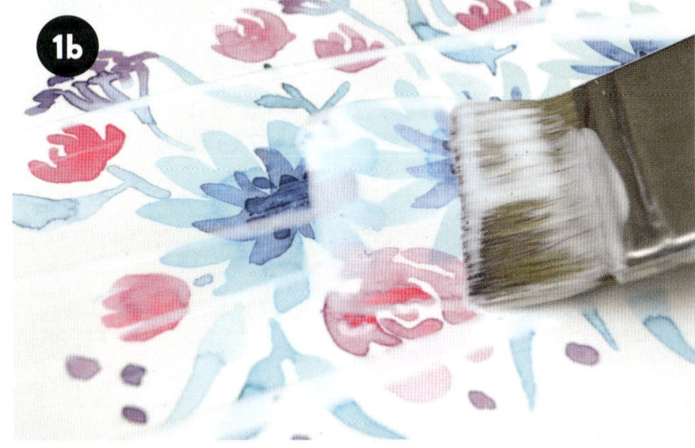

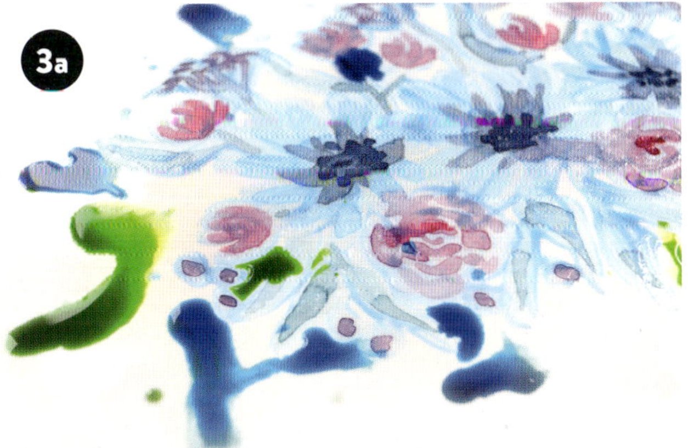

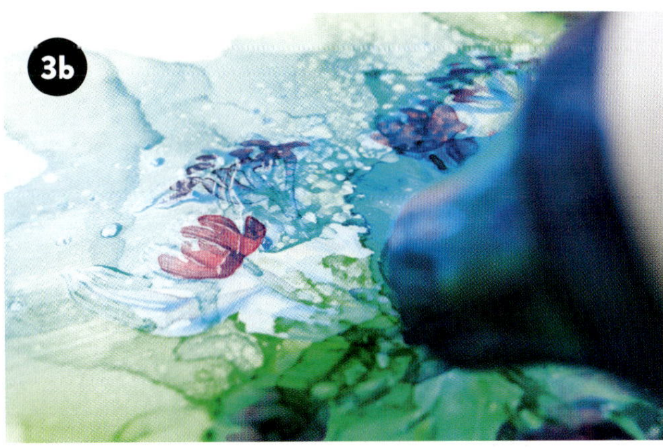

1 I painted using watercolour on paper, let it dry and sealed it with clear varnish applied with a wide, fine-hair paintbrush. Seal the painting surface with acrylic binder, using a small roller to prevent brush marks. Apply one or two layers then let it dry completely.

2 Now cover your chosen features with masking fluid. Let it dry before you paint with the alcohol ink.

3 I recommend you work with diluted alcohol ink. Use the Swivel and then Wispy techniques to quickly achieve all-over effects. When removing the masking fluid, areas covered with too much dye could smudge. You can avoid this by using mixed alcohol ink over completely dry paint. Should streaks occur, clean them away with kitchen towel soaked in alcohol.

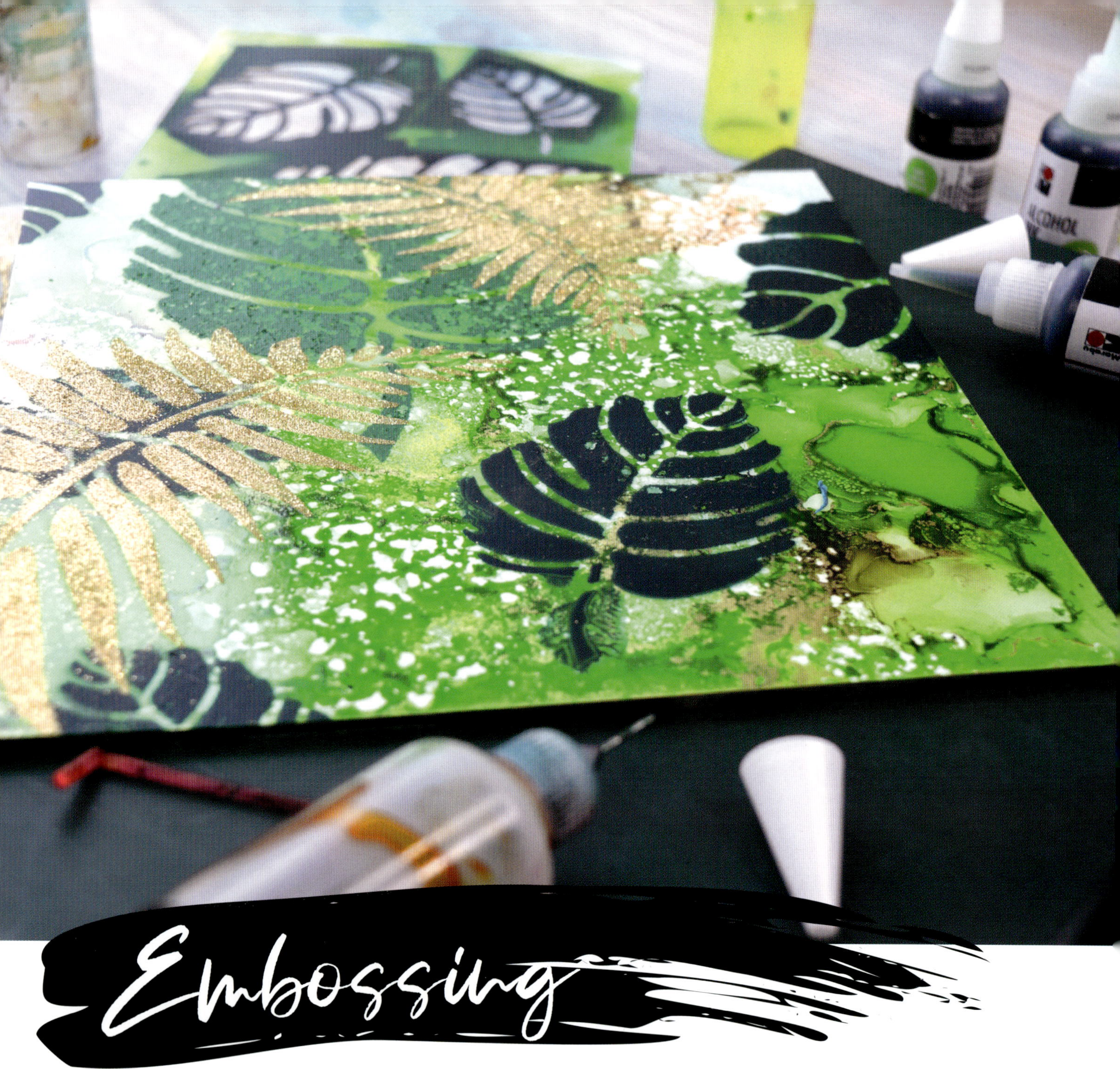

Embossing

Another mixed media combination I love is embossing – a really cool relief technique for which you will need a piece of equipment that you already have: a hot-air blower. The only other supply you need is an inexpensive embossing powder. Using the powder, you can add sublime reliefs to your alcohol ink art that, depending on the pigment, can also glisten and sparkle.

YOU'LL NEED

- Embossing powder
- Embossing gel or spray glue
- Self-adhesive laser-cut or punched stencils (or use temporary spray adhesive)
- Heat-resistant painting surface
- Hot-air blower
- Spray bottle

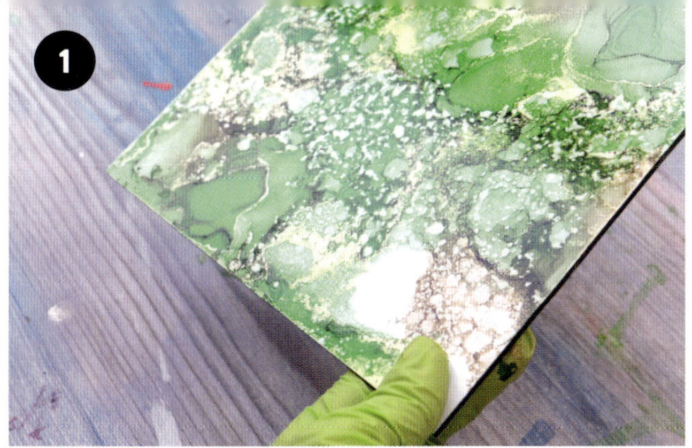

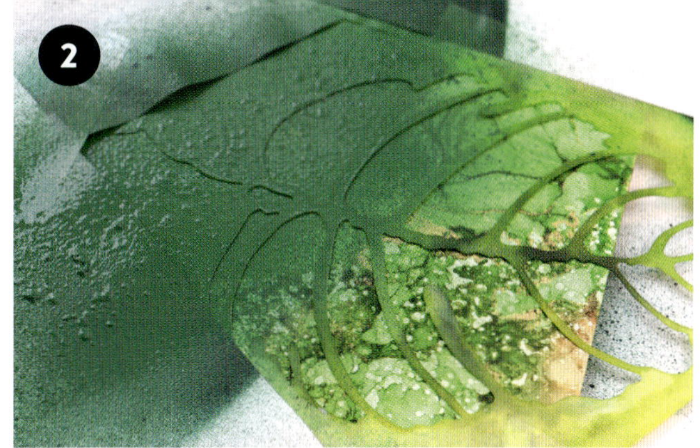

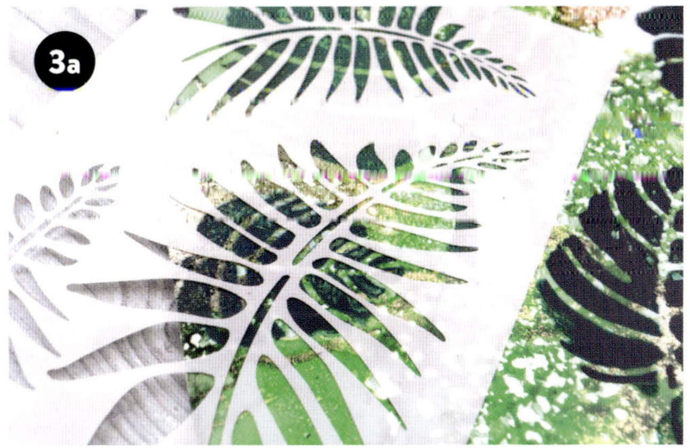

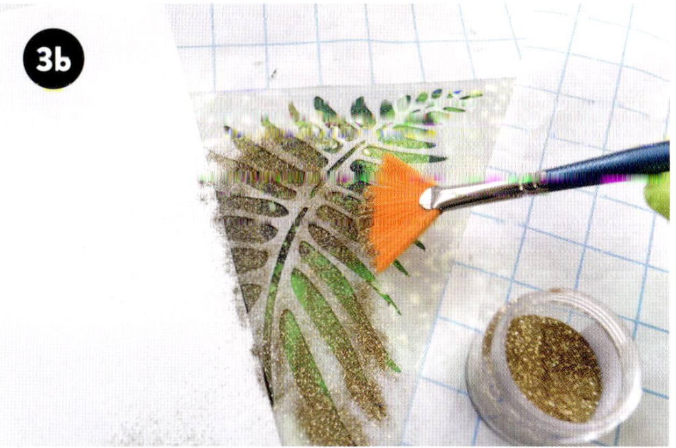

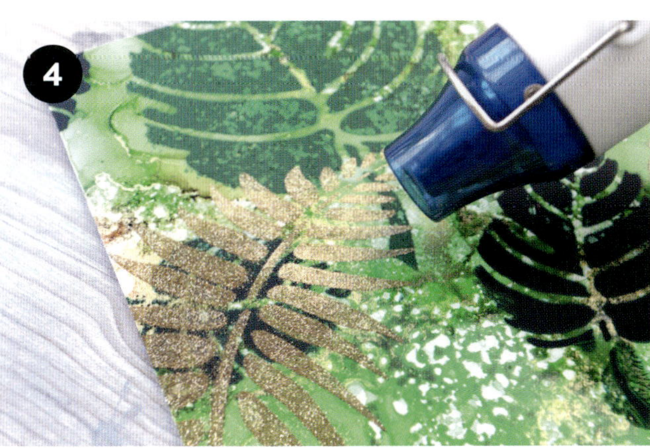

IMPORTANT NOTE

The painting surface should be heat resistant, as you have to get the hot-air blower very close to it to melt the embossing powder. Yupo paper would just melt away. I use heat-resistant aluminium panels that are primed white on one side. They're excellent surfaces and alcohol ink floats really well over them.

1 For this jungle artwork, I applied light green alcohol ink for the background layer using the Cloudy, Soak and Drops techniques.

2 I sprayed on Monstera (Swiss cheese plant) leaves using dark green alcohol ink in a spray bottle and stencils. Remove the stencil when the ink is dry.

3 To emboss, put the stencils on the painting surface again and either paint the gaps with embossing gel or apply a layer of spray glue. Then add the embossing powder (I used metallic gold) with a paintbrush until you have made a dense covering. I used a fern stencil to create the embossed areas.

4 Carefully remove the stencil and melt the powder with a hot-air blower. This will result in raised, metallic areas.

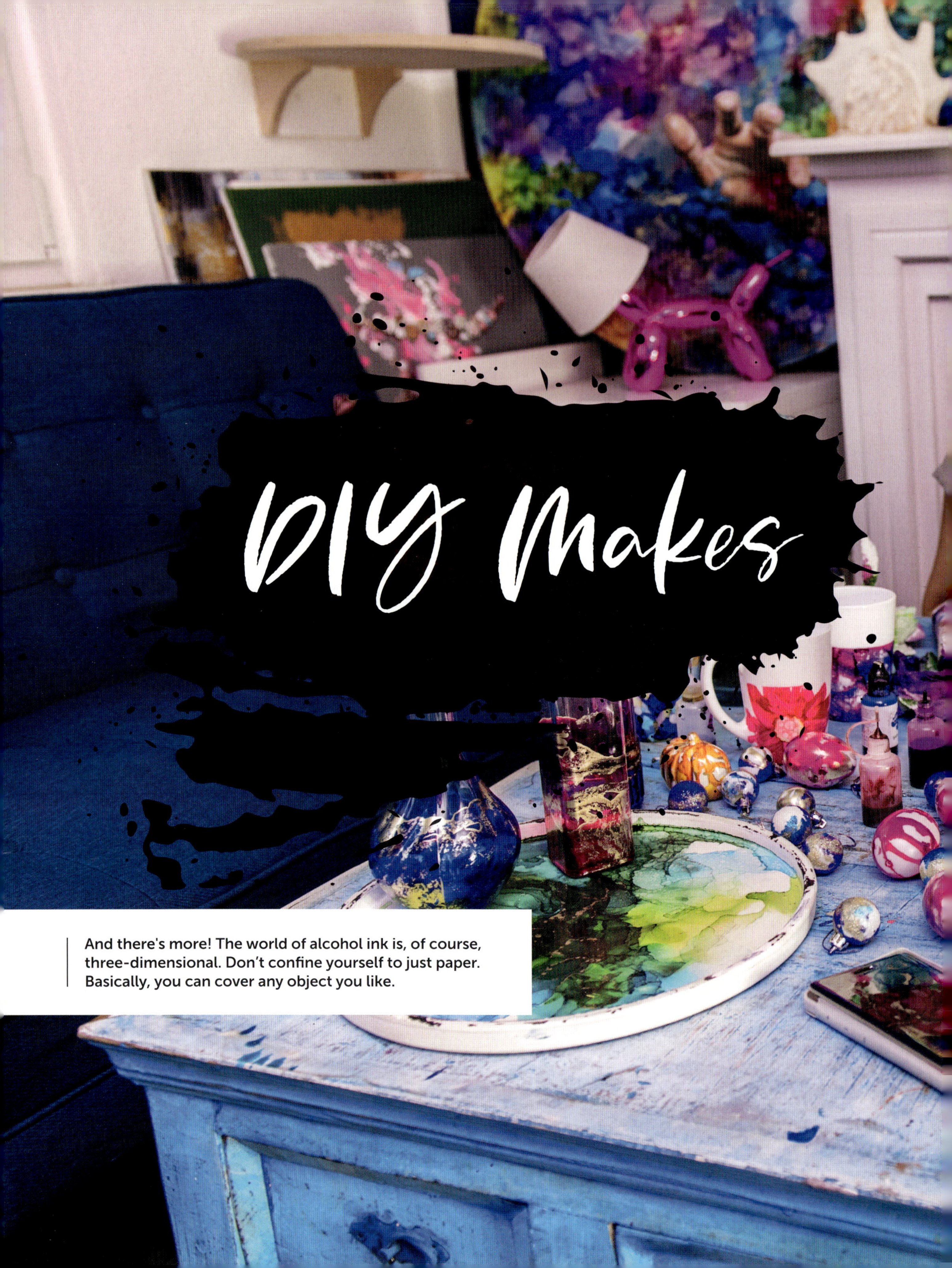

And there's more! The world of alcohol ink is, of course, three-dimensional. Don't confine yourself to just paper. Basically, you can cover any object you like.

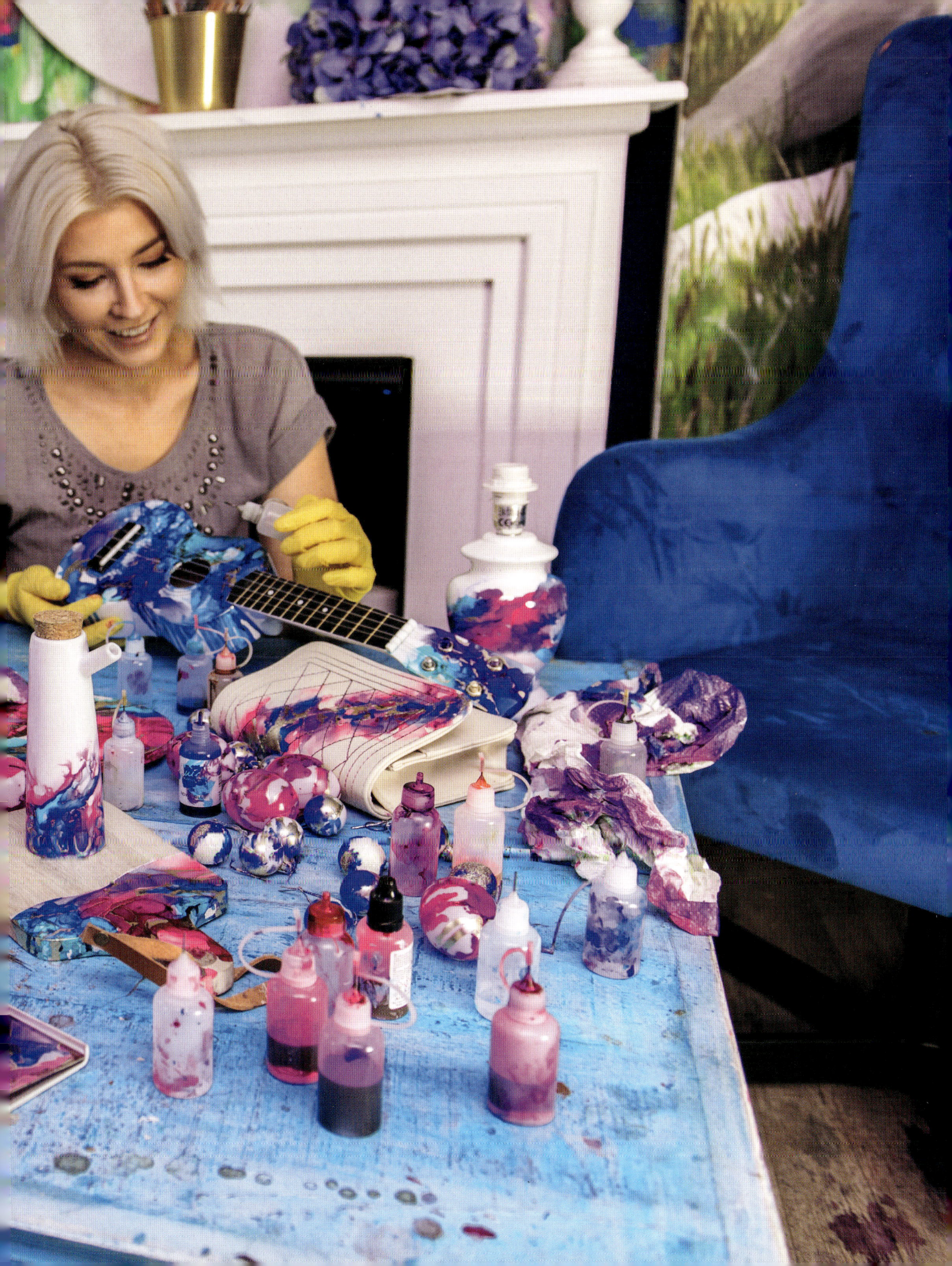

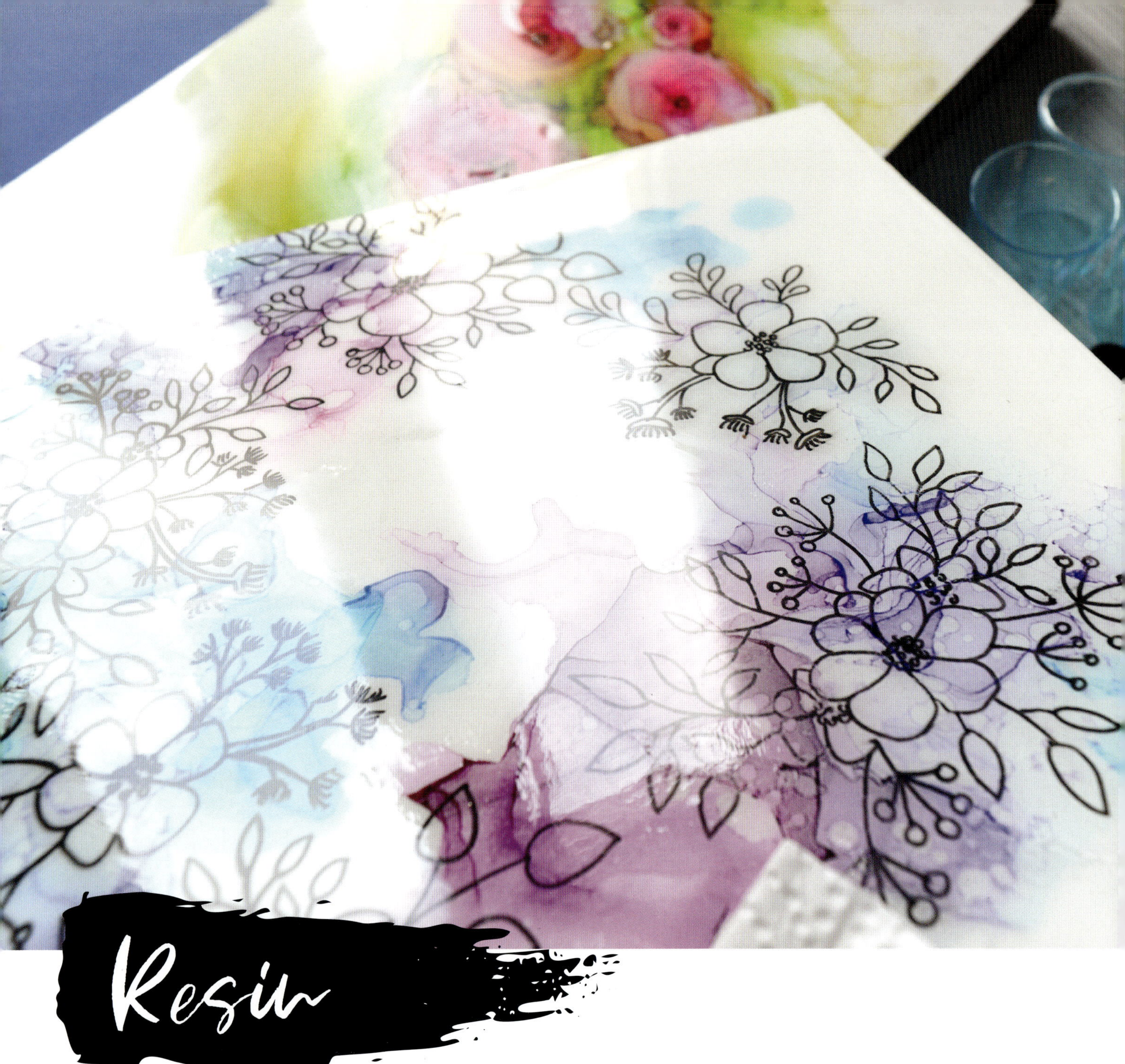

Resin

Finished alcohol ink paintings should be sealed with UV varnish to protect them from light. Clear varnish gives an additional protection and is important if you are going to add further painting on top of the sealed surface. In themselves, these safeguards are sufficient. However, for the very best results you should use epoxy resin.

YOU'LL NEED

- Epoxy resin set containing resin and hardener
- Digital kitchen scales and spirit level
- Small 'pedestals' e.g. old shot glasses of equal height
- Bowls or cups for the resin
- Rod for stirring
- Dust sheet, newspaper
- MDF board
- Spray glue

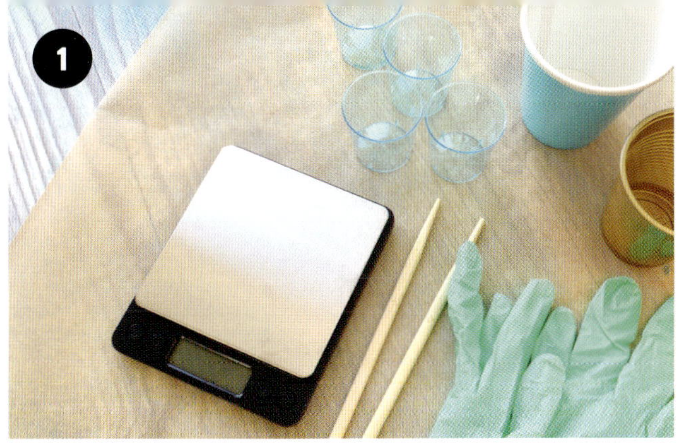

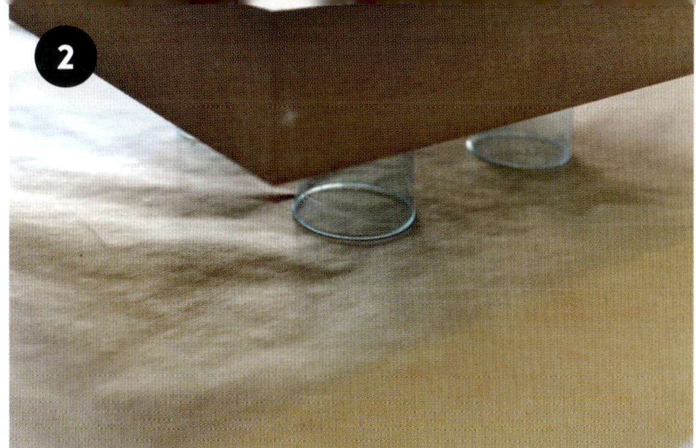

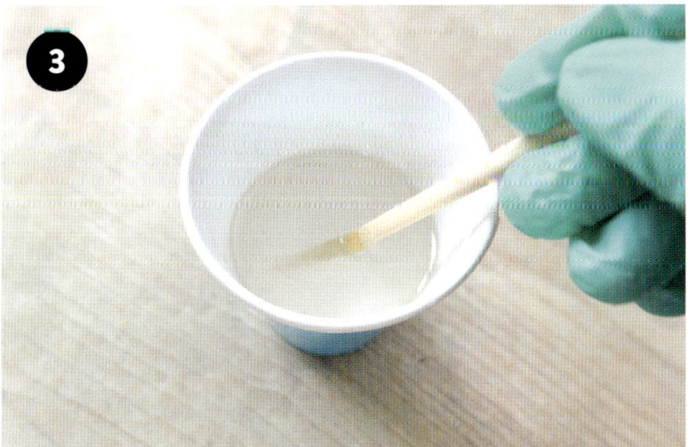

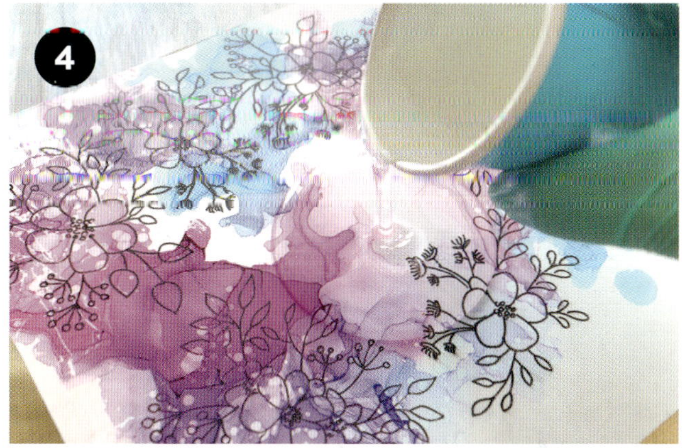

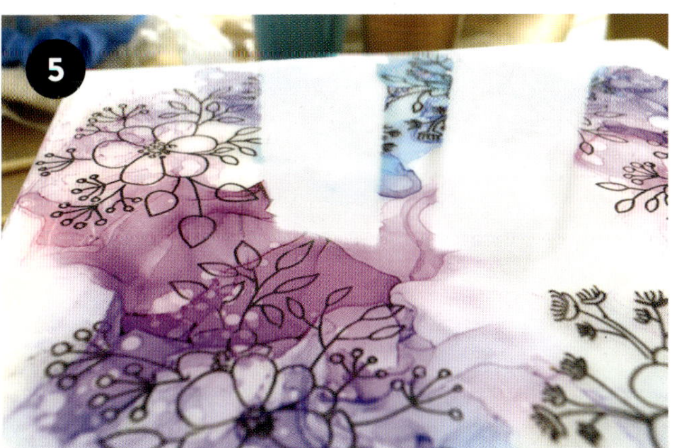

1 Have your tools and equipment to hand. To seal your painting with resin, fix it to a stable, rigid, warp-free, and perfectly level surface – this will be the artwork's backing. I pasted my paper neatly on to an MDF board using spray glue. Let the glue dry thoroughly.

2 Next you will need the small pedestals – place your artwork on them to raise the painting away from the table.

3 Put your gloves on to mix the resin. The ratio of resin to hardener can be found on the product instructions. Use the digital kitchen scales to weigh the amount accurately.

4 Stir this mixture very slowly until it turns from cloudy to clear. This may take a while, but stir slowly to avoid creating bubbles.

5 Pour the resin onto your painting. You may need to lift the artwork up and tilt it slightly so that everything is well distributed. Once done, place it flat on the pedestals and allow to dry for one or two days. Don't be tempted to touch it within the first 24 hours, as you'll leave marks. If the resin doesn't sufficiently cover the artwork the first time, you can pour another coat over the first.

6 The result is a painting with alcohol ink, set beneath a glossy surface of resin.

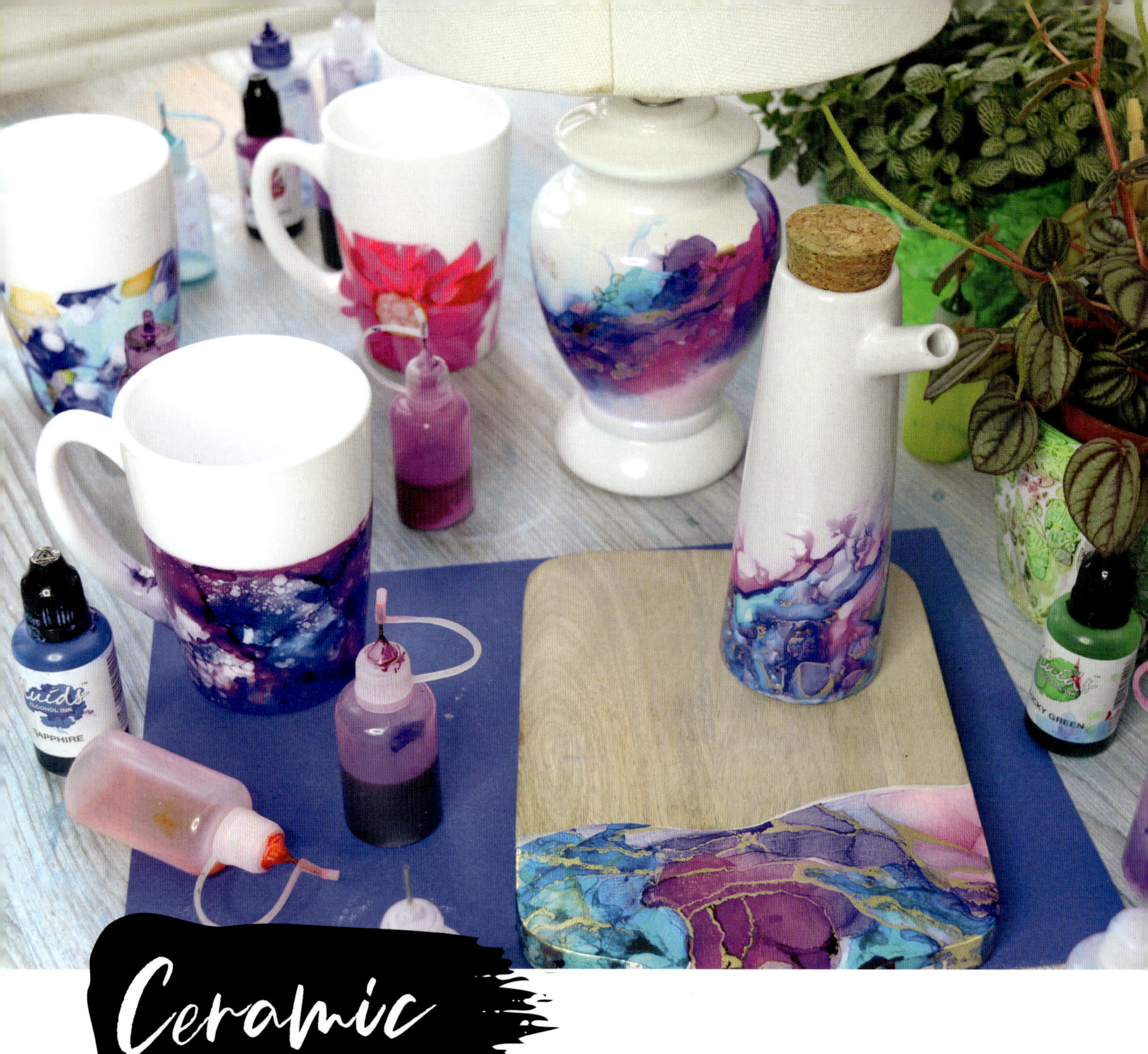

Ceramic

Any glazed ceramic item can be decorated with alcohol ink, allowing you to create personalised designer pieces from simple white objects. Here is another technique you can try with alcohol ink - achieving texture with cling film, this time on a decorative planter.

YOU'LL NEED

– Small hot-air blower or airbrush
– Light-coloured glazed ceramics
– Alcohol ink
– Isopropanol (alcohol) in a pipette or applicator bottle
– Special alcohol in a spray bottle
– UV clear varnish (optional)
– Cling film (plastic wrap)

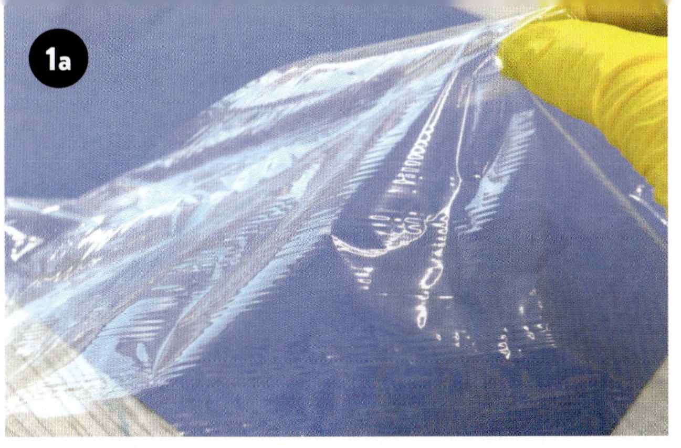
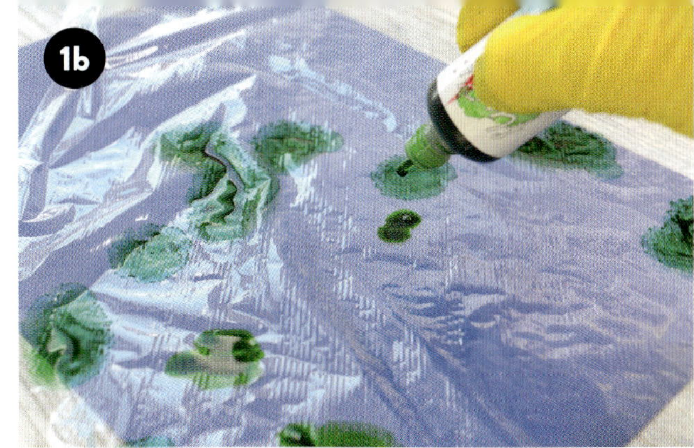

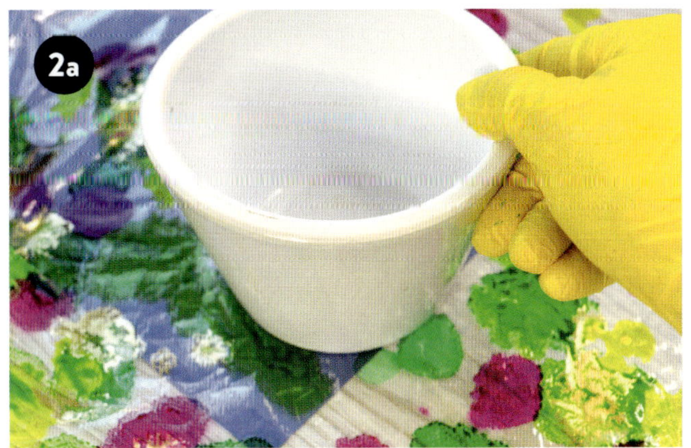
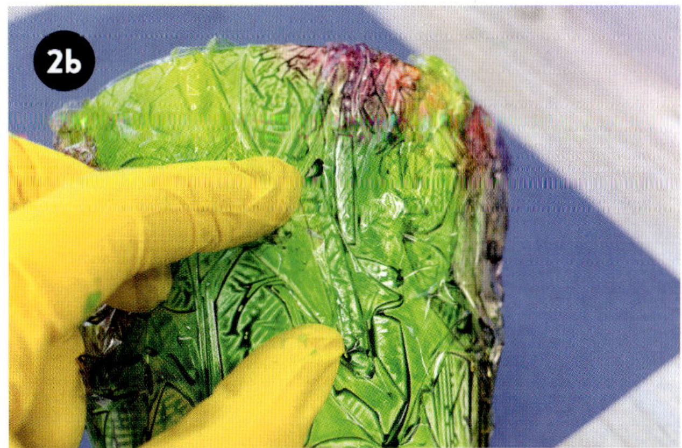

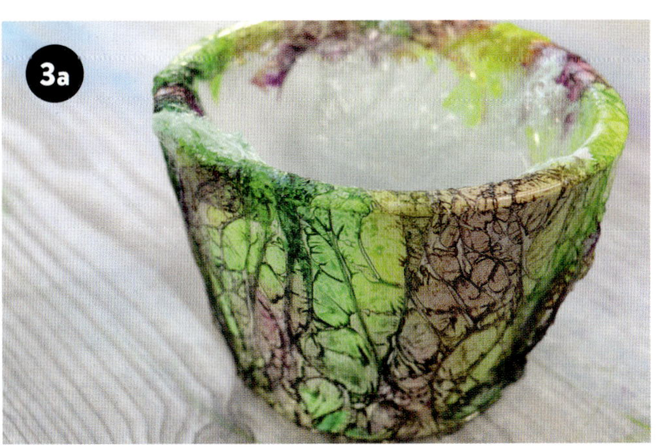
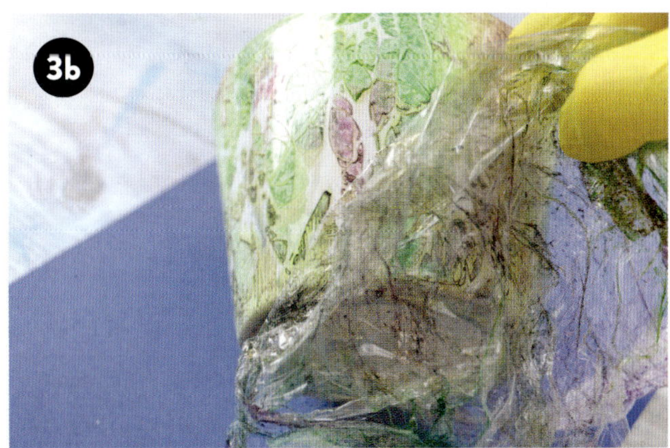

1. Lay out a large piece of cling film and sprinkle it with alcohol ink. It's best to choose related or analogous colours to avoid mixing patches of muddy colours.

2. Place the flower pot in the middle and wrap the cling film around it. Manipulate the plastic and deliberately create wrinkles, so that the ink accumulates in random patterns.

3. Allow your pot to dry overnight. The next day, remove the cling film and you're finished. Carefully seal the pot with UV clear varnish (optional).

PAINTING CROCKERY

Ceramic or glass cups and crockery can be decorated, but alcohol ink is not food-grade, and usually the same applies for the epoxy resin used. For safety, either don't use the cups for drinking or use food-grade epoxy resin.To make the cups suitable for hand washing, seal them in UV varnish then clear varnish and dunk them in food-grade epoxy resin to cover all the painting. Lift out and leave to drip dry.Even when resin-coated, these cups are not dishwasher safe.

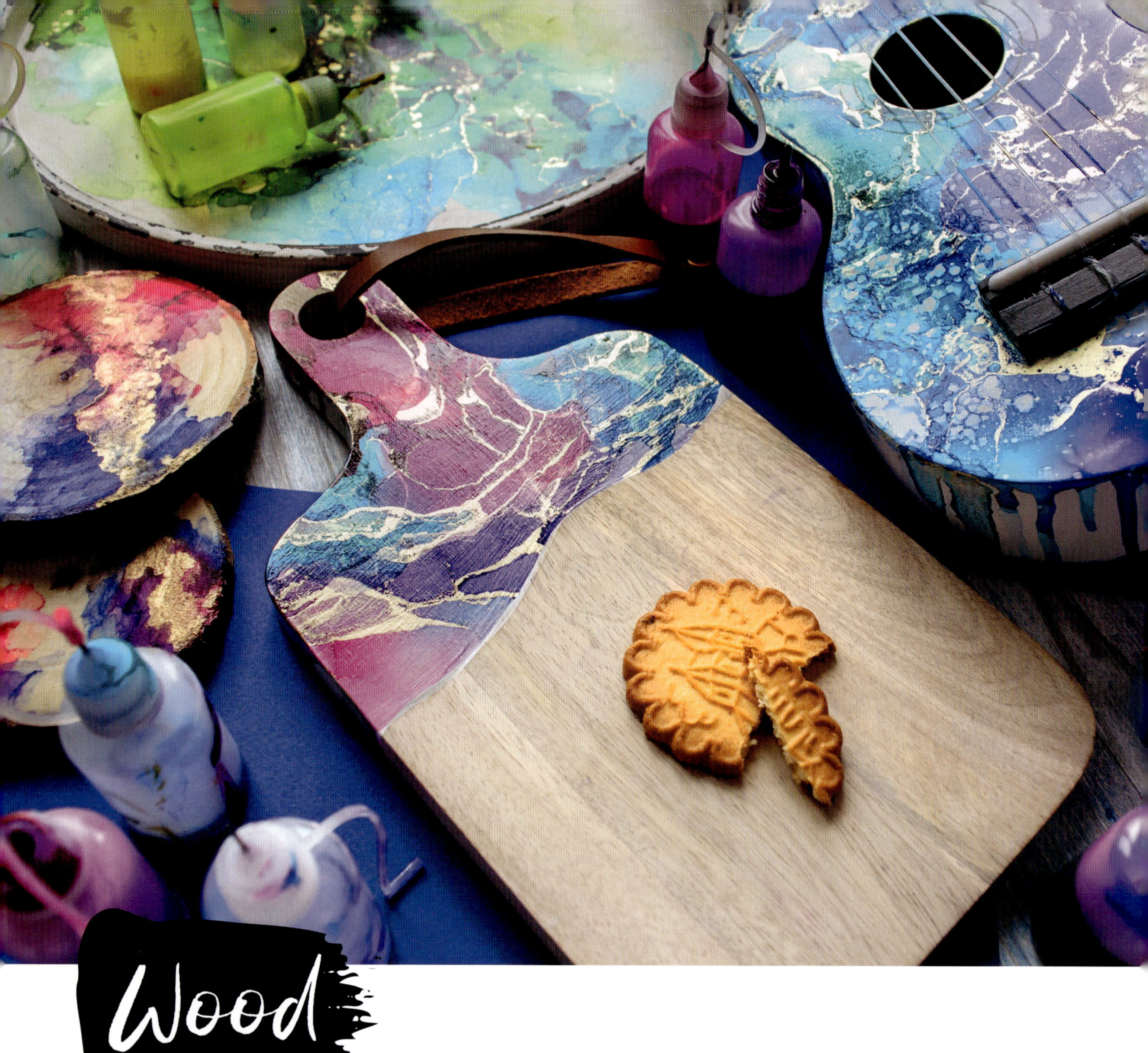

Wood

Brightly coloured alcohol ink also looks beautiful on wood. Most wooden objects are already treated but items that aren't can be primed and sealed in preparation for painting with alcohol ink.

YOU'LL NEED

- White gesso
- Acrylic binder
- Fine tip paintbrushes
- Masking fluid or tape
- Clear varnish or epoxy resin

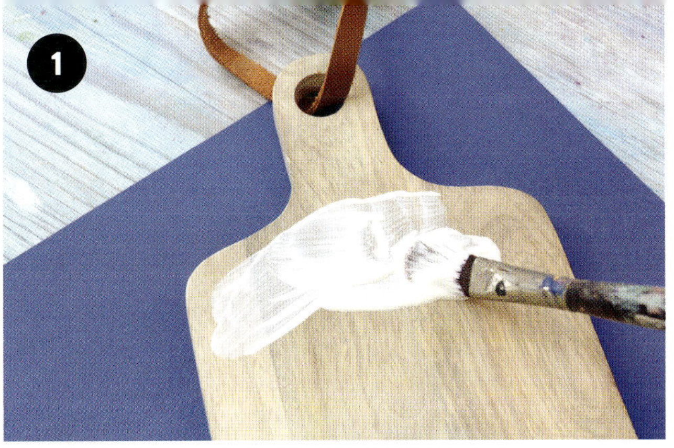

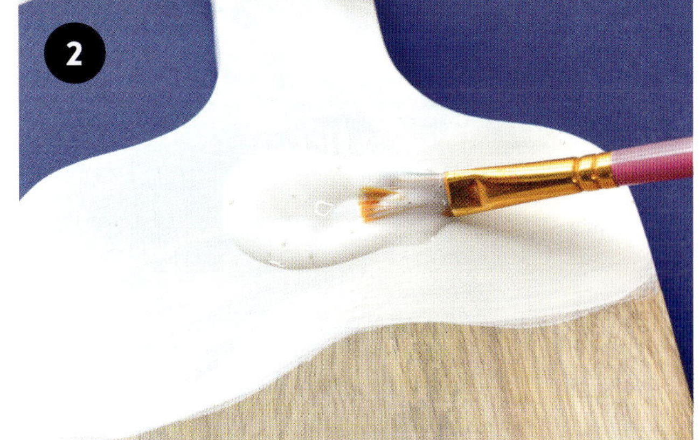

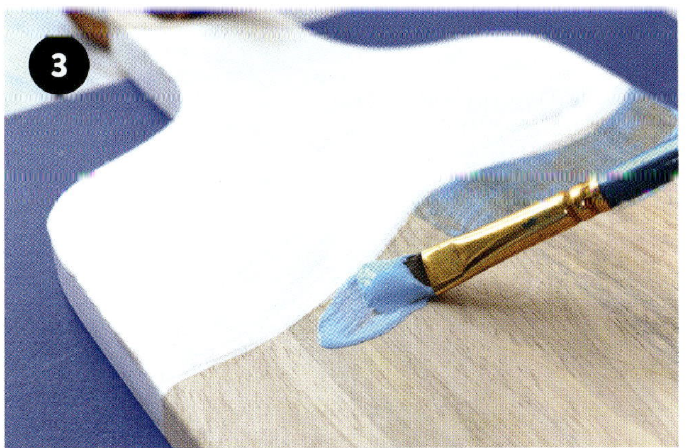

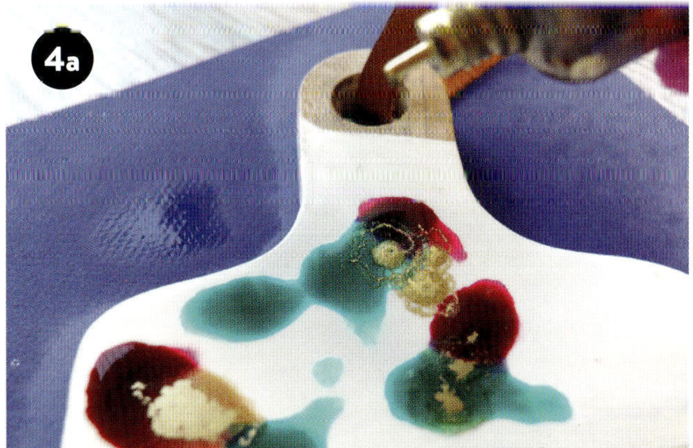

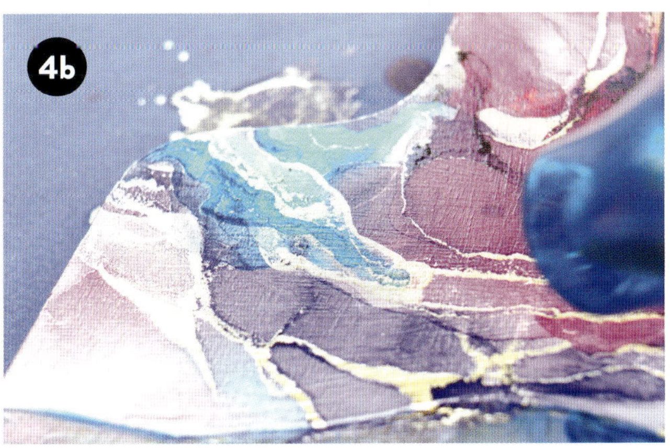

EVEN MORE IDEAS

MDF boards, which are generally ready-primed with white primer, are well suited for alcohol ink, as are all pieces of wood that have been painted. One of my favourite pieces is my blue and gold ukulele (see photo) – it's got to be the most beautiful one of its kind, don't you think?

1 Prime the area you have chosen to paint with alcohol ink with white gesso.

2 When the primer has dried, seal the surface with a clear acrylic binder.

3 To protect the rest of the surface of the wood, you can either mask it off or mark the edge with masking fluid.

4 In this example, I used the Cloudy technique with the Metallic technique. Once everything has dried thoroughly, you can seal the painted area with varnish or epoxy resin. If it's a purely decorative object, UV varnish is sufficient.

5 Remove the masking fluid and adhesive tape, and it's ready.

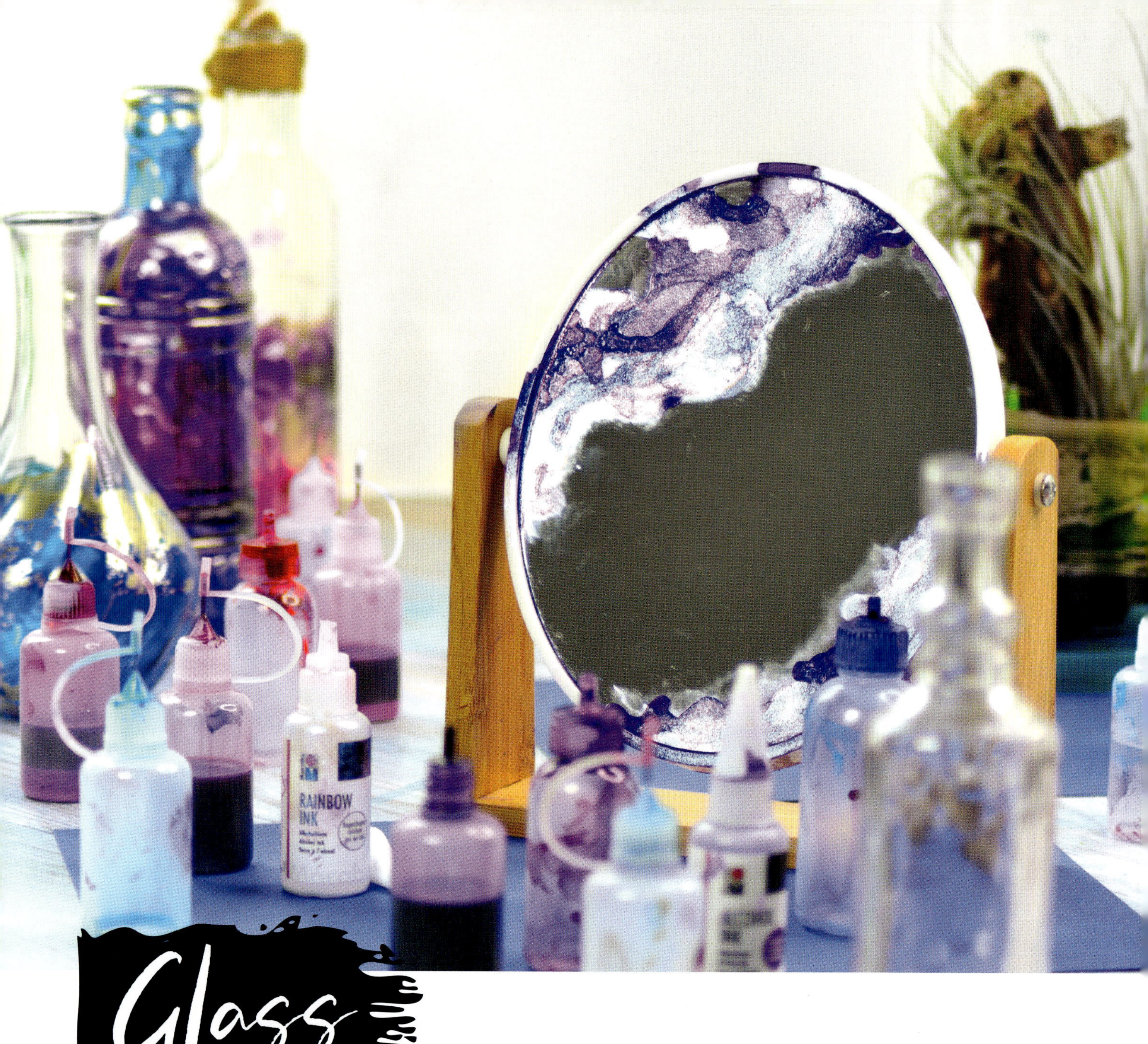

Transparent and coloured glass, as well as mirrors, are great for decorating with alcohol ink. Using metallic gold, you can create a very opulent effect.

YOU'LL NEED

- Small hot-air blower or airbrush
- Mirror
- Alcohol ink
- Isopropanol (alcohol) in a pipette or applicator bottle
- Kitchen towels for polishing

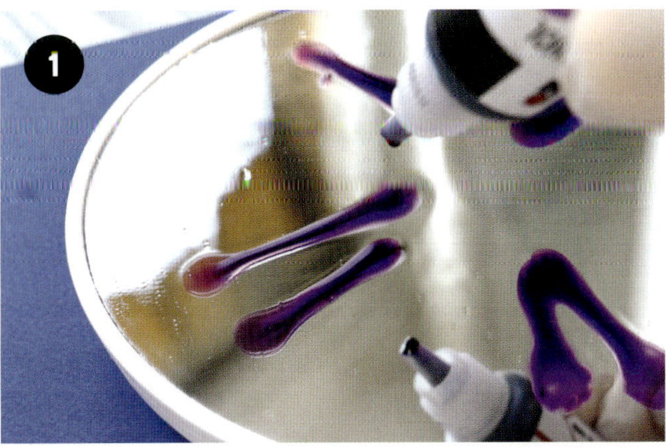

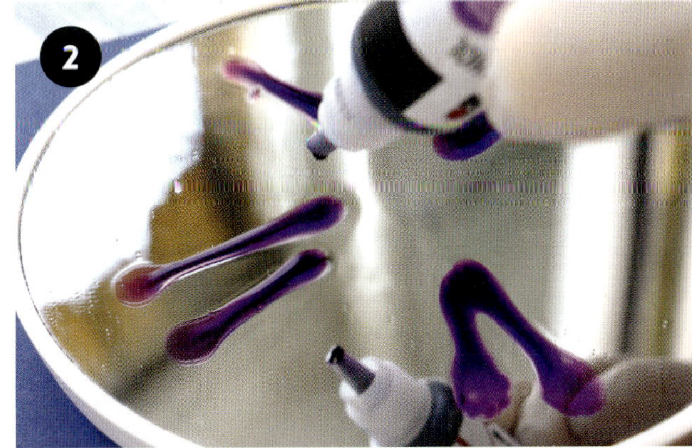

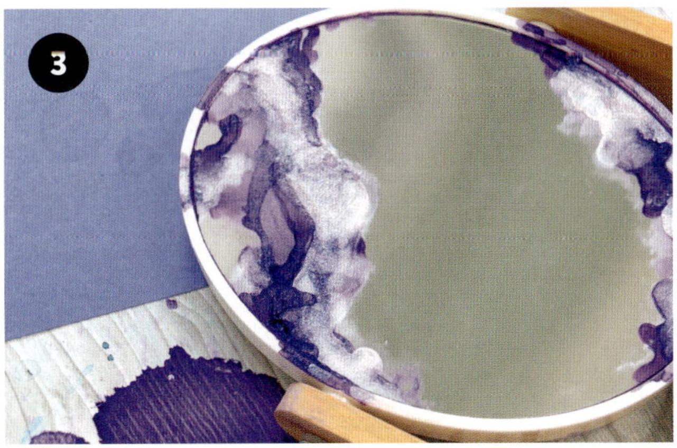

1 For this mirror, I sprayed the glass surface with alcohol, then painted it using purple alcohol ink.

2 To make the colour in some areas more intense, I applied more purple alcohol ink and added glittering colour effects. Remember that not every colour effect behaves like metallic colour. It's best to try things out on a piece of film first.

3 Messy edges will really stand out on a mirror – I wiped the clear area clean with a cloth soaked in alcohol. Don't seal the mirror as the spray would make the surface dull.

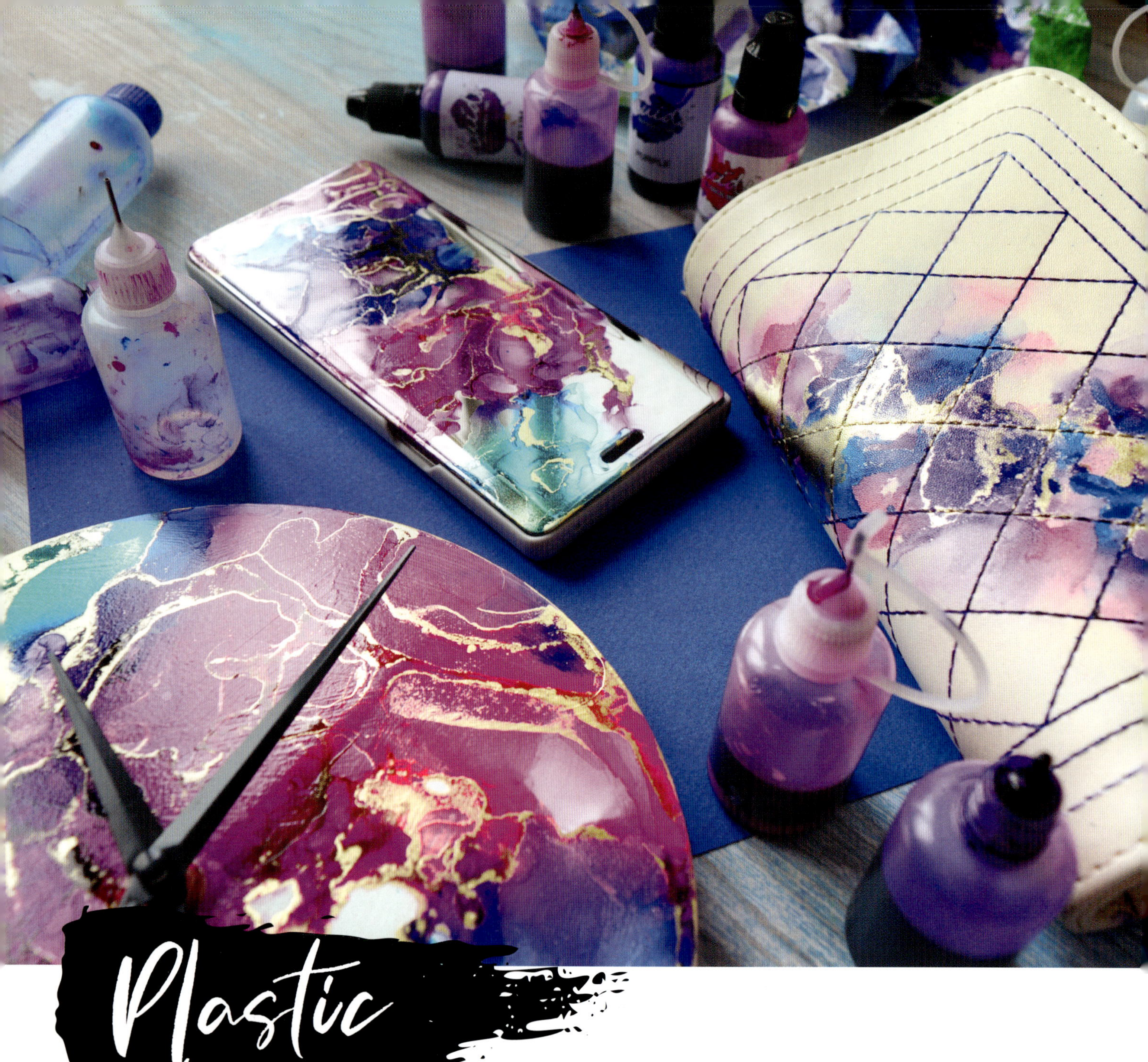

Plastic

The term plastic can cover a lot of things: from a plastic clock face to imitation leather, everything can be dyed with alcohol ink. Most of the time, the material does not need to be prepared. The approach for plastics is the same as for Yupo paper, the surfaces must be non-absorbent. I'll show you here with a bag made from faux leather.

YOU'LL NEED

- Small hot-air blower or airbrush
- Plastic object (pale in colour)
- Alcohol ink
- Isopropanol (alcohol) in a pipette or applicator bottle
- UV clear varnish spray (matt)

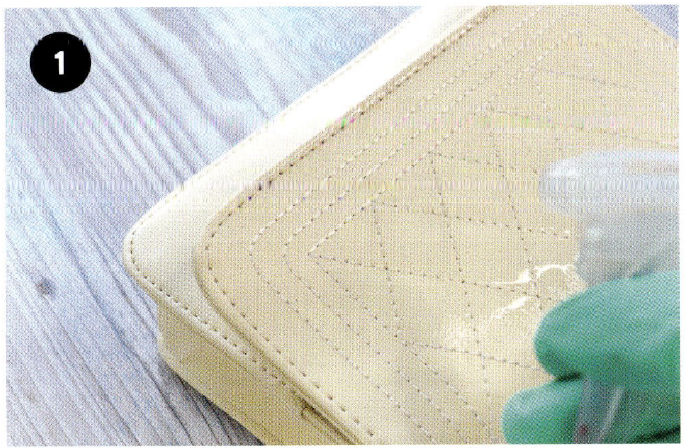

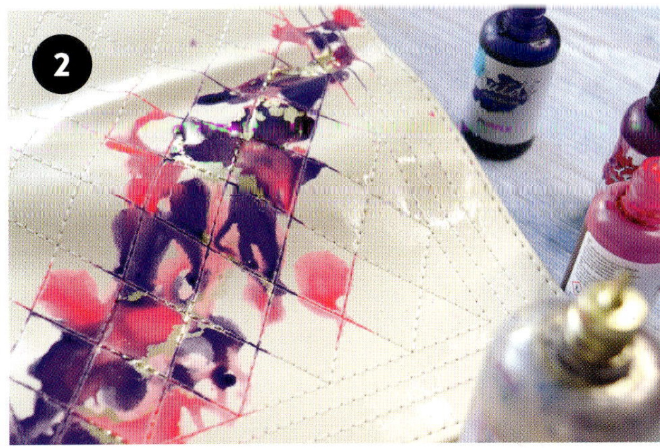

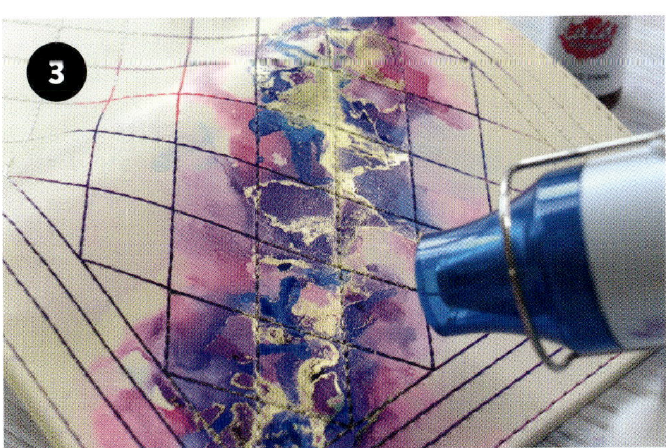

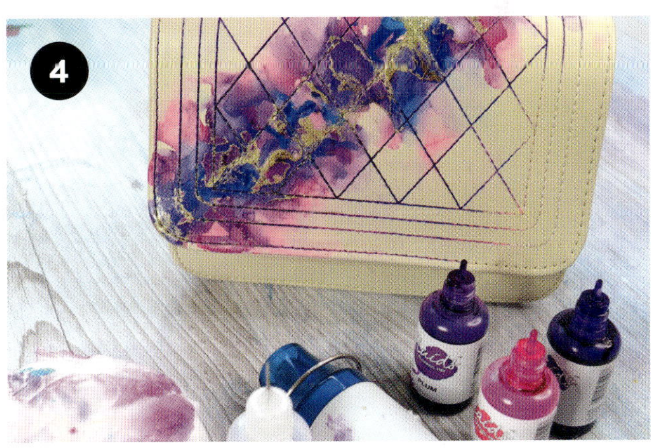

1 Spray the surface with alcohol to help the ink float more easily.

2 Next apply the alcohol inks using simple Cloudy and Wispy techniques.

3 It takes a bit of skill due to the uneven surface, but bit by bit, with patience, you'll get the effect you want.

4 Finally, you can spray matt UV varnish over it. Bags and items decorated in this way should nevertheless be used carefully. Suitability for everyday use must be judged individually depending on the material. This bag is holding up well so far!

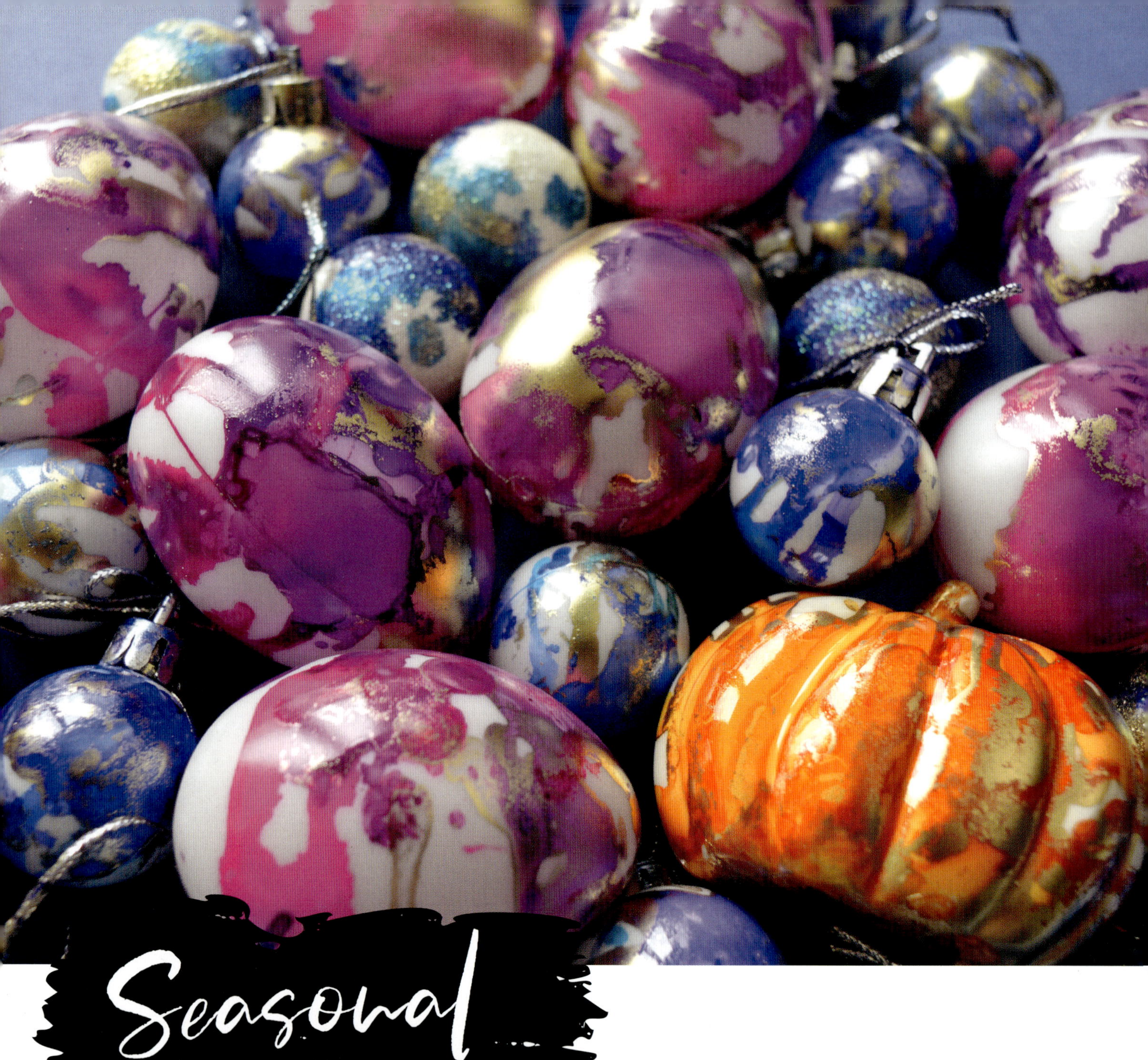

Seasonal

Let's not overlook the many occasions for celebration during the year! This book would be incomplete without mentioning that Christmas baubles and Easter eggs can also be decorated with alcohol ink. I tend to paint these small objects in groups and sprinkle them with alcohol ink. It's easy and the result is really effective.

YOU'LL NEED

- Small hot-air blower or airbrush
- All kinds of decorations made from materials previously mentioned in the book
- Alcohol ink
- Isopropanol (alcohol) in a pipette or applicator bottle
- UV clear varnish or acrylic binder for non-plastic decorations

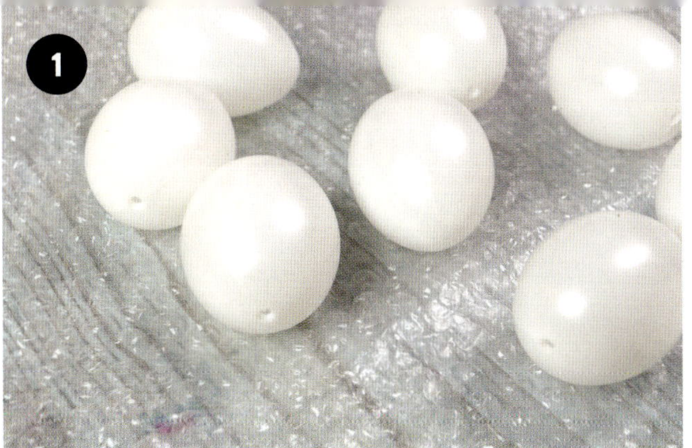

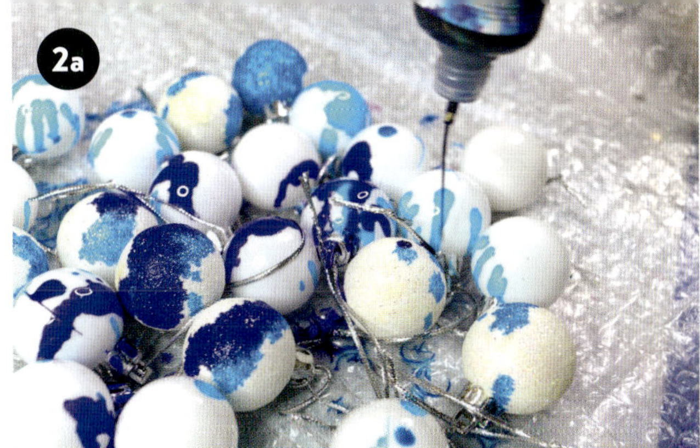

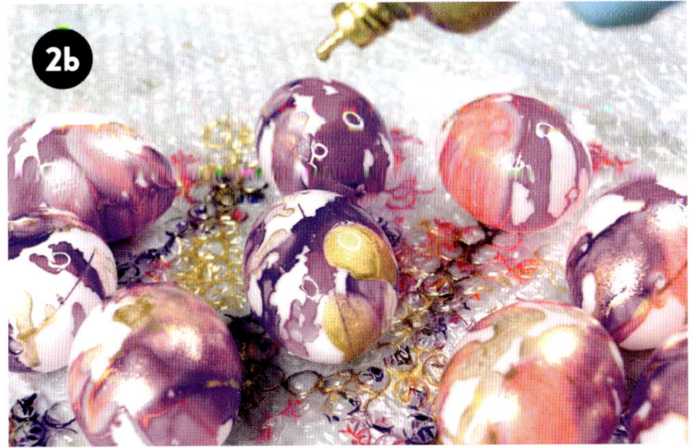

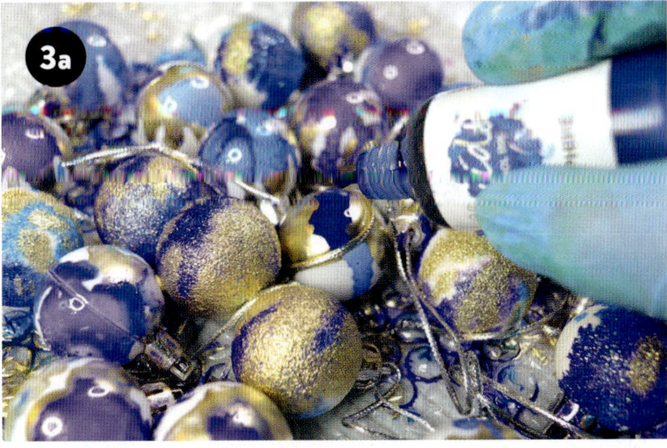

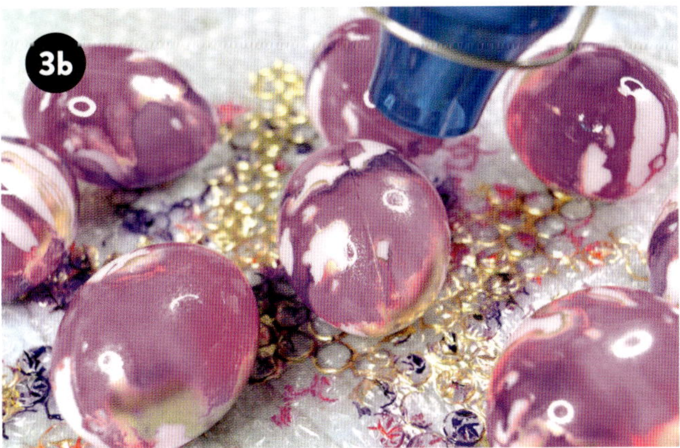

1   You'll need a base that prevents the decorations from rolling away. Bubble wrap is good for this.

2   Simply drip alcohol ink over the eggs and baubles, then add some metallic alcohol ink.

3   With the hot-air blower, dry the pieces, moving them around to cover all the surface. This will distribute the colour. And that's it!

TIP

You can also apply alcohol ink in a more controlled way by masking off areas and applying the ink with a paintbrush. Just get cracking – creativity comes when you're having fun!

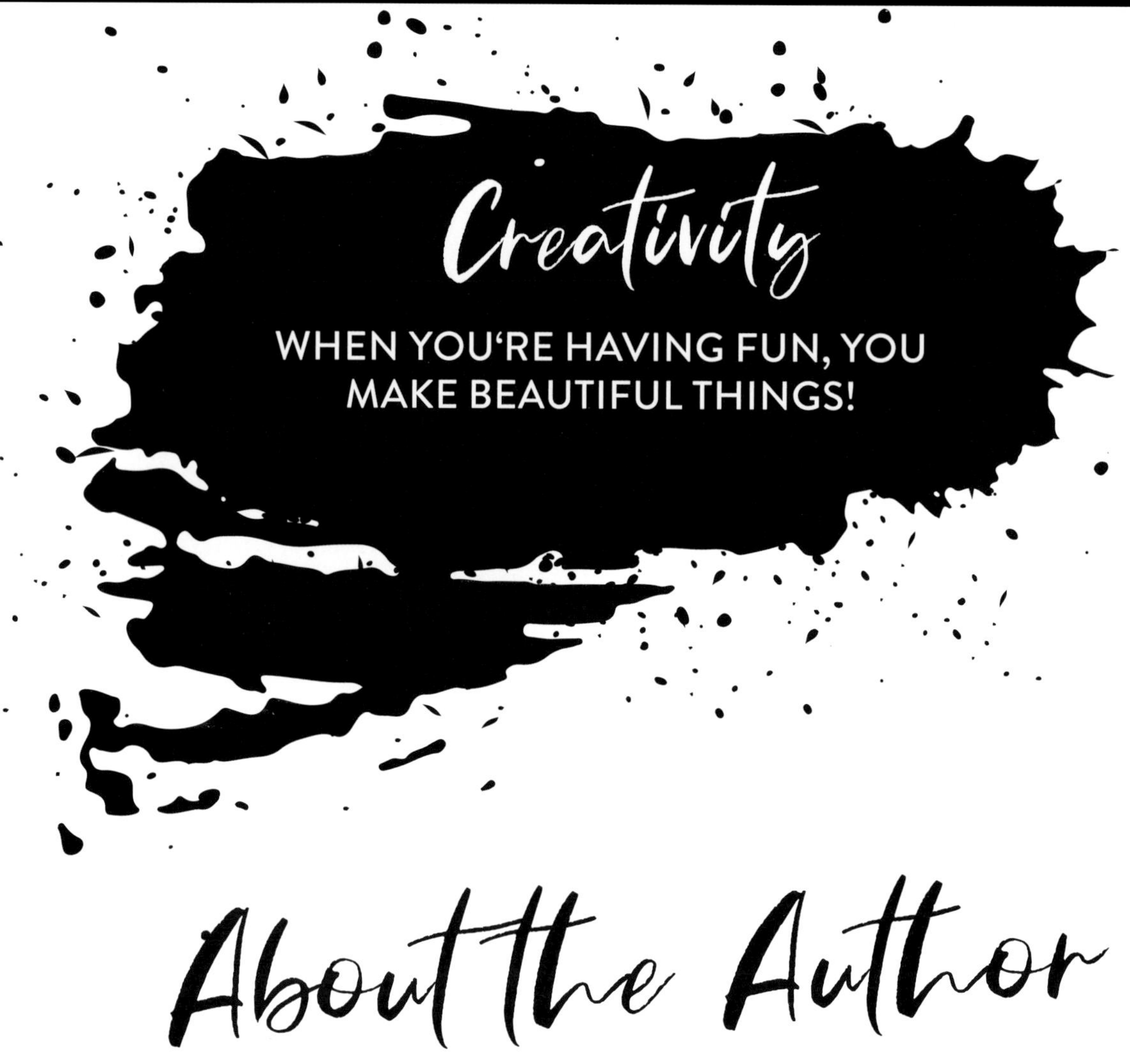

About the Author

Desirée Delâge is an artist from Cologne, Germany., where she she runs her teaching studio. She also has the creative blog Krigelkragel, where she shared painting advice and techniques, and offers online courses in addition to live workshops. Desirée originally worked as a visual designer. Today, she exhibits her mixed media artwork and invests 100% of her time in the many facets of creative work in art. In 2019, she also completed further education in art therapy.

BLOG, PAINTING SCHOOL AND COMMISSIONED WORK

WEBSITE	INSTAGRAM	FACEBOOK	YOUTUBE
www.krigelkragel.com	@krigelkragel	desiree.delage.artstudio	Krigelkragel

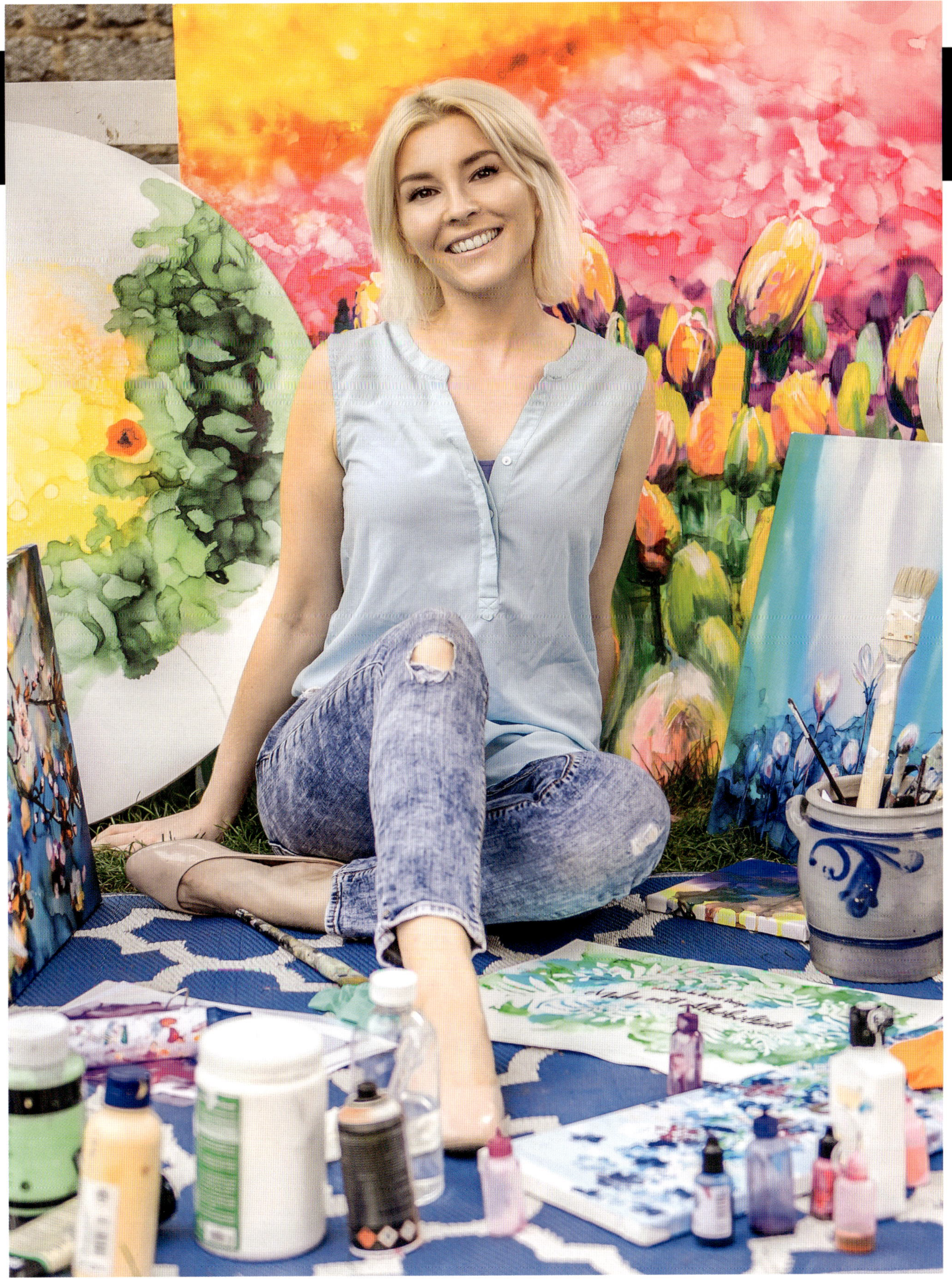

Acknowledgements

The fact that I was allowed to write this wonderful book is such a gift for me. An unexpected dream come true. The project has re-energised me after several misfortunes and losses.

I should like to thank EMF publishing house for accepting my proposal for the subject, despite the relative lack of knowledge around alcohol ink at the time.

I have shared this book project with the following people:

FILIZ
Favourite person in the blogger world. Girlfriend. Thank you for always being reachable by phone, listening and keeping my secret! Thank you.

https://www.blogger-coaching.de

LESLIE
Photographer. Thank you for your beautiful portrait photography. With you, taking beautiful photos is easy.

FRANZISKA
Thank you for always lending an ear and for letting me just do things. It was a pleasure to work with you.

YOU UP THERE
I would also like to mention you, because who knows, maybe someone is watching me from above while I'm typing? That would be nice. I wish I could show you this. You're with me in my heart.

THANKS ALSO TO MY SPONSORS:

MARABU ...
Thank you for a great selection of alcohol inks.

OCTOPUS FLUIDS ...
Thank you for a great selection of alcohol inks.

My special thanks go in particular to my lovely little online community. Writing and painting was, in retrospect, a rather lonely activity, which occupied me fully because of the tight schedule. Unfortunately, I couldn't and didn't want to speak all of the time. Thank you for staying, despite my days and months of online absence. I'm very happy that I've already been able to inspire a few of you to use alcohol ink and that you're intrepidly reaching for the mask. You're simply fantastic!

A thousand thanks also to YOU! Thank you for buying this book, supporting me on my social media channels, painting together with us and sharing it with everyone (#krigelkragel). Thanks to you, I can pursue my calling and do what I love. Thank you!

Index

A DAVID AND CHARLES BOOK

© 2020 Edition Michael Fischer GmbH, Donnersbergstr. 7, 86859 Igling, Germany
This translation of ALCOHOL INK first published in Germany by Edition Michael Fischer GmbH in 2020 is published by arrangement with Silke Bruenink Agency, Munich, Germany

Text and Designs © DESIRÉE DELÂGE 2020
Layout and Photography © Silvia Keller/ 2020 Edition Michael Fischer GmbH

First published in Germany in 2020

Desirée Delâge has asserted her right to be identified as author of this work in accordance with the Copyright, Designs and Patents Act, 1988.

All rights reserved. No part of this publication may be reproduced in any form or by any means, electronic or mechanical, by photocopying, recording or otherwise, without prior permission in writing from the publisher.

Readers are permitted to reproduce any of the designs in this book for their personal use and without the prior permission of the publisher. However, the designs in this book are copyright and must not be reproduced for resale.

The author and publisher have made every effort to ensure that all the instructions in the book are accurate and safe, and therefore cannot accept liability for any resulting injury, damage or loss to persons or property, however it may arise.

Names of manufacturers and product ranges are provided for the information of readers, with no intention to infringe copyright or trademarks.

A catalogue record for this book is available from the British Library.

ISBN-13: 9781446308349 paperback
ISBN-13: 9781446379868 EPUB

This book has been printed on paper from approved suppliers and made from pulp from sustainable sources.

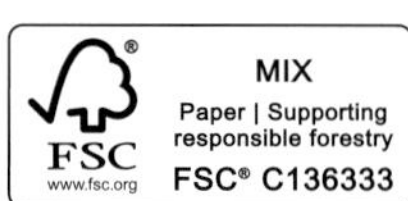

Printed in China through Asia Pacific Offset for:
David and Charles, Ltd
Suite A, Tourism House, Pynes Hill, Exeter, EX2 5WS

10 9 8 7 6 5

Cover, layout & setting: Silvia Keller
Editor and editing: Dr Franziska Klorer
Photos: Leslie Lorenz and Desirée Delâge
Translator: Network Languages Ltd.

David and Charles publishes high-quality books on a wide range of subjects. For more information visit www.davidandcharles.com.

Share your makes with us on social media using #dandcbooks and follow us on Facebook and Instagram by searching for @dandcbooks.

Layout of the digital edition of this book may vary depending on reader hardware and display settings.